PENGUIN ⓟ CLASSICS

THE POWER OF
NONVIOLENT RESISTANCE

MOHANDAS KARAMACHAND GANDHI (1869–1948) was a pre-eminent leader of the Indian national movement and his nonviolent resistance inspired and continues to inspire generations struggling to redefine freedom and enlarge its ambit. His conception of nonviolence included the structural nature of violence inherent in poverty and impediments placed by ascribed identities in the fulfillment of human vocation. Truth and nonviolence, though as old as the mountains, found in Gandhi a practitioner unceasingly engaged in search of a state where one is freed from the impulse to lie and to violate others. Mahatma Gandhi was married to Kastur Gandhi and they had four sons. He was assassinated on January 30, 1948, as he walked to offer prayers.

TRIDIP SUHRUD is a scholar, writer, and translator who works on the intellectual and cultural history of modern Gujarat and the Gandhian intellectual tradition. As the director and chief editor of the Sabarmati Ashram Preservation and Memorial Trust (2012–2017), he was responsible for creating the world's largest digital archive on Gandhi—the Gandhi Heritage Portal. His translations include the critical edition of *Hind Swaraj*; Narayan Desai's four-volume biography of Gandhi, *My Life Is My Message*; and the four-volume epic Gujarati novel, *Sarasvatichandra*. His most recent work is a critical edition of Gandhi's autobiography *The Story of My Experiments with Truth* in two languages, Gujarati and English. He is presently translating the diaries of Manu Gandhi, covering the period between 1942 and 1948, compiling a series "Letters to Gandhi"—of unpublished correspondence to Gandhi—and working on an eight-volume compendium of testimonies of indigo cultivators of Champaran. He is the provost of CEPT University and director of Lalbhai Dalpatbhai Institute of Indology, Ahmedabad, and serves as chairman of the Governing Council of MICA.

D1111634

M. K. GANDHI

The Power of Nonviolent Resistance

SELECTED WRITINGS

Edited with an Introduction by
TRIDIP SUHRUD

PENGUIN BOOKS

PENGUIN BOOKS

An imprint of Penguin Random House LLC
penguinrandomhouse.com

Published in Penguin Books 2019

Selections from this collection are from *The Collected Works of Mahatma Gandhi*
by Mahatma Gandhi. 100 volumes. New Delhi: Publications Division,
Ministry of Information and Broadcasting, 1956–1994.

Library of Congress Control Number: 2019942772

ISBN 9780143134152 (paperback)
ISBN 9780525505891 (ebook)

Printed in the United States of America
1 3 5 7 9 10 8 6 4 2

Set in Sabon LT Pro

Contents

IV. THE PRACTICE

V. THE POLITICS

VI. LETTER TO HITLER

VII. CONUNDRUMS OF AHIMSA

VIII. DARK NIGHT OF THE SOUL

Introduction

A SMALL, STILL VOICE

The more he took to violence, the more he receded from Truth.[1]

Mohandas Karamchand Gandhi (1869–1948) described "ahimsa,"[2] nonviolence or more accurately love, as the "supreme duty." This essay seeks to understand the necessity of nonviolence in Gandhi's life and thought.

Toward the end of his life, Gandhi was asked by a friend to resume writing his autobiography and write a "treatise on the science of ahimsa." What the friend wanted were accounts of Gandhi's striving for truth and his quest for nonviolence, and since these were the two most significant forces that moved Gandhi, the friend wanted Gandhi's exposition on the practice of truth and love and his philosophical understanding of both. Gandhi was not averse to writing about himself or his quest. He had written—moved by what he called *Antaryami*, the dweller within—his autobiography, *An Autobiography or the Story of My Experiments with Truth*.[3] Even in February 1946 when this exchange occurred he was not philosophically opposed to writing about the self. However, he left the possibility of the actual act of writing to the will of God.

On the request for the treatise on the "science[4] of ahimsa" he was categorical in his refusal. His unwillingness stemmed from two different grounds: one of inability and the other of impossibility.

He argued that as a person whose domain of work was action, it was beyond his powers to do so. "To write a treatise on
the science of ahimsa is beyond my powers. I am not built for
academic writings. Action is my domain, and what I understand, according to my lights, to be my duty, and what comes
my way, I do. All my action is actuated by the spirit of service."[5] He suggested that anyone who had the capacity to systematize ahimsa into a science should do so, but added a
proviso: "if it lends itself to such treatment."[6] Gandhi went on
to argue that a cohesive account of even his own striving for
nonviolence, his numerous experiments with ahimsa both
within the realms of the spiritual and the political, the personal and the collective, could be attempted only after his
death, as anything done before that would be necessarily incomplete. Gandhi was prescient. He was to conduct the most
vital and most moving experiment with ahimsa after this, and
he was to experience the deepest doubts about both the nature
of nonviolence and its efficacy after this. With the violence in
large parts of the Indian subcontinent from 1946 onward,
Gandhi began to think deeply about the commitment of people
and political parties to collective nonviolence. In December
1946 Gandhi made the riot-ravaged village of Sreerampore his
home and then began a barefoot march through the villages of
East Bengal.

This was not the impossibility that he alluded to. He believed that just as it was impossible for a human being to get a
full grasp of truth (and of truth as God), it was equally impossible for humans to get a vision of ahimsa that was complete.
He said: "If at all, it could only be written after my death. And
even so let me give the warning that it would fail to give a complete exposition of ahimsa. No man has been able to describe
God fully. The same holds true of ahimsa."[7]

Gandhi believed that just as it was given to him only to strive
to have a glimpse of truth, he could only endeavor to soak his
being in ahimsa and translate it in action.

It is important for us to understand why it was a necessity of
life for Gandhi to strive for nonviolence. This striving is cap-

tured by the epigram with which this essay begins. Violence takes us away from ourselves; it makes us forget our humanity, our vocation, and our limits, and for Gandhi such amnesia can only lead to destruction of self and others. The following section seeks to explain the complex set of arguments and practices through which Gandhi elucidated the relationship between nonviolence, self-recognition, and freedom. For Gandhi freedom—both collective and personal—is predicated upon an incessant search to know oneself. This self-recognition, Gandhi believed, eluded all those who were practitioners and votaries of violence.

Gandhi described violence as "brute force" (*sharir bal* or *top bal*, in Gujarati) and nonviolence as "soul force" (*atma bal* or *daya bal*, in Gujarati).[8] The distance between the two, between the beastly and the human, is marked by nonviolence. The idea of brute force locates violence in the body and the instruments that the body can command to cause injury or to inflict death. It connotes pure instrumentality. By locating violence within the realm of the beastly, Gandhi clearly points out the absence of the conscience, of the normative. He wrote: "Nonviolence is the law of our species as violence is the law of the brute. The spirit lies dormant in the brute and he knows no law but that of physical might. The dignity of man requires obedience to a higher law—to the strength of the spirit."[9] The term "soul force" is indicative of the working of the conscience, of the human ability to *discern* the path of rectitude and act upon this judgment. In a speech given before the members of the Gandhi Seva Sangh in 1938, he brought this distinction sharply into focus: "Physical strength is called brute force. We are born with such strength. . . . But we are born as human beings in order that we may realize God who dwells within our hearts. This is the basic distinction between us and the beasts. . . . Along with the human form, we also have human power—that is the power of nonviolence. We can have an insight into the mystery of the soul force. In that consists our humanity."[10] Gandhi clearly indicates two aspects: One, that nonviolence is a unique human capacity; it is because we are capable of restraint, of nonaggression, of ahimsa that we are human. Two,

to be human is to fulfill the human vocation, which is to realize the God—Truth as God—who dwells in our hearts. This
was Gandhi's principle quest. In his autobiography, Gandhi
clarified the nature of his pursuit. He wrote: "What I want to
achieve—what I have been striving and pining to achieve these
thirty years—is self-realization, to see God face-to-face, to attain moksha. I live and move and have my being in pursuit of
this goal."[11] He worshipped *Satya Narayan*, God as Truth. He
did not ever claim that he had indeed found Him, or seen Him
face-to-face. But Gandhi was seeking this absolute truth and
was "prepared to sacrifice the things dearest to me in pursuit
of this quest."[12] Although Gandhi never claimed to have seen
God face-to-face, he could imagine that state: "One who has
realized God is freed from sin forever. He has no desire to be
fulfilled. Not even in his thoughts will he suffer from faults,
imperfections, or impurities. Whatever he does will be perfect
because he does nothing himself but the God within him does
everything. He is completely merged in Him."[13]

This state was for Gandhi the state of perfect self-realization,
of perfect self-knowledge. It was a moment of revelation, a moment when the self was revealed to him. Although he believed
that such perfect knowledge may elude him so long as he was
imprisoned in the mortal body, he did make an extraordinary
claim. This was his claim to hear what he described as a
"small, still voice" or the "inner voice." He used various terms
such as 'the voice of God,' 'of conscience,' 'the inner voice,'
'the voice of Truth,' or 'the small, still voice.'[14] He made this
claim often and declared that he was powerless before the irresistible voice, that his conduct was guided by his voice. The
nature of this inner voice and Gandhi's need and ability to listen to the voice becomes apparent when we examine his invocation of it.

The first time he invoked the authority of this inner voice in
India was at a public meeting in Ahmedabad, where he suddenly declared his resolve to fast. The day was February 15,
1918. Twenty-two days prior to this date, Gandhi had been
leading the strike of the workers at the textiles mills of

Ahmedabad. The mill workers had taken a pledge to strike until their demands were met. They appeared to be going back on their pledge. Gandhi described his sudden resolve thus: "One morning—it was at a mill hands' meeting—while I was groping and unable to see my way clearly, the light came to me. Unbidden and all by themselves the words came to my lips: 'unless the strikers rally,' I declared to the meeting, 'and continue to strike till a settlement is reached or till they leave the mills altogether, I will not touch any food.'"[15]

He was to repeatedly speak of the inner voice in similar metaphors: of darkness that enveloped him, his groping, churning, wanting to find a way forward and the moment of light, of knowledge when the voice spoke to him. Gandhi sought the guidance of his inner voice not only in the spiritual realm, a realm that was incommunicable and known only to him and his maker, but also in the political realm. He called off the noncooperation movement against the British in February 1922 in response to the prompting of his inner voice. His famous Dandi March also came to him through the voice speaking from within. Gandhi's search for a moral and spiritual basis for political action was anchored in his claim that one could and ought to be guided by the voice of truth speaking from within. This made his politics deeply spiritual. Gandhi expanded the scope of the inner voice to include the political realm. Gandhi's ideas of civilization and swaraj[16] were rooted in this possibility of knowing oneself. In 1909, Gandhi wrote his most important philosophical work, the *Hind Swaraj*.[17] Gandhi argued in the *Hind Swaraj* that modern Western civilization in fact decivilized[18] itself and characterized it as a "black-age" or satanic civilization. Civilization in the modern sense had no place for either religion or morality. He wrote: "Its true test lies in the fact that people living under it make bodily welfare the object of life."[19] Modern civilization had shifted the locus of judgment outside the human being. It had made not right conduct but objects the measure of human worth. In so doing, it had closed the possibility of knowing oneself. True civilization, on the other hand, was rooted in this very possibility. He wrote: "Civilization is that mode of conduct which points out to man the path of duty. Performance of duty and observance of morality are convertible terms. To observe morality is to attain mastery over our mind and passions. So doing, we know ourselves."[20] This act of knowing oneself is not only the basis of spiritual life but also of political life. He defined swaraj thus: "It is swaraj when we learn to rule ourselves."[21] This act of ruling oneself meant the control of mind and passions, of observance of morality, and of knowing the right and true path. Gandhi's idea and practice of satyagraha with its invocation of the soul force is based on this. Satyagraha requires not only the purity of means and ends but also the purity of the practitioner. Satyagraha in the final instance is based on the recognition of one's own conscience, on one's ability to listen to one's inner voice and submit to it.

Gandhi knew that his invocation of the inner voice was beyond comprehension and beyond his capacity to explain. He asked: "After all, does one express, can one express, all one's thoughts to others?"[22] Many tried to dissuade him from the fast in submission to the inner voice. Not all were convinced of his claim to hear the inner voice. It was argued that what he heard was not the voice of God but was a hallucination, that Gandhi was deluding himself and that his imagination had become overheated by long years of living within the cramped prison walls.

Gandhi remained steadfast and refuted the charge of self-delusion or hallucination. He said that "not the unanimous verdict of the whole world against me could shake me from the belief that what I heard was the true Voice of God."[23] He argued that his claim was beyond both proof and reason. The only proof he could probably provide was the fact that he had survived the fiery ordeal. It was a moment that he had been preparing himself for. He felt that his submission to God as Truth was so complete, at least in that particular instance of fasting, that he had no autonomy left. All his acts were prompted by the inner voice. It was a moment of perfect surrender. Such a moment of total submission transcends reason.

He wrote in a letter: "Of course, for me personally it transcends reason, because I feel it to be a clear will from God. My
position is that there is nothing just now that I am doing of my
own accord. He guides me from moment to moment."[24]

This extraordinary confession of perfect surrender perturbed many. The source of this discomfort is clear. Gandhi's
claim to hear the inner voice was neither unique nor exclusive.
The validity and legitimacy of such a claim was recognized in
the spiritual realm. The idea of perfect surrender was integral
to and consistent with the ideals of religious life. Although
Gandhi never made the claim of having seen God face-to-face,
having attained self-realization, the inner voice was for him
the voice of God. He said: "The inner voice is the voice of the
Lord."[25] But it was not a voice that came from a force outside
of him. Gandhi made a distinction between an outer force and
a power beyond us. A power beyond us has its locus within us.
It is superior to us, not subject to our command or willful action, but it is still located within us. He explained the nature of
this power. "Beyond us" means a "power that is beyond our
ego."[26] According to Gandhi, one acquires the capacity to hear
this voice when the "ego is reduced to zero."[27] Reducing the
ego to zero for Gandhi meant an act of total surrender to *Satya
Narayan*, God as Truth. This surrender required the subjugation of human will, of individual autonomy. It is when a person loses autonomy that conscience emerges. Conscience is an
act of obedience, not willfulness. He said: "Willfulness is not
conscience. . . . Conscience is the ripe fruit of strictest discipline. . . . Conscience can reside only in a delicately tuned
breast."[28] He knew what a person with conscience could be
like. "A conscientious man hesitates to assert himself, he is always humble, never boisterous, always compromising, always
ready to listen, ever willing, even anxious to admit mistakes."[29]
A person without this tender breast delicately tuned to the
working of the conscience cannot hear the inner voice or, more
dangerously, may in fact hear the voice of the ego. This capacity did not belong to everyone as a natural gift or a right available in equal measure. What one required was a cultivated

capacity to discern the inner voice as distinct from the voice of the ego, as "one cannot always recognize whether it is the voice of Rama or Ravana."[30]

What was this ever-wakefulness that allowed him to hear the call of truth as distinct from the voice of untruth? How does one acquire the fitness to wait upon God? He had likened this preparation to an attempt to empty the sea with a drain as small as the point of a blade of grass. Yet it had to be as natural as life itself. He created a regimen of spiritual discipline that enabled him to search himself through and through. As part of his spiritual training, he formulated what he called the *Ekadash Vrata*, Eleven Vows or Observances.[31] The ashram,[32] or a community of co-religionists, was constituted by their abiding faith in these *vrata* and by their act of prayer. Prayer was the very core of Gandhi's life. Medieval devotional poetry sung by Pandit Narayan Moreshwar Khare moved him. He drew sustenance from Mira and Charlie Andrews's rendition of "When I Survey the Wondrous Cross," while young Olive Doke healed him with "Lead Kindly Light." He recited the *Gita* every day. What was this intense need for prayer? What allowed him to claim that he was not a man of learning but a man of prayer? He knew that mere repetition of the Ramanama was futile if it did not stir his soul. A prayer for him had to be a clear response to the hunger of the soul. What was the hunger that moved his being?

His was a passionate cry of the soul hungering for union with the divine. He saw his communion with God as that of a master and a slave in perpetual bondage; prayer was the expression of the intense yearning to merge in the Master. Prayer was the expression of the definitive and conscious longing of the soul; it was his act of waiting upon Him for guidance. His want was to feel the utterly pure presence of the divine within. Only a heart purified and cleansed by prayer could be filled with the presence of God, where life became one long continuous prayer, an act of worship. Prayer was for him the final reliance upon God to the exclusion of all else. He knew that only when a person lives constantly in the sight of God, when he or she regards each thought with God as witness and its Master, could one feel Rama dwelling in the heart at every moment. Such a prayer could only be offered in the spirit of nonattachment, *anasakti*. Moreover, when the God that he sought to realize is truth, prayer though externalized was in essence directed inward. Because truth is not merely that which we are expected to speak. It is that which alone is, it is that of which all things are made, it is that which subsists by its own power, which alone is eternal. Gandhi's intense yearning was that such truth should illuminate his heart. Prayer was a plea, a preparation, a cleansing that enabled him to hear his inner voice. The *Ekadash Vrata* allowed for this waiting upon God. The act of waiting meant to perform one's actions in a desireless or detached manner. The *Gita* describes this state as a state of *sthitpragnya*, literally the one whose intellect is secure. The state of *sthitpragnya* was for Gandhi not only a philosophical ideal but a personal aspiration. The Gita describes this state as a condition of *sthitpragnya*. A *sthitpragnya* is one who puts away "all the cravings that arise in the mind and finds comfort for himself only from the atman";[33] and one "whose senses are reined in on all sides from their objects"[34] so that the mind is "untroubled in sorrows and longeth not for joys, who is free from passion, fear and wrath";[35] who knows attachment nowhere; only such a brahmachari can be in the world "moving among sense objects with the sense weaned from likes and dislikes and brought under the control of the atman."[36] This detachment or self-effacement allowed Gandhi to dwell closer to Him. It made possible an act of surrender and allowed him to claim: "I have been a willing slave to this most exacting master for more than half a century. His voice has been increasingly audible as years have rolled by. He has never forsaken me even in my darkest hour. He has saved me often against myself and left me not a vestige of independence. The greater the surrender to Him, the greater has been my joy."[37] What he craved was this absence of independence, the lack of autonomy, because that would finally allow him to see God face-to-face. He knew that he had not attained this state and perhaps would never attain it so long as his body remained, as "no one can be called a mukta while he is alive."[38]

In this we have an understanding of Gandhi's experiment and his quest. His quest is to know himself, to attain moksha, that is, to see God (Truth) face-to-face. In order to fulfill his quest, he must be an ashramite, a satyagrahi,[39] and a seeker after swaraj. Swaraj had deep resonance during India's struggle for freedom, and it continues to have both political and philosophical salience. Swaraj is composed of two terms, "swa" (self) and "raj" (rule). Swaraj is thus self-rule; Gandhi used it in two very different ways: self-rule and rule over the self. He added two other practices to this search. One was fasting, the other brahmacharya. Brahmacharya quite often is used in a limited sense of chastity or celibacy (including celibacy within marriage). Gandhi initially began with this sense, but as he thought deeper and struggled with a state devoid of sexual desire, he began to understand the root meaning of the term. "Brahma" is truth and "charya" is conduct. In the root sense, conduct that leads one to truth is brahmacharya. Fasting in its original sense is not mortification of the flesh but *Upvas*, to dwell closer to Him. *Upvas* is widely used to denote various acts of fasting. In the root sense, it is to dwell closer to God, wherein one of the modes of being close to God is fasting. In this sense, there could be no fast without a prayer and indeed no prayer without a fast. Such a fast was both penance and self-purification.

The ultimate practice of self-purification is the practice of brahmacharya. For Gandhi the realization of truth and self-gratification appears a contradiction in terms. From this emanates not only brahmacharya but also three other observances: control of the palate; aparigraha, or nonacquisition; and asteya, or non-stealing. The idea of nonacquisition has a place in all ascetic traditions of the world. Gandhi gave the term a profound ecological sense. It is only by nonacquisition that the earth could produce for the needs of all. Gandhi extended the meaning of the term "asteya." He argued that to possess in excess of what one needs is an act of theft. He further argued that anyone who eats without performing bodily labor also commits an act of theft. Such bodily labor had to be performed in the service of others, which he termed as sacrificial labor.

This was his understanding of the biblical injunction of living by the "sweat of one's brow."

Brahmacharya, described as a mahavrata, a difficult observance or a great endeavor, came to Gandhi as a necessary observance at a time when he had organized an ambulance corps during the Zulu rebellion in South Africa. He realized that service of the community was not possible without the observance of brahmacharya. In 1906, at the age of thirty-seven, Gandhi took the vow of brahmacharya.

He had begun experimenting with food and diet as a student in England. It was much later that he was to comprehend the relationship between brahmacharya and the control of the palate.

These observances and strivings of self-purification were not without a purpose. He was later to feel that they were secretly preparing him for satyagraha.[40] It would take him several decades, but through his observances, his experiments, Gandhi developed insights into the interrelatedness of truth, ahimsa, and brahmacharya. He came to regard the practice of brahmacharya in thought, word, and deed as essential for the search for truth and the practice of ahimsa. Gandhi, by making the observance of brahmacharya essential for truth and ahimsa, made it central to the practice of satyagraha and the quest for swaraj. Satyagraha involves the recognition of truth and the steadfast adherence to it; it requires self-sacrifice and self-suffering. It is predicated upon the use of pure, and that is nonviolent means by a person cleansed through self-purification. Satyagraha and swaraj are both modes of self-recognition. This understanding allowed Gandhi to expand the conception of brahmacharya itself. He began with a popular and restricted notion in the sense of chastity and celibacy, including celibacy in marriage. He expanded this notion to mean observance in thought, word, and deed. However, it is only when he began to recognize the deeper and fundamental relationship that brahmacharya shared with satyagraha, ahimsa, and swaraj that Gandhi could go to the root of the term "brahmacharya." Charya or conduct adopted in search of Brahma, that truth is brahmacharya. In this sense brahmacharya is not denial or control over one sense, but an attempt to bring all senses in harmony with one another. Brahmacharya so conceived and practiced becomes that mode of conduct that leads to truth, knowledge, and hence moksha. Thus, the ability to hear the inner voice, a voice that is "perfect knowledge or realization of truth,"[41] is an experiment in brahmacharya.

Gandhi was acutely and painfully aware of the fact that "it is impossible for us to realize perfect truth so long as we are imprisoned in this mortal frame."[42] If perfect truth was an unattainable quest, so was the attainment of perfect brahmacharya. What was given to us, Gandhi argued, was to perfect the means to truth or brahmacharya. The means for him was the practice of ahimsa or love. Gandhi asserted that ahimsa be regarded as the means to be within our grasp. This places nonviolence in a different category. Nonviolence is for Gandhi attainable and hence it becomes the duty of those seeking truth to practice nonviolence.

It is the capacity to hear the inner voice that for Gandhi reveals the distance he has traversed in his quest. Each invocation of the inner voice indicated to him his submission to God. This listening required proximity with oneself. This proximity could be attained through the practice of ahimsa. Violence on the other hand increased the distance in this quest for self-realization. Violence is to be abjured for this reason. Gandhi clearly stated this aspect of violence: "the more he took to violence, the more he receded from truth."[43] Ahimsa is a necessity and a supreme duty for Gandhi in this sense. It made possible the realization of God, if not face-to-face, then through the mediation of the small, still voice speaking from within and pointing out to him the path of duty.

This selection in no way seeks to present the "science of ahimsa." However, it is an attempt to capture something of Gandhi's incessant striving to comprehend ahimsa, to soak his being with it, to practice it both as personal virtue and political ethic, to foster a community of coworkers, to seek resolution of the violence inherent in structurally unequal human relations and also of wars between nations. Also it hopes to represent the myriad ways and forms in which Gandhi communicated his ideas. Gandhi wrote letters and essays, gave speeches, and answered questions. The ninety-seven volumes of his collected writings bear testimony to Gandhi's literary flair, the creative ways in which he employed each of the literary forms—save the novel—to convey his strivings and kindle our collective conscience. All of the selections presented in this book are from *The Collected Works of Mahatma Gandhi* (CWMG). There are one hundred volumes, of which ninety-seven contain his writings or speeches, that could be authenticated with a source. Each item is referenced to the volume and page number(s) of the *CWMG*.

This book is divided into eight sections. This division is done despite the awareness that for Gandhi the field of nonviolence was indivisible; its manifestations and practice had to move like an unbroken thread to form the warp and weft through which he sought to weave the tapestry that was his life.

The book includes selections from his philosophical writings, statements before courts, and letters to his associates and adversaries and even those who were not acquaintances—like Adolf Hitler. Some of these selections are deeply spiritual while others go into the nitty-gritty of political movements and the conduct of civil resisters, and debate the questions of the Great War or the ethics of causing harm to monkeys and dogs.

The last item, an excerpt from a talk with Manu Gandhi included in this anthology's final section, "Dark Night of the Soul," bears attention.

It captures the moment when "light" seemed to have penetrated "the dark night of the soul" that Gandhi experienced. It captures the moment when consolation reappears, faith stands firm. In it Gandhi speaks of his desire to give one final demonstration of his striving for truth and nonviolence, and his hope, his aspiration to embrace death—violent death—as a devotee.

That this desire was fulfilled, that Gandhi stopped three bullets in their path of hate and obtained a death that he wished for, is also a fulfillment of our political destiny; that as people we are called upon to bear witness to the violent deaths of our exemplars.

TRIDIP SUHRUD

NOTES

1. M. K. Gandhi, *From Yeravda Mandir*, translated from the original Gujarati by Valji Govindji Desai (Ahmedabad: Navajivan, 1932/2003), p. 5.

2. "Ahimsa" is usually translated as nonviolence or non-killing, but Gandhi was aware that these were inadequate translations of the term. He believed that the Christian idea of love best captured the various meanings that he attributed to the term "ahimsa." Hence, in his *From Yeravda Mandir*, the term "ahimsa" has been translated as "love."

3. M. K. Gandhi, *An Autobiography or The Story of My Experiments with Truth: A Critical Edition*, introduced and annotated by Tridip Suhrud (New Haven and London: Yale University Press, 2018, and New Delhi: Penguin Random House India, 2018).

4. The term "science" indicated a Sanskrit term *Shastra*, which would also translate as scripture. We should remember that both "science" and "scripture" have authority in their domains.

5. M. K. Gandhi, *The Collected Works of Mahatma Gandhi* (*CWMG*), vol. 83 (New Delhi: Publications Division, Government of India), p. 180.

6. Ibid.

7. Ibid.

8. The most systematic exposition of these two terms occurs for the first time in Gandhi's 1909 text *Hind Swaraj*.

9. *CWMG*, vol. 18, p. 133.

10. *CWMG*, vol. 66, pp. 420–21.

11. M. K. Gandhi, *An Autobiography or The Story of My Experiments with Truth*, translated from the original Gujarati by Mahadev Desai (Ahmedabad: Navajivan, 1927/1999), p. x.

12. Ibid., p. xi.

13. *CWMG*, vol. 55, p. 255.

14. Ibid.

15. Gandhi, *An Autobiography* [Suhrud], p. 665.

16. There is no English substitute that captures the full range of meanings that the word "swaraj" invokes. It has been loosely translated as freedom (which presupposes slavery) and self- or home-rule (which presupposes political subjugation). Gandhi himself preferred to use the term "swaraj."

17. M. K. Gandhi, *Hind Swaraj*. First published in 1909, Gandhi translated it into English, which was published in 1911. All references hereafter to *Hind Swaraj* are from the thirteenth reprint published in 2000 by the Navajivan Press, Ahmedabad.

18. The Gujarati term that he used was *"kudhar,"* literally the wrong way.

19. *Hind Swaraj*, p. 31.

20. Ibid., p. 53.

21. Ibid., p. 56.

22. Ibid.

23. *CWMG*, vol. 55, p. 256.

24. *CWMG*, vol. 52, p. 244.

25. Ibid., vol. 53, p. 483.

26. Ibid.

27. Ibid.

28. Ibid., vol. 25, pp. 23–24.

29. Ibid.

30. Ibid., vol. 52, p. 130.

31. These eleven vows are truth, ahimsa or love (also called non-violence), brahmacharya or chastity, control of the palate, non-stealing, nonpossession or poverty, bread labor, fearlessness, removal of untouchability, tolerance or equality of all religions, and swadeshi or promotion of native goods.

32. Gandhi explained the ashram as a community of co-religionists. This ancient institution came to be transformed by Gandhi. His ashram did not recognize any distinction of caste, gender, or race, and bodily labor was mandated for all members.

33. Bhagavad Gita, discourse II: verse 55. "Atman" is often translated as soul. Gandhi's preferred usage was "spirit" or the "dweller within."

34. Ibid., verse 68.

35. Ibid., verse 56.

36. Ibid., 64. Brahmachari is literally the one who practices brahmacharya and often refers to the celibate one.

37. *CWMG*, vol. 55, p. 121.

38. Ibid., vol. 37, p. 116. "Mukta" means free; in this context, one who is free from the cycle of birth-death-rebirth.

39. Satyagrahi is one who is steadfast to truth. Quite often it is used to denote a civil resister. In this essay it is used in the former sense.

40. Gandhi, *An Autobiography* [Suhrud], p. 345.

41. *CWMG*, vol. 56, p. 182.

42. M. K. Gandhi, *From Yeravda Mandir*, p. 5.

43. Ibid.

The Power of
Nonviolent Resistance

I.

FOUNDATION

Gandhi's insistence that nonviolence is not only an ancient virtue that we should aspire to cultivate but the very foundation of modern polity and society remains one of his most enduring of strivings. This section presents some of the foundational interventions through which Gandhi explained his conduct and laid bare the intricacies of nonviolent action. The selection opens with Gandhi's speech at the Empire Theatre in Johannesburg on September 11, 1906, the day regarded as the advent of satyagraha and closes with Gandhi's testimony on the duty of disloyalty at a trial in Ahmedabad.

1.
The Advent of Satyagraha

The meeting was duly held on September 11, 1906. It was attended by delegates from various places in the Transvaal. But I must confess that even I myself had not then understood all the implications of the resolutions* I had helped to frame; nor had I gauged all the possible conclusions to which they might lead. The old Empire Theatre was packed from floor to ceiling. I could read in every face the expectation of something strange to be done or to happen. Mr. Abdul Gani, Chairman of the Transvaal British Indian Association, presided. He was one of

* For the text of the resolutions see the next item.

the oldest Indian residents of the Transvaal, and partner and
manager of the Johannesburg branch of the well-known firm
of Mamad Kasam Kamrudin. The most important among the
resolutions passed by the meeting was the famous Fourth Resolution by which the Indians solemnly determined not to submit to the Ordinance in the event of its becoming law in the
teeth of their opposition and to suffer all the penalties attach-
ing to such non-submission. I fully explained this resolution to
the meeting and received a patient hearing. The business of the
meeting was conducted in Hindi or Gujarati; it was impossible
therefore that anyone present should not follow the proceedings. For the Tamils and Telugus who did not know Hindi
there were Tamil and Telugu speakers who fully explained everything in their respective languages. The resolution was duly
proposed, seconded, and supported by several speakers one of
whom was Sheth Haji Habib. He, too, was a very old and experienced resident of South Africa and made an impassioned
speech. He was deeply moved and went so far as to say that we
must pass this resolution with God as witness and must never
yield a cowardly submission to such degrading legislation. He
then went on solemnly to declare in the name of God that he
would never submit to that law, and advised all present to do
likewise. Others also delivered powerful and angry speeches in
supporting the resolution. When in the course of his speech
Sheth Haji Habib came to the solemn declaration, I was at
once startled and put on my guard. Only then did I fully realize my own responsibility and the responsibility of the community. The community had passed many a resolution before and
amended such resolutions in the light of further reflection or
fresh experience. There were cases in which resolutions passed
had not been observed by all concerned. Amendments in resolutions and failure to observe resolutions on the part of persons agreeing thereto are ordinary experiences of public life all
the world over. But no one ever imports the name of God into
such resolutions. In the abstract there should not be any distinction between a resolution and an oath taken in the name of
God. When an intelligent man makes a resolution deliberately
he never swerves from it by a hairsbreadth. With him his reso-

lution carries as much weight as a declaration made with God as witness does. But the world takes no note of abstract principles and imagines an ordinary resolution and an oath in the name of God to be poles asunder. A man who makes an ordinary resolution is not ashamed of himself when he deviates from it, but a man who violates an oath administered to him is not only ashamed of himself but is also looked upon by society as a sinner. This imaginary distinction has struck such a deep root in the human mind that a person making a statement on oath before a judge is held to have committed an offense in law if the statement is proved to be false and receives drastic punishment. Full of these thoughts as I was, possessing as I did much experience of solemn pledges, having profited by them, I was taken aback by Sheth Haji Habib's suggestion of an oath. I thought out the possible consequences of it in a moment. My perplexity gave place to enthusiasm. And although I had no intention of taking an oath or inviting others to do so, when I went to the meeting I warmly approved of the Sheth's suggestion. But at the same time it seemed to me that the people should be told of all the consequences and should have explained to them clearly the meaning of a pledge. And if even then they were prepared to pledge themselves, they should be encouraged to do so; otherwise, I must understand that they were not still ready to stand the final test. I therefore asked the president for permission to explain to the meeting the implications of Sheth Haji Habib's suggestion. The president readily granted it and I rose to address the meeting. I give below a summary of my remarks just as I can recall them now: "I wish to explain to this meeting that there is a vast difference between this resolution and every other resolution we have passed up to date and that there is a wide divergence also in the manner of making it. It is a very grave resolution we are making, as our existence in South Africa depends upon our fully observing it. The manner of making the resolution suggested by our friend is as much of a novelty as of a solemnity. I did not come to the meeting with a view to getting the resolution passed in that manner, which redounds to the credit of Sheth Haji Habib as well as it lays a burden of responsibility upon him. I tender my congratulations to him. I deeply appreciate his suggestion, but if you adopt it you too will share his responsibility. You must understand what is this responsibility, and as an adviser and servant of the community, it is my duty fully to explain it to you.

"We all believe in one and the same God, the differences of nomenclature in Hinduism and Islam notwithstanding. To pledge ourselves or to take an oath in the name of that God or with Him as witness is not something to be trifled with. If having taken such an oath we violate our pledge we are guilty before God and man. Personally I hold that a man who deliberately and intelligently takes a pledge and then breaks it forfeits his manhood. And just as a copper coin treated with mercury not only becomes valueless when detected but also makes its owner liable to punishment, in the same way a man who lightly pledges his word and then breaks it becomes a man of straw and fits himself for punishment here as well as hereafter. Sheth Haji Habib is proposing to administer an oath of a very serious character. There is no one in this meeting who can be classed as an infant or as wanting in understanding. You are all well advanced in age and have seen the world; many of you are delegates and have discharged responsibilities in a greater or lesser measure. No one present, therefore, can ever hope to excuse himself by saying that he did not know what he was about when he took the oath.

"I know that pledges and vows are, and should be, taken on rare occasions. A man who takes a vow every now and then is sure to stumble. But if I can imagine a crisis in the history of the Indian community of South Africa when it would be in the fitness of things to take pledges, that crisis is surely now. There is wisdom in taking serious steps with great caution and hesitation. But caution and hesitation have their limits, and we have now passed them. The government has taken leave of all sense of decency. We would only be betraying our unworthiness and cowardice, if we cannot stake our all in the face of the conflagration which envelops us and sit watching it with folded hands. There is no doubt, therefore, that the present is a proper occasion for taking pledges. But every one of us must think out for himself if he has the will and the ability to pledge himself.

Resolutions of this nature cannot be passed by a majority vote. Only those who take a pledge can be bound by it. This pledge must not be taken with a view to producing an effect on outsiders. No one should trouble to consider what impression it might have upon the local government, the imperial government, or the government of India. Everyone must only search his own heart, and if the inner voice assures him that he has the requisite strength to carry him through, then only should he pledge himself and then only will his pledge bear fruit.

"A few words now as to the consequences. Hoping for the best, we may say that if a majority of the Indians pledge themselves to resistance and if all who take the pledge prove true to themselves, the ordinance may not be passed and, if passed, may be soon repealed. It may be that we may not be called upon to suffer at all. But if on the one hand a man who takes a pledge must be a robust optimist, on the other hand he must be prepared for the worst. Therefore I want to give you an idea of the worst that might happen to us in the present struggle. Imagine that all of us present here numbering three thousand at the most pledge ourselves. Imagine again that the remaining ten thousand Indians take no such pledge. We will only provoke ridicule in the beginning. Again, it is quite possible that in spite of the present warning some or many of those who pledge themselves may weaken at the very first trial. We may have to go to jail, where we may be insulted. We may have to go hungry and suffer extreme heat or cold. Hard labor may be imposed upon us. We may be flogged by rude warders. We may be fined heavily and our property may be attached and held up to auction if there are only a few resisters left. Opulent today, we may be reduced to abject poverty tomorrow. We may be deported. Suffering from starvation and similar hardships in jail, some of us may fall ill and even die. In short, therefore, it is not at all impossible that we may have to endure every hardship that we can imagine, and wisdom lies in pledging ourselves on the understanding that we shall have to suffer all that and worse. If someone asks me when and how the struggle may end, I may say that if the entire community manfully stands the test, the end will be near. If many of us fall back under storm and stress, the struggle will be prolonged. But I can boldly declare, and with certainty, that so long as there is even a handful of men true to their pledge, there can only be one end to the struggle, and that is victory.

"A word about my personal responsibility. If I am warning you of the risks attendant upon the pledge, I am at the same time inviting you to pledge yourselves, and I am fully conscious of my responsibility in the matter. It is possible that a majority of those present here may take the pledge in a fit of enthusiasm or indignation but may weaken under the ordeal, and only a handful may be left to face the final test. Even then there is only one course open to someone like me, to die but not to submit to the law. It is quite unlikely but even if everyone else flinched, leaving me alone to face the music, I am confident that I would never violate my pledge. Please do not misunderstand me. I am not saying this out of vanity, but I wish to put you, especially the leaders upon the platform, on your guard. I wish respectfully to suggest it to you that if you have not the will or the ability to stand firm even when you are perfectly isolated, you must not only not take the pledge yourselves but you must declare your opposition before the resolution is put to the meeting and before its members begin to take pledges and you must not make yourselves parties to the resolution. Although we are going to take the pledge in a body, no one should imagine that default on the part of one or many can absolve the rest from their obligation. Everyone should fully realize his responsibility, then only pledge himself independently of others and understand that he himself must be true to his pledge even unto death, no matter what others do."

CWMG, vol. 29, *Satyagraha in South Africa*, pp. 86–90

2.
Resolutions Passed at the Meeting

RESOLUTION I

This mass meeting of British Indians here assembled, respectfully urges the Honourable the President and Members of the Legislative Council of the Transvaal not to pass the Draft Asiatic Ordinance to amend Law No. 3 of 1885, now before that Honourable House, in view of the facts that:

(1) It is, so far as the Indian community of the Transvaal is concerned, a highly contentious measure.

(2) It subjects the British Indian community of the Transvaal to degradation and insult totally undeserved by its past history.

(3) The present machinery is sufficient for checking the alleged influx of Asiatics.

(4) The statements as to the alleged influx are denied by the British Indian community.

(5) If the Honourable House is not satisfied with the denial, this meeting invites [an] open, judicial, and British enquiry into the question of the alleged influx.

RESOLUTION II

This mass meeting of British Indians here assembled respectfully protests against the Draft Asiatic Law Amendment Ordinance now being considered by the Legislative Council of the Transvaal, and humbly requests the local Government and the

Imperial Authorities to withdraw the Draft Ordinance, for the reasons that:

(1) It is manifestly in conflict with the past declarations of His Majesty's representatives.

(2) It recognises no distinction between British and alien Asiatics.

(3) It reduces British Indians to a status lower than that of the aboriginal races of South Africa and the Coloured people.

(4) It renders the position of British Indians in the Transvaal much worse than under Law 3 of 1885, and, therefore, than under the Boer regime. 1 In accordance with Resolution V, copies of Resolutions II, III and IV were sent to the Secretary of State for India through the Governor of the Transvaal, who was also requested to telegraph their substance to the Viceroy of India. Vide p. 423 and Cd. 3308 issued in February 1907.

(5) It sets up a system of passes and espionage unknown in any other British territory.

(6) It brands the communities to which it is applied as criminals or suspects.

(7) The alleged influx of unauthorised British Indians into the Transvaal is denied.

(8) If such denial is not accepted, a judicial, open and British enquiry should be instituted before such drastic and uncalled for legislation is enforced.

(9) The measure is otherwise un-British and unduly restricts the liberty of inoffensive British subjects and constitutes a compulsory invitation to British Indians in the Transvaal to leave the country.

(10) This meeting further and especially requests the Right Honourable the Secretary of State for the Colonies and the Right Honourable the Secretary of State for India to suspend the Royal sanction and to receive a deputation on behalf of the British Indian community of the Transvaal in connection with this Draft Ordinance.

RESOLUTION III

This meeting hereby appoints a delegation with power from the Committee of the British Indian Association to add to its membership or to change its personnel, to proceed to England and to lay before the Imperial Authorities the complaint of the British Indian community of the Transvaal regarding the Draft Asiatic Law Amendment Ordinance.

RESOLUTION IV

In the event of the Legislative Council, the local Government, and the Imperial Authorities rejecting the humble prayer of the British Indian community of the Transvaal in connection with the Draft Asiatic Law Amendment Ordinance, this mass meeting of British Indians here assembled solemnly and regretfully resolves that, rather than submit to the galling, tyrannous, and un-British requirements laid down in the above Draft Ordinance, every British Indian in the Transvaal shall submit himself to imprisonment and shall continue so to do until it shall please His Most Gracious Majesty the King-Emperor to grant relief.

RESOLUTION V

This meeting desires the Chairman to forward copy of the first resolution to the Honourable the President and Members of the Legislative Council, and copies of all the resolutions to the

Honourable the Colonial Secretary, to His Excellency the Acting Lieutenant-Governor, and to His Excellency the High
Commissioner, and to request His Excellency the High Commissioner to cable the text of resolutions Nos. 2, 3 and 4 to the
Imperial Authorities.

CWMG, vol. 5, pp. 422–23

3.
Excerpts from *Hind Swaraj*

CHAPTER XVI: BRUTE FORCE*

READER: This is a new doctrine, that what is gained through
fear is retained only while the fear lasts. Surely, what is given
will not be withdrawn?

EDITOR: Not so. The Proclamation of 1857 was given at
the end of a revolt, and for the purpose of preserving peace.
When peace was secured and people became simpleminded, its
full effect was toned down. If I cease stealing for fear of punishment, I would recommence the operation as soon as the fear
is withdrawn from me. This is almost a universal experience.
We have assumed that we can get men to do things by force
and, therefore, we use force.

READER: Will you not admit that you are arguing against
yourself? You know that what the English obtained in their
own country they obtained by using brute force. I know you
have argued that what they have obtained is useless, but that
does not affect my argument. They wanted useless things and
they got them. My point is that their desire was fulfilled. What
does it matter what means they adopted? Why should we not
obtain our goal, which is good, by any means whatsoever, even

* This and the following chapter "Passive Resistance" are from MKG's
philosophical seed text *Hind Swaraj*, written in 1909.

by using violence? Shall I think of the means when I have to deal with a thief in the house? My duty is to drive him out anyhow. You seem to admit that we have received nothing, and that we shall receive nothing, by petitioning. Why, then, may we not do so by using brute force? And, to retain what we may receive, we shall keep up the fear by using the same force to the extent that it may be necessary. You will not find fault with a continuance of force to prevent a child from thrusting its foot into fire? Somehow or other we have to gain our end.

EDITOR: Your reasoning is plausible. It has deluded many. I have used similar arguments before now. But I think I know better now, and I shall endeavor to undeceive you. Let us first take the argument that we are justified in gaining our end by using brute force because the English gained theirs by using similar means. It is perfectly true that they used brute force and that it is possible for us to do likewise, but by using similar means we can get only the same thing that they got. You will admit that we do not want that. Your belief that there is no connection between the means and the end is a great mistake. Through that mistake even men who have been considered religious have committed grievous crimes. Your reasoning is the same as saying that we can get a rose through planting a noxious weed. If I want to cross the ocean, I can do so only by means of a vessel; if I were to use a cart for that purpose, both the cart and I would soon find the bottom. "As is the God, so is the votary" is a maxim worth considering. Its meaning has been distorted and men have gone astray. The means may be likened to a seed, the end to a tree; and there is just the same inviolable connection between the means and the end as there is between the seed and the tree. I am not likely to obtain the result flowing from the worship of God by laying myself prostrate before Satan. If, therefore, anyone were to say: "I want to worship God; it does not matter that I do so by means of Satan," it would be set down as ignorant folly. We reap exactly as we sow. The English in 1833 obtained greater voting power by violence. Did they by using brute force better appreciate their duty? They wanted the right of voting, which they obtained by using physical force. But real rights are a result of performance of duty; these rights they have not obtained. We, therefore, have before us in England the force of everybody wanting and insisting on his rights, nobody thinking of his duty. And, where everybody wants rights, who shall give them to whom? I do not wish to imply that they do no duties. They don't perform the duties corresponding to those rights; and as they do not perform that particular duty, namely, acquire fitness, their rights have proved a burden to them. In other words, what they have obtained is an exact result of the means they adopted. They used the means corresponding to the end. If I want to deprive you of your watch, I shall certainly have to fight for it; if I want to buy your watch, I shall have to pay you for it; and if I want a gift I shall have to plead for it; and, according to the means I employ, the watch is stolen property, my own property, or a donation. Thus we see three different results from three different means. Will you still say that means do not matter? Now we shall take the example given by you of the thief to be driven out. I do not agree with you that the thief may be driven out by any means. If it is my father who has come to steal I shall use one kind of means. If it is an acquaintance I shall use another; and in the case of a perfect stranger I shall use a third. If it is a white man, you will perhaps say you will use means different from those you will adopt with an Indian thief. If it is a weakling, the means will be different from those to be adopted for dealing with an equal in physical strength; and if the thief is armed from top to toe, I shall simply remain quiet. Thus we have a variety of means between the father and the armed man. Again, I fancy that I should pretend to be sleeping whether the thief was my father or that strong-armed man. The reason for this is that my father would also be armed and I should succumb to the strength possessed by either and allow my things to be stolen. The strength of my father would make me weep with pity; the strength of the armed man would rouse in me anger and we should become enemies. Such is the curious situation. From these examples we may not be able to agree as to the means to be adopted in each case. I myself seem clearly to see what should be done in all these cases, but the remedy may frighten you. I therefore hesitate to place it before you. For the time being I will leave you to guess it, and if you cannot, it is clear you will have to adopt different means in each case. You will also have seen that any means will not avail to drive away the thief. You will have to adopt means to fit each case. Hence it follows that your duty is not to drive away the thief by any means you like.

Let us proceed a little further. That well-armed man has stolen your property; you have harbored the thought of his act; you are filled with anger; you argue that you want to punish that rogue, not for your own sake, but for the good of your neighbors; you have collected a number of armed men, you want to take his house by assault; he is duly informed of it, he runs away; he too is incensed. He collects his brother robbers and sends you a defiant message that he will commit robbery in broad daylight. You are strong, you do not fear him, you are prepared to receive him. Meanwhile, the robber pesters your neighbors. They complain before you. You reply that you are doing all for their sake, you do not mind that your own goods have been stolen. Your neighbors reply that the robber never pestered them before, and that he commenced his depredations only after you declared hostilities against him. You are between Scylla and Charybdis. You are full of pity for the poor men. What they say is true. What are you to do? You will be disgraced if you now leave the robber alone. You, therefore, tell the poor men: "Never mind. Come, my wealth is yours, I will give you arms, I will teach you how to use them; you should belabor the rogue; don't you leave him alone." And so the battle grows; the robbers increase in numbers; your neighbors have deliberately put themselves to inconvenience. Thus the result of wanting to take revenge upon the robber is that you have disturbed your own peace; you are in perpetual fear of being robbed and assaulted; your courage has given place to cowardice. If you will patiently examine the argument, you will see that I have not overdrawn the picture. This is one of the means. Now let us examine the other. You set this armed robber down as an ignorant brother; you intend to reason with him at a suitable opportunity: you argue that he is, after all, a fellow man; you do not know what prompted him to steal. You, therefore, decide that, when you can, you will destroy the man's motive for stealing. Whilst you are thus reasoning with yourself, the man comes again to steal. Instead of being angry with him, you take pity on him. You think that this stealing habit must be a disease with him. Henceforth, you, therefore, keep your doors and windows open, you change your sleeping place, and you keep your things in a manner most accessible to him. The robber comes again and is confused as all this is new to him; nevertheless, he takes away your things. But his mind is agitated. He inquires about you in the village; he comes to learn about your broad and loving heart; he repents; he begs your pardon, returns you your things, and leaves off the stealing habit. He becomes your servant, and you find for him honorable employment. This is the second method. Thus, you see, different means have brought about totally different results. I do not wish to deduce from this that robbers will act in the above manner or that all will have the same pity and love like you, but I only wish to show that fair means alone can produce fair results, and that, at least in the majority of cases, if not indeed in all, the force of love and pity is infinitely greater than the force of arms. There is harm in the exercise of brute force, never in that of pity. Now we will take the question of petitioning. It is a fact beyond dispute that a petition, without the backing of force, is useless. However, the late Justice Ranade used to say that petitions served a useful purpose because they were a means of educating people. They give the latter an idea of their condition and warn the rulers. From this point of view, they are not altogether useless. A petition of an equal is a sign of courtesy; a petition from a slave is a symbol of his slavery. A petition backed by force is a petition from an equal and, when he transmits his demand in the form of a petition, it testifies to his nobility. Two kinds of force can back petitions. "We shall hurt you if you do not give this" is one kind of force; it is the force of arms, whose evil results we have already examined. The second kind of force can thus be stated: "If you do not concede our demand, we shall be no longer your petitioners. You can govern us only so long as we remain the governed; we shall no longer have any dealings with you." The force implied in this may be described as love force, soul force, or, more popularly but less accurately, passive resistance. This force is indestructible. He who uses it perfectly understands his position. We have an ancient proverb which literally means "One negative cures thirty-six diseases." The force of arms is powerless when matched against the force of love or the soul. Now we shall take your last illustration, that of the child thrusting its foot into fire. It will not avail you. What do you really do to the child? Supposing that it can exert so much physical force that it renders you powerless and rushes into fire, then you cannot prevent it. There are only two remedies open to you—either you must kill it in order to prevent it from perishing in the flames or you must give your own life because you do not wish to see it perish before your very eyes. You will not kill it. If your heart is not quite full of pity, it is possible that you will not surrender yourself by preceding the child and going into the fire yourself. You, therefore, helplessly allow it to go into the flames. Thus, at any rate, you are not using physical force. I hope you will not consider that it is still physical force, though of a low order, when you would forcibly prevent the child from rushing toward the fire if you could. That force is of a different order and we have to understand what it is.

Remember that, in thus preventing the child, you are minding entirely its own interest, you are exercising authority for its sole benefit. Your example does not apply to the English. In using brute force against the English you consult entirely your own, that is the national, interest. There is no question here either of pity or of love. If you say that the actions of the English, being evil, represent fire, and that they proceed to their actions through ignorance, and that therefore they occupy the position of a child and that you want to protect such a child, then you will have to overtake every evil action of that kind by whomsoever committed and, as in the case of the evil child, you will have to sacrifice yourself. If you are capable of such immeasurable pity, I wish you well in its exercise.

CHAPTER XVII: PASSIVE RESISTANCE

READER: Is there any historical evidence as to the success of what you have called soul force or truth force? No instance seems to have happened of any nation having risen through soul force. I still think that the evildoers will not cease doing evil without physical punishment.

EDITOR: The poet Tulsidas has said: "Of religion, pity, or love, is the root, as egotism of the body. Therefore, we should not abandon pity so long as we are alive." This appears to me to be a scientific truth. I believe in it as much as I believe in two and two being four. The force of love is the same as the force of the soul or truth. We have evidence of its working at every step. The universe would disappear without the existence of that force. But you ask for historical evidence. It is, therefore, necessary to know what history means. The Gujarati equivalent means: "It so happened." If that is the meaning of history, it is possible to give copious evidence. But, if it means the doings of kings and emperors, there can be no evidence of soul force or passive resistance in such history. You cannot expect silver ore in a tin mine. History, as we know it, is a record of the wars of the world, and so there is a proverb among Englishmen that a nation which has no history, that is, no wars, is a happy nation. How kings played, how they became enemies of one another, how they murdered one another, is found accurately recorded in history, and if this were all that had happened in the world, it would have been ended long ago. If the story of the universe had commenced with wars, not a man would have been found alive today. Those people who have been warred against have disappeared as, for instance, the natives of Australia of whom hardly a man was left alive by the intruders. Mark, please, that these natives did not use soul force in self-defense, and it does not require much foresight to know that the Australians will share the same fate as their victims. "Those that take the sword shall perish by the sword." With us the proverb is that professional swimmers will find a watery grave. The fact that there are so many men still alive in the world shows that it is based not on the force of arms but on the force of truth or love. Therefore, the greatest and most un-impeachable evidence of the success of this force is to be found in the fact that, in spite of the wars of the world, it still lives on. Thousands, indeed tens of thousands, depend for their exis-tence on a very active working of this force. Little quarrels of millions of families in their daily lives disappear before the ex-ercise of this force. Hundreds of nations live in peace. History does not and cannot take note of this fact. History is really a record of every interruption of the even working of the force of love or of the soul. Two brothers quarrel; one of them repents and reawakens the love that was lying dormant in him; the two again begin to live in peace; nobody takes note of this. But if the two brothers, through the intervention of solicitors or some other reason take up arms or go to law—which is another form of the exhibition of brute force—their doings would be imme-diately noticed in the press, they would be the talk of their neighbors and would probably go down to history. And what is true of families and communities is true of nations. There is no reason to believe that there is one law for families and an-other for nations. History, then, is a record of an interruption of the course of nature. Soul force, being natural, is not noted in history.

READER: According to what you say, it is plain that in-stances of this kind of passive resistance are not to be found in history. It is necessary to understand this passive resistance more fully. It will be better, therefore, if you enlarge upon it.

EDITOR: Passive resistance is a method of securing rights by personal suffering; it is the reverse of resistance by arms. When I refuse to do a thing that is repugnant to my conscience, I use soul force. For instance, the government of the day has passed a law which is applicable to me. I do not like it. If by using violence I force the government to repeal the law, I am employing what may be termed body force. If I do not obey the law and accept the penalty for its breach, I use soul force. It involves sacrifice of self. Everybody admits that sacrifice of self is infinitely superior to sacrifice of others. Moreover, if this kind of force is used in a cause that is unjust, only the person using it suffers. He does not make others suffer for his mistakes. Men have before now done many things which were subsequently found to have been wrong. No man can claim that he is absolutely in the right or that a particular thing is wrong because he thinks so, but it is wrong for him so long as that is his deliberate judgment. It is therefore meet that he should not do that which he knows to be wrong, and suffer the consequence whatever it may be. This is the key to the use of soul force.

READER: You would then disregard laws—this is rank disloyalty. We have always been considered a law-abiding nation. You seem to be going even beyond the extremists. They say that we must obey the laws that have been passed, but that if the laws be bad, we must drive out the lawgivers even by force.

EDITOR: Whether I go beyond them or whether I do not is a matter of no consequence to either of us. We simply want to find out what is right and to act accordingly. The real meaning of the statement that we are a law-abiding nation is that we are passive resisters. When we do not like certain laws, we do not break the heads of lawgivers but we suffer and do not submit to the laws. That we should obey laws whether good or bad is a newfangled notion. There was no such thing in former days. The people disregarded those laws they did not like and suffered the penalties for their breach. It is contrary to our manhood if we obey laws repugnant to our conscience. Such teaching is opposed to religion and means slavery. If the government were to ask us to go about without any clothing, should we do so? If I were a passive resister, I would say to them that I would have nothing to do with their law. But we have so forgotten ourselves and become so compliant that we do not mind any degrading law. A man who has realized his manhood, who fears only God, will fear no one else. Man-made laws are not necessarily binding on him. Even the government does not expect any such thing from us. They do not say: "You must do such and such a thing," but they say: "If you do not do it, we will punish you." We are sunk so low that we fancy that it is our duty and our religion to do what the law lays down. If man will only realize that it is unmanly to obey laws that are unjust, no man's tyranny will enslave him. This is the key to self-rule or home rule. It is a superstition and ungodly thing to believe that an act of a majority binds a minority. Many examples can be given in which acts of majorities will be found to have been wrong and those of minorities to have been right. All reforms owe their origin to the initiation of minorities in opposition to majorities. If among a band of robbers a knowledge of robbing is obligatory, is a pious man to accept the obligation? So long as the superstition that men should obey unjust laws exists, so long will their slavery exist. And a passive resister alone can remove such a superstition. To use brute force, to use gunpowder, is contrary to passive resistance, for it means that we want our opponent to do by force that which we desire but he does not. And if such a use of force is justifiable, surely he is entitled to do likewise by us. And so we should never come to an agreement. We may simply fancy, like the blind horse moving in a circle round a mill, that we are making progress. Those who believe that they are not bound to obey laws which are repugnant to their conscience have only the remedy of passive resistance open to them. Any other must lead to disaster.

READER: From what you say I deduce that passive resistance is a splendid weapon of the weak, but that when they are strong they may take up arms.

EDITOR: This is gross ignorance. Passive resistance, that is, soul force, is matchless. It is superior to the force of arms. How, then, can it be considered only a weapon of the weak? Physical-force men are strangers to the courage that is requisite in a passive resister. Do you believe that a coward can ever disobey a law that he dislikes? Extremists are considered to be advocates of brute force. Why do they, then, talk about obeying laws? I do not blame them. They can say nothing else. When they succeed in driving out the English and they themselves become governors, they will want you and me to obey their laws. And that is a fitting thing for their constitution. But a passive resister will say he will not obey a law that is against his conscience, even though he may be blown to pieces at the mouth of a cannon. What do you think? Wherein is courage required—in blowing others to pieces from behind a cannon, or with a smiling face to approach a cannon and be blown to pieces? Who is the true warrior?—he who keeps death always as a bosom friend, or he who controls the death of others? Believe me that a man devoid of courage and manhood can never be a passive resister. This, however, I will admit: that even a man weak in body is capable of offering this resistance. One man can offer it just as well as millions. Both men and women can indulge in it. It does not require the training of an army; it needs no jujitsu. Control over the mind is alone necessary, and when that is attained, man is free like the king of the forest and his very glance withers the enemy. Passive resistance is an all-sided sword, it can be used anyhow; it blesses him who uses it and him against whom it is used. Without drawing a drop of blood it produces far-reaching results. It never rusts and cannot be stolen. Competition between passive resisters does not exhaust. The sword of passive resistance does not require a scabbard. It is strange indeed that you should consider such a weapon to be a weapon merely of the weak.

READER: You have said that passive resistance is a specialty of India. Have cannons never been used in India?

EDITOR: Evidently, in your opinion, India means its few princes. To me it means its teeming millions on whom depends the existence of its princes and our own. Kings will always use their kingly weapons. To use force is bred in them. They want to command, but those who have to obey commands do not want guns: and these are in a majority throughout the world. They have to learn either body force or soul force. Where they learn the former, both the rulers and the ruled become like so many madmen; but where they learn soul force, the commands of the rulers do not go beyond the point of their swords, for true men disregard unjust commands. Peasants have never been subdued by the sword, and never will be. They do not know the use of the sword, and they are not frightened by the use of it by others. That nation is great which rests its head upon death as its pillow. Those who defy death are free from all fear. For those who are laboring under the delusive charms of brute force, this picture is not overdrawn. The fact is that, in India, the nation at large has generally used passive resistance in all departments of life. We cease to cooperate with our rulers when they displease us. This is passive resistance. I remember an instance when, in a small principality, the villagers were offended by some command issued by the prince. The former immediately began vacating the village. The prince became nervous, apologized to his subjects, and withdrew his command. Many such instances can be found in India. Real home rule is possible only where passive resistance is the guiding force of the people. Any other rule is foreign rule.

READER: Then you will say that it is not at all necessary for us to train the body?

EDITOR: I will certainly not say any such thing. It is difficult to become a passive resister unless the body is trained. As a rule, the mind, residing in a body that has become weakened by pampering, is also weak, and where there is no strength of mind there can be no strength of soul. We shall have to improve our physique by getting rid of infant marriages and luxurious living. If I were to ask a man with a shattered body to face a cannon's mouth, I should make a laughingstock of myself.

READER: From what you say, then, it would appear that it is not a small thing to become a passive resister, and, if that is so, I should like you to explain how a man may become one.

EDITOR: To become a passive resister is easy enough, but it is also equally difficult. I have known a lad of fourteen years become a passive resister; I have known also sick people do likewise; and I have also known physically strong and otherwise happy people unable to take up passive resistance. After a great deal of experience it seems to me that those who want to become passive resisters for the service of the country have to observe perfect chastity, adopt poverty, follow truth, and cultivate fearlessness. Chastity is one of the greatest disciplines without which the mind cannot attain requisite firmness. A man who is unchaste loses stamina, becomes emasculated and cowardly. He whose mind is given over to animal passions is not capable of any great effort. This can be proved by innumerable instances. What, then, is a married person to do is the question that arises naturally; and yet it need not. When a husband and wife gratify the passions, it is no less an animal indulgence on that account. Such an indulgence, except for perpetuating the race, is strictly prohibited. But a passive resister has to avoid even that very limited indulgence because he can have no desire for progeny. A married man, therefore, can observe perfect chastity. This subject is not capable of being treated at greater length. Several questions arise: How is one to carry one's wife with one, what are her rights, and other similar questions. Yet those who wish to take part in a great work are bound to solve these puzzles. Just as there is necessity for chastity, so is there for poverty. Pecuniary ambition and passive resistance cannot well go together. Those who have money are not expected to throw it away, but they are expected to be indifferent about it. They must be prepared to lose every penny rather than give up passive resistance. Passive resistance has been described in the course of our discussion as truth force. Truth, therefore, has necessarily to be followed and that at any cost. In this connection, academic questions such as whether a man may not lie in order to save a life, etc., arise, but these questions occur only to those who wish to justify lying. Those who want to follow truth every time are not placed in such a quandary; and if they are, they are still saved from a false position. Passive resistance cannot proceed a step without fearlessness. Those alone can follow the path of passive resistance who are free from fear, whether as to their possessions, false honor, their relatives, the government, bodily injuries, or death. These observances are not to be abandoned in the belief that they are difficult. Nature has implanted in the human breast ability to cope with any difficulty or suffering that may come to man unprovoked. These qualities are worth having, even for those who do not wish to serve the country. Let there be no mistake, as those who want to train themselves in the use of arms are also obliged to have these qualities more or less. Everybody does not become a warrior for the wish. A would-be warrior will have to observe chastity and to be satisfied with poverty as his lot. A warrior without fearlessness cannot be conceived of. It may be thought that he would not need to be exactly truthful, but that quality follows real fearlessness. When a man abandons truth, he does so owing to fear in some shape or form. The above four attributes, then, need not frighten anyone. It may be as well here to note that a physical-force man has to have many other useless qualities which a passive resister never needs. And you will find that whatever extra effort a swordsman needs is due to lack of fearlessness. If he is an embodiment of the latter, the sword will drop from his hand that very moment. He does not need its support. One who is free from hatred requires no sword. A man with a stick suddenly came face-to-face with a lion and instinctively raised his weapon in self-defense. The man saw that he had only prated about fearlessness when there was none in him. That moment he dropped the stick and found himself free from all fear.

4.
Excerpts from *From Yeravda Mandir*

I deal first with truth,* as the Satyagraha Ashram owes its very existence to the pursuit and the attempted practice of truth. The word *"satya"* is derived from *"sat,"* which means that which is. *Satya* means a state of being. Nothing is or exists in reality except Truth. That is why *sat* or *satya* is the right name for God. In fact, it is more correct to say that Truth is God than to say that God is Truth. But as we cannot do without a ruler or a general, the name God is and will remain more current. On deeper thinking, however, it will be realized that *sat*

---

* This and the other discourses on the Ashram vows contained in the letters to Narandas Gandhi were written during MKG's imprisonment in 1930 following the civil disobedience movement, known as the Salt March, and first appeared in book form under the title *Mangal Prabhat* (*Tuesday Morning* or *Auspicious Morning*). The translation is reproduced from *From Yeravda Mandir*, with a few changes to bring it into conformity with the Gujarati. MKG states in the preface to the booklet that he had gone through it carefully and revised the translation in places.

or *satya* is the only correct and fully significant name for God. And where there is Truth, there also is knowledge which is true. Where there is no Truth, there can be no true knowledge. That is why the word "chit" or "knowledge" is associated with the name of God. And where there is true knowledge, there is always *ananda*, bliss. There sorrow has no place. And even as Truth is eternal, so is the bliss derived from it. Hence we know God as Sat-chit-*ananda*, one who combines in Himself Truth, knowledge, and bliss. Devotion to this Truth is the sole justification for our existence. All our activities should be centered in truth. Truth should be the very breath of our life. When once this stage in the pilgrim's progress is reached, all other rules of correct living will come without effort and obedience to them will be instinctive. But without Truth it is impossible to observe any principles or rules in life. Generally speaking, [observance of the law of] Truth is understood merely to mean that we must speak the truth. But we in the Ashram should understand the word "*satya*" or Truth in a much wider sense. There should be Truth in thought, Truth in speech, and Truth in action. To the man who has realized this Truth in its fullness, nothing else remains to be known, because, as we have seen above, all knowledge is necessarily included in it. What is not included in it is not Truth, and so not true knowledge; and there can be no real bliss without true knowledge. If we once learn how to apply this never-failing test of Truth, we will at once be able to find out what is worth doing, what is worth seeing, what is worth reading. But how is one to realize this Truth, which may be likened to the philosopher's stone or the cow of plenty? By *abhyasa*, single-minded devotion, and *vairagya*, indifference to all other interests in life—replies the Bhagavad Gita. Even so, what may appear as truth to one person will often appear as untruth to another person. But that need not worry the seeker. Where there is honest effort, it will be realized that what appear to be different truths are like the countless and apparently different leaves of the same tree. Does not God Himself appear to different individuals in different aspects? Yet we know that He is one. But Truth is the right designation of God. Hence there is nothing wrong in every man following Truth according to his lights. Indeed it is his duty to do so. Then if there is a mistake on the part of anyone so following Truth, it will be automatically set right. For the quest of Truth involves *tapascharya*, self-suffering, sometimes even unto death. There can be no place in it for even a trace of self-interest. In such selfless search for Truth, nobody can lose his bearings for long. Directly he takes to the wrong path he stumbles and is thus redirected to the right path. Therefore the pursuit of Truth is true *bhakti*, devotion. Such *bhakti* is "a bargain in which one risks one's very life." It is the path that leads to God. There is no place in it for cowardice, no place for defeat. It is the talisman by which death itself becomes the portal to life eternal. But now we have come to the borderline beyond which lies ahimsa. We shall discuss it next week. In this connection, it would be well to ponder over the lives and examples of Harishchandra, Prahlad, Ramachandra, Imam Hasan, and Imam Husain, the Christian saints, etc. How beautiful it would be if all of us, young and old, men and women, meditated, till next week, on these thoughts at all hours of the day, whether working, eating, drinking, or playing, and were rewarded with innocent sleep? God as Truth has been for me, at any rate, a treasure beyond price. May He be so to every one of us.

CWMG, vol. 44, pp. 40–42

The path of Truth is as narrow as it is straight. Even so is that of ahimsa. It is like balancing oneself on the edge of a sword. With concentration an acrobat can walk on a rope. But the concentration required to tread the path of Truth and ahimsa is far greater. The slightest inattention brings one tumbling to the ground. One can realize truth and ahimsa only by ceaseless striving. But it is impossible for us to realize perfect truth so long as we are imprisoned in this mortal frame. We can only visualize it in our imagination. We cannot, through the instrumentality of this ephemeral body, see face-to-face truth, which is eternal. That is why in the last resort we must depend on faith. It appears that the impossibility of full realization of truth in this mortal body led some ancient seeker after truth to the appreciation of ahimsa. The question which confronted him was: "Shall I bear with those who create difficulties for me, or shall I destroy them?" The seeker realized that he who went on destroying others did not make headway but simply stayed where he was, while the man who suffered those who created difficulties marched ahead and at times even took the others with him. The first act of destruction taught him that the truth which was the object of his quest was not outside himself but within. Hence the more he took to violence, the more he receded from truth. For in fighting the imagined enemy without, he neglected the enemy within. We punish thieves because we think they harass us. They may leave us alone; but they will only transfer their attentions to another victim. This other victim, however, is also a human being, ourselves in a different form, and so we are caught in a vicious circle. The trouble from thieves continues to increase, as they think it is their business to steal. In the end we see that it is better to tolerate the thieves than to punish them. The forbearance may even bring them to their senses. By tolerating them we realize that thieves are not different from ourselves, they are our brethren, our friends, and may not be punished. But whilst we may bear with the thieves, we may not endure the infliction. That would only induce cowardice. So we realize a further duty. Since we regard the thieves as our kith and kin, they must be made to realize the kinship. And so we must take pains to devise ways and means of winning them over. This is the path of ahimsa. It may entail continuous suffering and the cultivating of endless patience. Given these two conditions, the thief is bound in the end to turn away from his evil ways and we shall get a clearer vision of truth. Thus step by step we learn how to make friends with all the world; we realize the greatness of God, of Truth. Our peace of mind increases in spite of suffering; we become braver and more enterprising; we understand more clearly the difference between what is everlasting and what is not; we learn how to distinguish between what is our duty and what is not. Our pride melts away and we become humble. Our worldly attachments diminish and likewise the evil within us diminishes from day to day. Ahimsa is not the crude thing it has been made to appear. Not to hurt any living thing is no doubt a part of ahimsa. But it is its least expression. The principle of ahimsa is hurt by every evil thought, by undue haste, by lying, by hatred, by wishing ill of anybody. It is also violated by our holding on to what the world needs. But the world needs even what we eat day by day. In the place where we stand there are millions of microorganisms to whom the place belongs and who are hurt by our presence there. What should we do then? Should we commit suicide? Even that is no solution, if we believe, as we do, that so long as the spirit is attached to the flesh, on every destruction of the body it weaves for itself another. The body will cease to be only when we give up all attachment to it. This freedom from all attachment is the realization of God as Truth. Such realization cannot be attained in a hurry. Realizing that this body does not belong to us, that it is a trust handed over to our charge, we should make the right use of it and progress toward our goal. I wished to write something which would be easy for all to understand, but I find that I have written a difficult discourse. However, no one who has thought even a little about ahimsa should find any difficulty in understanding what I have written. It is perhaps clear from the foregoing that without ahimsa it is not possible to seek and find Truth. Ahimsa and truth are so intertwined that it is practically impossible to disentangle and separate them. They are like the two sides of a coin, or rather of a smooth unstamped metallic disk. Who can say which is the obverse and which is the reverse? Nevertheless, ahimsa is the means and Truth is the end. Means to be means must always be within our reach, and so ahimsa becomes our supreme duty and Truth becomes God for us. If we take care of the means, we are bound to reach the end sooner or later. If we resolve to do this, we shall have won the battle. Whatever difficulties we encounter, whatever apparent reverses we sustain, we should not lose faith but should ever repeat one mantra: "Truth exists, it alone exists. It is the only God and there is but one way of realizing it; there is but one means and

that is ahimsa. I will never give it up. May the God that is
Truth, in whose name I have taken this pledge, give me the
strength to keep it."

CWMG, vol. 44, pp. 57–59

5.
Excerpts from *History of the Satyagrah Ashram*

TRUTH

Whenever someone was found telling a lie in the Ashram, effective steps were taken to deal with the situation as symptom-
atic of a serious disease. The Ashram does not believe in
punishing wrongdoers, so much so that hesitation is felt even
in asking them to leave the institution. Three lines of preven-
tive action were therefore adopted. The first thing attended to
was the purity of the principal workers in charge, the idea
being that if they were free from fault, the atmosphere about
them was bound to be affected by their innocence. Untruth
cannot stand before truth like darkness before the light of the
sun. Secondly, we had recourse to confession. If someone was
found practicing untruth, the fact was brought to the notice of
the congregation. This is a very useful measure if it is judi-
ciously adopted. But one has to be careful about two things.
The public confession must not be tainted by even a trace of
force; and the confession should not lead to the person confess-
ing taking leave of all sense of shame. If he comes to believe
that mere confession has washed off his sin, he is no longer
ashamed of it at all. There should be an ever-present consciousness of the fact that the least little untruth is a dangerous thing.
Thirdly, the worker in charge of the Ashram as well as the
wrongdoer would fast as a matter of penance. Of course it is a
matter for the wrongdoer himself to decide whether or not he
should undertake a fast. But as for the worker in charge, he is

clearly responsible for intentional and unintentional wrongdoing in his institution. Untruth is more poisonous and more subtle than any poison gas whatever, but it dare not enter where the head of the institution is wide awake and has a spiritual outlook on life. Still, if it is found to have effected an entrance, it is a warning to the principal worker, who may be sure that he must bear his share of responsibility for this infection. I for one believe that spiritual acts have clearly defined results precisely like combinations or processes in the natural sciences. Only as we have no such means of measurement in the former case as in the latter, we are not ready to believe or we only half-heartedly believe in the spiritual influences. Again, we are inclined to be lenient to ourselves with the result that our experiments are unsuccessful and we tend to move only in a circle like the oil miller's bullock. Thus untruth gets a long lease of life, and at last we reach the melancholy conclusion that it is unavoidable. And what is unavoidable easily becomes necessary, so that not truth but untruth increases its own prestige. When therefore untruth was discovered in the Ashram, I readily pleaded guilty for it myself. That is to say, I have not still attained truth as defined by me. It may be due to ignorance, but it is clear that I have not fully understood truth and therefore neither even thought it out nor declared it, still less practiced it. But granting all this, was I to leave the Ashram and resort to some Himalayan cave and impose silence upon myself? That would be sheer cowardice. The quest of truth cannot be prosecuted in a cave. Silence makes no sense where it is necessary to speak. One may live in a cave in certain circumstances, but the common man can be tested only in society. What then is the remedy to be tried to get rid of untruth? The only answer which suggests itself to me is bodily penance, that is fasting and the like. Bodily penance has a threefold influence, first over the penitent, secondly over the wrongdoer, and thirdly over the congregation. The penitent becomes more alert, examines the innermost recesses of his own heart, and takes steps to deal with any personal weakness that he may discover. If the wrongdoer has any pity, he becomes conscious of his own fault, is ashamed of it, and resolves never to sin anymore in the future. The congregation takes a course of self-introspection.

But bodily penance is only a means to an end, not an end in itself. By itself it cannot bring an erring person to the right path. It is profitable only if it is accompanied by a certain line of thinking, which is as follows: Man tends to become a slave of his own body and engages in many activities and commits many sins for the sake of physical enjoyment. He should therefore mortify the flesh whenever there is an occasion of sin. A man given to physical enjoyment is subject to delusion. Even a slight renunciation of enjoyment in the shape of food will probably be helpful in breaking the power of that delusion. Fasting in order to produce this effect must be taken in its widest sense as the exercise of control over all the organs of sense with a view to the purification of oneself or others. Merely giving up food does not amount to a fast. And fasting for health is no fasting at all in this sense. I have also found that frequent fasting tends to rob it of its efficacy, for then it becomes almost a mechanical process without any background of thought. Every fast therefore should be undertaken after due deliberation. I have noted one special effect of fasting in my own case. I have fasted frequently; therefore my coworkers are nervous and afraid that a fresh fast may place my life in danger. This fear makes them observe certain rules. I consider this an undesirable consequence of fasting. I do not, however, think that self-control practiced on account of such fear does any harm. This fear is inspired by love, and therefore it is a good thing if a person steers clear of wrongdoing even under the influence of such fear. Deliberate and voluntary reformation is, of course, very desirable, but it is only to be welcomed if a person avoids sin because he is afraid of causing pain to elders, as it involves no use of brute force. There are many cases of reformation undertaken primarily only to please one's dear ones becoming a permanent feature of men's lives. One painful consequence of fasting must be taken into account. People sometimes do not avoid sin but only try to hide it for fear that someone else may fast if he comes to know of it. I hold that penance is necessary in certain cases and it has benefited the Ashram on the whole. But one who undertakes it must possess certain qualifications:

1. The wrongdoer should have love for the penitent. The penitent may have love for the wrongdoer; but if the wrongdoer is unaware of it or adopts an inimical attitude toward the penitent, penance for him is out of the question. As he regards himself as an enemy of the penitent, he hates the latter. There is therefore a possibility of the fast affecting him in a manner contrary to all expectations, or acting as brute force employed against him and thus regarded by him as a form of coercion. Moreover, if everyone is supposed to be entitled to undertake penance for the failings of others who do not stand in a special relation to him, there would be no end to the program of penance. Penance for the sins of the whole world might befit a mahatma (great soul), but here we are concerned with the common man.

2. The penitent himself must be one of the parties wronged. That is to say, one should not do penance for a failing with which he is not in any way concerned. Thus, suppose A and B are friends. B is a member of the Ashram, but A has nothing to do with it. B has wronged the Ashram. Here A has neither the duty nor the right to undertake a penance for B's fault. His interference might even complicate the situation both for the Ashram and B. He may not even possess the necessary material to pronounce a judgment on B's conduct. By agreeing to B's admission to the Ashram, A must be regarded as having transferred to the Ashram his responsibility for B's good conduct.

3. A penitent for another's wrongdoing must himself be guiltless of similar misconduct. "The pot may not call the kettle black."

4. The penitent must otherwise also be a man of purity and appear such to the wrongdoer. Penance for another's wrongdoing presupposes purity; and if the guilty man has no respect for the

penitent, the latter's fast might easily have an unhealthy effect
upon him.

5. The penitent must not have any personal interest to serve.
Thus, if A has promised to pay B ten rupees, nonpayment of it
is a fault. But B may not perform penance for A's failure to redeem his promise.

6. The penitent must not have any anger in him. If a father
commences a fast in anger for a fault of his son, that is not penance. There should be nothing but compassion in penance, the
object being the purification of oneself as well as of the guilty
person.

7. The wrong act must be patent, accepted as such by all and
spiritually harmful, and the doer must be aware of its nature.
There should be no penance for inferential guilt, as it might at
times have dangerous consequences. There should be no room
for doubt as regards the fault. Moreover, one should not do
penance for an act which he alone regards as wrong. It is possible that what one holds to be wrong today he might regard as
innocent tomorrow. So the wrong must be one that is accepted
as such by society. For instance, I might regard the nonwearing
of khadi to be very wrong. But my coworker might see nothing
wrong in it, or might not attach much importance to it, and so
might or might not wear it as he wishes. If I regard this as a
wrong and fast for it, that is not penance but coercion. There
can be no penance also where the wrongdoer is not conscious
of having done anything wrong. The discussion of this topic is
necessary for an institution in which there is no place for punishment or which always strives to act in a religious spirit. In
such institutions the penance on the part of the heads of the
Ashram takes the place of penal measures. It would be impossible to maintain its purity in any other way. Punishment and
disciplinary action might make for an outer show of orderli-
ness and progress, but that is all. On the other hand, penance
preserves the institution both internally and externally and
makes the institution firmer day by day. Hence the necessity

for some such rules as those given above. Fasts and such other penance have been undertaken in the Ashram. Still, it is far, far indeed, from its ideal of truth, and therefore, as we shall see later on, we now call it by the name of Udyoga Mandir (Temple of Industry). But we can certainly say that the men in charge of the Ashram are wide awake, fully conscious of their imperfections and constantly trying to make sure that untruth does not find a foothold anywhere. But in an institution to which new members are being admitted from time to time, and that too only on trust, and which is frequented by men from all provinces of India and some foreign countries, it is no easy thing to keep all of them on the straight and narrow path. But if only the men at the top are true to themselves, the Ashram is sure to stand the test, no matter how hard it is. There is no limit to the potency of truth, as there is a limit to the power of an individual seeker. But if he is wide awake and is striving constantly, there is no limit to his power as well.

CWMG, vol. 50, pp. 193–97

AHIMSA OR LOVE

The greatest difficulties perhaps were encountered as regards the observance of ahimsa. There are problems of Truth, but it is not very hard to understand what Truth is. But in understanding ahimsa we every now and then find ourselves out of our depth. Ahimsa was discussed in the Ashram at greater length than any other subject. Even now the question often arises whether a particular act is violent or nonviolent. And even if we know the distinction between violence and nonviolence, we are often unable to satisfy the demand of nonviolence on account of weakness, which cannot easily be overcome. Ahimsa means not to hurt any living creature by thought, word, or deed, even for the supposed benefit of that creature. To observe this principle fully is impossible for men, who kill a number of living beings large and small as they breathe or blink or till the land. We catch and hurt snakes or scorpions for fear of being bitten and leave them in some out-of-the-way place if we do not kill them. Hurting them in this way may be unavoidable, but [it] is clearly *himsa* as defined above. If I save the food I eat or the clothes I wear or the space I occupy, it is obvious that these can be utilized by someone else whose need is greater than mine. As my selfishness prevents him from using these things, my physical enjoyment involves violence to my poorer neighbor. When I eat cereals and vegetables in order to support life, that means violence done to vegetable life. Surrounded thus as I am by violence on all sides, how am I to observe nonviolence? Fresh difficulties are bound to arise at every step as I try to do so. The violence described above is easily recognized as such. But what about our being angry with one another? A teacher inflicting corporal punishment on his pupils, a mother taking her children to task, a man losing his temper in his intercourse with equals, all these are guilty of violence, and violence of a bad type, which is not easy to tackle. Violence is there where there is attachment on the one hand and dislike on the other. How are we to get rid of it? The first lesson therefore that we in the Ashram must learn is that although to sever some person's head from his body for the sake of the country or the family or oneself is indeed a violent act, the subtle violence involved in injuring the feelings of other people day in and day out is possibly very much worse than that. Murders committed in the world will seem to be numerous when considered by themselves and not so numerous when compared with the number of deaths due to other causes; but the subtle violence involved in daily loss of temper and the like defies all attempts at calculation. We are constantly striving in the Ashram to deal with all these kinds of violence. All of us realize our own weakness. All of us, including myself, are afraid of snakes, for instance. We therefore as a rule catch them and put them out of harm's way. But if someone kills a snake out of fear, he is not taken to task. There was once a snake in the cowshed and it was impossible to catch it where it was. It was a risky thing to keep the cattle there; the men also were afraid of working thereabouts. Maganlal Gandhi felt helpless and permitted them to kill that snake. I approved of his action when he told me about it. I believe that

even if I had been there on the spot, I could not have done anything other than what he did. My intellect tells me that I must
treat even a snake as my kinsman and at the risk of losing my
life I must hold the snake in my hands and take it away from
those who are afraid of it. But in my heart I do not harbor the
necessary love, fearlessness, and readiness to die of snakebite. I
am trying to cultivate all these qualities but have not still succeeded in the attempt. It is possible that if I am attacked by a
snake, I may neither resist nor kill it. But I am not willing to
place anyone else's life in danger. Once in the Ashram the monkeys made a terrible nuisance of themselves and did extensive
damage to the crops. The watchman tried to frighten them by
making a show of hurling stones from a sling but in vain. He
then actually threw stones and injured and crippled one of
the monkeys. I thought this even worse than killing it. I therefore held discussions with coworkers in the Ashram, and finally
we took the decision that if we could not get rid of the monkeys
by gentle means short of wounding them, we must kill one or
two of them and end the nuisance. Before this decision was
taken there was a public discussion in the columns of Navajivan, which may be consulted by the curious.* No one outside
India thinks that one should not kill even a violent animal.
Some individuals like Saint Francis observed this rule, but the
common people did not, so far as I am aware. The Ashram believes in the principle, but it is a pity that we have not succeeded
in putting it into practice. We have not still acquired the art of
doing this. It is possible that many men will have to lay down
their lives before this art is mastered. For the present it is only a
consummation devoutly to be wished for. The principle has
long been accepted in India but the practice is very imperfect on
account of our laziness and self-deception. Mad dogs are killed
in the Ashram, the idea being that they die after much suffering
and never recover. Our people torture mad dogs instead of killing them and deceive themselves into thinking that they observe
nonviolence. As a matter of fact, they only indulge in greater
violence. Nonviolence sometimes calls upon us to put an end to

* Vide vol. 37, pp. 32–33, and vol. 38, pp. 72–73.

the life of a living being. For instance, a calf in the Ashram
dairy was lame and had developed terrible sores; it could not
eat and breathed with difficulty. After three days' argument
with myself and my coworkers, I had poison injected into its
body and thus put an end to its life.* That action was nonviolent, because it was wholly unselfish inasmuch as the sole purpose was to achieve the calf's relief from pain. It was a surgical
operation, and I should do exactly the same thing with my
child, if he were in the same predicament. Many Hindus were
shocked at this, but their reaction to the incident only betrays
their ignorance of the nature of ahimsa, which has for us long
ceased to be a living faith, and has been degraded into formali-
ties complied with when not very inconvenient. Here we must
take leave of the Ashram experiments with ahimsa as regards
subhuman species. Ahimsa as regards subhuman life is from
the Ashram point of view an important aspect but still only one
aspect of this comprehensive principle. Our dealings with our
fellow men are still more important than that. The commonest
form of human intercourse is either violent or nonviolent. For-
tunately for humanity, nonviolence pervades human life and is
observed by men without special effort. If we had not borne
with one another, mankind would have been destroyed long
ago. Ahimsa would thus appear to be the law of life, but we are
not thus far entitled to any credit for observing it. Whenever
there is a clash of ephemeral interests, men tend to resort to violence. But with a deliberate observance of nonviolence, a person
experiences a second birth or "conversion." We in the Ashram
are out to observe ahimsa intelligently. In so doing we meet
with numerous obstacles, disappointments, and trials of faith.
We may not be satisfied with observing ahimsa in deed only.
Not to think badly of anyone, not to wish ill to him though we
have suffered at his hands, not to hurt him even in thought,-this
is an uphill task, but therein lies the acid test of our ahimsa.
Thieves have visited the Ashram from outside, and there have
been thieves in the Ashram itself. But we do not believe in inflicting punishment on them. We do not inform the police; we

* Vide vol. 37, pp. 310–15, and vol. 38, pp. 139–40.

put up with the losses as best we may. This rule has been in-fringed at times. A thief was once caught red-handed by day. The Ashramite who caught him bound him with a rope and treated him contemptuously. I was in the Ashram at the time. I went to the thief, rebuked him, and set him free. But as a matter of fact ahimsa demands from us something more than this. We must find out and apply methods which would put a stop to thieving altogether. For one thing we must diminish the num-ber of our "possessions" so as not to tempt others. Secondly, we must bring about a reformation in the surrounding villages. And thirdly, the Ashram ministry should be extended in scope so that the bad as well as the good would learn to look upon the settlement as their own. We thus find that it is impossible for a man with "possessions" to observe ahimsa even in the gross meaning of that term. A man of property must adopt measures for its security involving the punishment of whoever tries to steal it. Only he can observe ahimsa who holds nothing as his own and works away in a spirit of total detachment. If there are many such individuals and organizations in society, violence will not be much in evidence. As gunpowder has a large place in a society based on violence and a soldier who can handle it with skill becomes entitled to honor and rewards, even so in a nonviolent society self-suffering and self-control are its "muni-tions of war," and persons endowed with these qualities are its natural protectors. The world at large has not still accepted ahimsa in this sense. India has accepted it more or less but not in a comprehensive manner. The Ashram holds that ahimsa should be universal in scope, and that society can be built upon the foundations of ahimsa. It conducts experiments with this end in view, but these have not been very successful. I have been unable to cite in this chapter much that would hearten the votary of ahimsa. This does not apply, of course, to ahimsa as applied to politics, to which I propose to devote a separate chapter.*

* This proposed chapter remained unwritten.

6.
Excerpts from a Speech on Ashram Vows
at the YMCA, Madras*

VOW OF TRUTH

Not truth simply as we ordinarily understand it, that as far as possible we ought not to resort to a lie, that is to say, not truth which merely answers the saying "Honesty is the best policy"— implying that if it is not the best policy, we may depart from it. But here truth, as it is conceived, means that we have to rule our life by this law of truth at any cost. And in order to satisfy the definition, I have drawn upon the celebrated illustration of the life of Prahlad.† For the sake of truth, he dared to oppose his own father, and he defended himself, not by retaliation by paying his father back in his own coin, but in defense of truth, as he knew it; he was prepared to die without caring to return the blows that he had received from his father or from those who were charged with his father's instructions. Not only that: He would not in any way even parry the blows. On the contrary, with a smile on his lips, he underwent the innumerable tortures to which he was subjected, with the result that, at last, truth rose triumphant, not that Prahlad suffered the tortures because he knew that someday or other in his very lifetime he would be able to demonstrate the infallibility of the law of truth. That fact was there; but if he had died in the midst of torture, he would still have adhered to truth. That is the truth that I would like us to follow. There was an incident I noticed yesterday. It was a trifling incident, but I think these trifling incidents are like straws which show which way the wind is blowing. The

---

* The speech was given on February 16, 1916.

† Prahlad, a character from the *Puranas*, was a devotee of God persecuted by his unbelieving father, the demon-king, Hiranyakashipu. MKG often spoke of him as an ideal satyagrahi.

incident was this: I was talking to a friend who wanted to talk to me aside, and we were engaged in a private conversation. A third friend dropped in and he politely asked whether he was intruding. The friend to whom I was talking said: "Oh, no, there is nothing private here." I felt taken aback a little, because, as I was taken aside, I knew that so far as this friend was concerned, the conversation was private. But he immediately, out of politeness, I would call it overpoliteness, said there was no private conversation and that he (the third friend) could join. I suggest to you that this is a departure from my definition of truth. I think that the friend should have, in the gentlest manner possible, but still openly and frankly, said: "Yes, just now, as you properly say, you would be intruding," without giving the slightest offense to the person if he was himself a gentleman—and we are bound to consider everybody to be a gentleman unless he proves to be otherwise. But I may be told that the incident, after all, proves the gentility of the nation. I think that it is overproving the case. If we continue to say these things out of politeness, we really become a nation of hypocrites. I recall a conversation I had with an English friend. He was comparatively a stranger. He is a principal of a college and has been in India for several years. He was comparing notes with me, and he asked me whether I would admit that we, unlike most Englishmen, would not dare to say "No" when it was "No" that we meant. And I must admit that I immediately said "Yes." I agree with that statement. We do hesitate to say "No" frankly and boldly, when we want to pay due regard to the sentiments of the person whom we are addressing. In this Ashram, we make it a rule that we must say "No" when we mean "No," regardless of consequences. This, then, is the first rule.

Then we come to the DOCTRINE OF AHIMSA.

Literally speaking, ahimsa means non-killing. But to me it has a world of meaning and takes me into realms much higher, infinitely higher, than the realm to which I would go, if I merely understood by ahimsa non-killing. Ahimsa really means that you may not offend anybody, you may not harbor an uncharitable thought even in connection with one who may consider himself

to be your enemy. Pray notice the guarded nature of this thought;
I do not say "whom you consider to be your enemy," but "who
may consider himself to be your enemy." For one who follows
the doctrine of ahimsa, there is no room for an enemy; he de-
nies the existence of an enemy. But there are people who consider
themselves to be his enemies, and he cannot help that circum-
stance. So it is held that we may not harbor an evil thought even
in connection with such persons. If we return blow for blow, we
depart from the doctrine of ahimsa. But I go further. If we resent
a friend's action or the so-called enemy's action, we still fall short
of this doctrine. But when I say we should not resent, I do not say
that we should acquiesce; but by resenting I mean wishing that
some harm should be done to the enemy, or that he should be put
out of the way, not even by any action of ours, but by the action
of somebody else, or, say, by divine agency. If we harbor even
this thought, we depart from this doctrine of ahimsa. Those who
join the Ashram have to literally accept that meaning. That does
not mean that we practice that doctrine in its entirety. Far from
it. It is an ideal which we have to reach, and it is an ideal to be
reached even at this very moment, if we are capable of doing so.
But it is not a proposition in geometry to be learnt by heart: it
is not even like solving difficult problems in higher mathematics;
it is infinitely more difficult than solving those problems. Many
of you have burnt the midnight oil in solving those problems. If
you want to follow out this doctrine, you will have to do much
more than burn the midnight oil. You will have to pass many a
sleepless night, and go through many a mental torture and agony
before you can reach, before you can even be within measurable
distance of this goal. It is the goal, and nothing less than that,
you and I have to reach if we want to understand what a religious
life means. I will not say much more on this doctrine than this:
that a man who believes in the efficacy of this doctrine finds in
the ultimate stage, when he is about to reach the goal, the whole
world at his feet, not that he wants the whole world at his feet,
but it must be so. If you express your love—ahimsa—in such a
manner that it impresses itself indelibly upon your so-called
enemy, he must return that love. Another thought which comes
out of this is that, under this rule, there is no room for organized

assassinations, and there is no room for murders even openly committed, and there is no room for any violence even for the sake of your country, and even for guarding the honor of precious ones that may be under your charge. After all, that would be a poor defense of honor. This doctrine of ahimsa tells us that we may guard the honor of those who are under our charge by delivering ourselves into the hands of the man who would commit the sacrilege. And that requires far greater physical and mental courage than the delivering of blows. You may have some degree of physical power—I do not say courage—and you may use that power. But after that is expended, what happens? The other man is filled with wrath and indignation, and you have made him more angry by matching your violence against his; and when he has done you to death, the rest of his violence is delivered against your charge. But if you do not retaliate, but stand your ground, between your charge and the opponent, simply receiving the blows without retaliating, what happens? I give you my promise that the whole of the violence will be expended on you and your charge will be left unscathed. Under this plan of life, there is no conception of patriotism which justifies such wars as you witness today in Europe.

CWMG, vol. 13, pp. 227–29

7.
Speech at Benares Hindu University*

Friends, I wish to tender my humble apology for the long delay that took place before I was able to reach this place. And you

---

* The following is the full text of the speech delivered on February 6, 1916, on the occasion of the opening of the Benares Hindu University. MKG's speech so deeply perturbed the chairperson of the occasion, Mrs. Annie Besant, that she left the dais and, following her, the many rulers and princes of native states of India also left the meeting.

will readily accept the apology when I tell you that I am not responsible for the delay nor is any human agency responsible for it. [Laughter.] The fact is that I am like an animal on show and my keepers in their overkindness always manage to neglect a necessary chapter in this life and that is pure accident. In this case, they did not provide for the series of accidents that happened to us—to me, my keepers, and my carriers. Hence this delay. Friends, under the influence of the matchless eloquence of the lady [Mrs. Besant] who has just sat down, pray, do not believe that our university has become a finished product and that all the young men who are to come to the university that has yet to rise and come into existence, have also come and returned from it finished citizens of a great empire. Do not go away with any such impression and if you, the student world to which my remarks are supposed to be addressed this evening, consider for one moment that the spiritual life, for which this country is noted and for which this country has no rival, can be transmitted through the lip, pray believe me you are wrong. You will never be able merely through the lip to give the message that India, I hope, will one day deliver to the world. I myself have been "fed up" with speeches and lectures. I except the lectures that have been delivered here during the last two days from this category, because they were necessary. But I do venture to suggest to you that we have now reached almost the end of our resources in speechmaking, and it is not enough that our ears are feasted, that our eyes are feasted, but it is necessary that our hearts have got to be touched and that our hands and feet have got to be moved. We have been told during the last two days how necessary it is, if we are to retain our hold upon the simplicity of Indian character, that our hands and feet should move in unison with our hearts. But this is only by way of preface. I wanted to say it is a matter of deep humiliation and shame for us that I am compelled this evening under the shadow of this great college, in this sacred city, to address my countrymen in a language that is foreign to me. I know that if I was appointed an examiner to examine all those who have been attending during these two days this series of lectures, most of those who might be examined upon these lectures would fail. And why? Because they have not been touched. I was present at the sessions of the great Congress in the month of December. There was a much vaster audience, and will you believe me when I tell you that the only speeches that touched that huge audience in Bombay were the speeches that were delivered in Hindustani? In Bombay, mind you, not in Benares, where everybody speaks Hindi. But between the vernaculars of the Bombay presidency on the one hand, and Hindi on the other, no such great dividing line exists as there does between English and the sister languages of India; and the Congress audience was better able to follow the speakers in Hindi. I am hoping that this university will see to it that the youths who come to it will receive their instruction through the medium of their vernaculars. Our language is the reflection of ourselves, and if you tell me that our languages are too poor to express the best thought, then I say that the sooner we are wiped out of existence, the better for us. Is there a man who dreams that English can ever become the national language of India? [Cries of "Never."] Why this handicap on the nation? Just consider for one moment what an unequal race our lads have to run with every English lad. I had the privilege of a close conversation with some Poona professors. They assured me that every Indian youth, because he reached his knowledge through the English language, lost at least six precious years of life. Multiply that by the number of students turned out by our schools and colleges and find out for yourselves how many thousand years have been lost to the nation. The charge against us is that we have no initiative. How can we have any if we are to devote the precious years of our life to the mastery of a foreign tongue? We fail in this attempt also. Was it possible for any speaker yesterday and today to impress his audience as was possible for Mr. Higginbotham? It was not the fault of the previous speakers that they could not engage the audience. They had more than substance enough for us in their addresses. But their addresses could not go home to us. I have heard it said that after all it is English-educated India which is leading and which is doing all the things for the nation. It would be monstrous if it were otherwise. The only education we receive is English education. Surely we must show something for it. But suppose that we had been receiving during the past fifty years education through our vernaculars, what should we have had today? We should have today a free India, we should have our educated men, not as if they were foreigners in their own land but speaking to the heart of the nation; they would be working amongst the poorest of the poor, and whatever they would have gained during the past fifty years would be a heritage for the nation. [Applause.] Today even our wives are not the sharers in our best thought. Look at Professor Bose* and Professor Ray† and their brilliant researches. Is it not a shame that their researches are not the common property of the masses? Let us now turn to another subject. The Congress has passed a resolution about self-government and I have no doubt that the All-India Congress Committee and the Moslem League will do their duty and come forward with some tangible suggestions. But I, for one, must frankly confess that I am not so much interested in what they will be able to produce as I am interested in anything that the student world is going to produce or the masses are going to produce. No paper contribution will ever give us self-government. No amount of speeches will ever make us fit for self-government. It is only our conduct that will fit us for it. [Applause.] And how are we trying to govern ourselves? I want to think audibly this evening. I do not want to make a speech, and if you find me this evening speaking without reserve, pray consider that you are only sharing the thoughts of a man who allows himself to think audibly, and if you think that I seem to transgress the limits that courtesy imposes upon me, pardon me for the liberty I may be taking. I visited the Viswanath Temple last evening and as I was walking through those lanes, these were the thoughts that touched me. If a stranger dropped from above onto this great temple and he had to consider what we as Hindus were, would he not be justified in condemning us? Is not

* Sir J. C. Bose, F.R.S., botanist.

† Sir P. C. Ray, chemist.

this great temple a reflection of our own character? I speak feelingly as a Hindu. Is it right that the lanes of our sacred temple should be as dirty as they are? The houses round about are built anyhow. The lanes are tortuous and narrow. If even our temples are not models of roominess and cleanliness, what can our self-government be? Shall our temples be abodes of holiness, cleanliness, and peace as soon as the English have retired from India, either of their own pleasure or by compulsion, bag and baggage? I entirely agree with the president of the Congress that before we think of self-government, we shall have to do the necessary plodding. In every city there are two divisions, the cantonment and the city proper. The city mostly is a stinking den. But we are a people unused to city life. But if we want city life, we cannot reproduce the easygoing hamlet life. It is not comforting to think that people walk about the streets of Indian Bombay under the perpetual fear of dwellers in the storied buildings spitting upon them. I do a great deal of railway traveling. I observe the difficulty of third-class passengers. But the railway administration is by no means to blame for all their hard lot. We do not know the elementary laws of cleanliness. We spit anywhere on the carriage floor, irrespective of the thought that it is often used as sleeping space. We do not trouble ourselves as to how we use it; the result is indescribable filth in the compartment. The so-called better-class passengers overawe their less fortunate brethren. Among them I have seen the student world also. Sometimes they behave no better. They can speak English and they have worn Norfolk jackets and therefore claim the right to force their way in and command seating accommodation. I have turned the searchlight all over and as you have given me the privilege of speaking to you, I am laying my heart bare. Surely we must set these things right in our progress toward self-government. I now introduce you to another scene. His Highness the Maharajah, who presided yesterday over our deliberations, spoke about the poverty of India. Other speakers laid great stress upon it. But what did we witness in the great pandal in which the foundation ceremony was performed by the viceroy? Certainly a most gorgeous show, an exhibition of jewelry which made a splendid

feast for the eyes of the greatest jeweler who chose to come
from Paris. I compare with the richly bedecked noblemen the
millions of the poor. And I feel like saying to these noblemen:
"There is no salvation for India unless you strip yourselves of
this jewelry and hold it in trust for your countrymen in India."
["Hear, hear" and applause.] I am sure it is not the desire of the
king-emperor or Lord Hardinge that in order to show the truest loyalty to our king-emperor, it is necessary for us to ran-
sack our jewelry boxes and to appear bedecked from top to
toe. I would undertake at the peril of my life to bring to you a
message from King George himself that he expects nothing of
the kind. Sir, whenever I hear of a great palace rising in any
great city of India, be it in British India or be it in India which
is ruled by our great chiefs, I become jealous at once and I say:
"Oh, it is the money that has come from the agriculturists."
Over 75 percent of the population are agriculturists and Mr.
Higginbotham told us last night in his own felicitous language
that they are the men who grow two blades of grass in the
place of one. But there cannot be much spirit of self-government
about us if we take away or allow others to take away from
them almost the whole of the results of their labor. Our salvation can only come through the farmer. Neither the lawyers,
nor the doctors, nor the rich landlords are going to secure it.
Now, last but not the least, it is my bounden duty to refer to
what agitated our minds during these two or three days. All of
us have had many anxious moments while the viceroy was
going through the streets of Benares. There were detectives sta-
tioned in many places. We were horrified. We asked ourselves:
"Why this distrust? Is it not better that even Lord Hardinge
should die than live a living death?" But a representative of a
mighty sovereign may not. He might find it necessary even to
live a living death. But why was it necessary to impose these
detectives on us? We may foam, we may fret, we may resent,
but let us not forget that India of today in her impatience has
produced an army of anarchists. I myself am an anarchist, but
of another type. But there is a class of anarchists amongst us,
and if I was able to reach this class, I would say to them that
their anarchism has no room in India if India is to conquer the

conqueror. It is a sign of fear. If we trust and fear God, we shall have to fear no one, not maharajahs, not viceroys, not the detectives, not even King George. I honor the anarchist for his love of the country. I honor him for his bravery in being willing to die for his country; but I ask him: Is killing honorable? Is the dagger of an assassin a fit precursor of an honorable death? I deny it. There is no warrant for such methods in any scriptures. If I found it necessary for the salvation of India that the English should retire, that they should be driven out, I would not hesitate to declare that they would have to go, and I hope I would be prepared to die in defense of that belief. That would, in my opinion, be an honorable death. The bomb thrower creates secret plots, is afraid to come into the open, and when caught pays the penalty of misdirected zeal. I have been told: "Had we not done this, had some people not thrown bombs, we should never have gained what we have got with reference to the partition movement."* [Mrs. Besant: "Please stop it."] This was what I said in Bengal when Mr. Lyons presided at the meeting. I think what I am saying is necessary. If I am told to stop, I shall obey. [Turning to the chairman] I await your orders. If you consider that by my speaking as I am, I am not serving the country and the empire, I shall certainly stop. [Cries of "Go on."] [The chairman: "Please explain your object."] I am explaining my object. I am simply [Another interruption.] My friends, please do not resent this interruption. If Mrs. Besant this evening suggests that I should stop, she does so because she loves India so well, and she considers that I am erring in thinking audibly before you young men. But even so, I simply say this, that I want to purge India of the atmosphere of suspicion on either side; if we are to reach our goal, we should have an empire which is to be based upon mutual love and mutual trust. Is it not better that we talk under the shadow of this college than that we should be talking irresponsibly in our homes? I consider that it is much better that we talk these things openly. I have done so with excellent results before now.

* The partition of Bengal, which took place in 1905, was annulled in December 1911.

I know that there is nothing that the students are not discussing. There is nothing that the students do not know. I am therefore turning the searchlight toward ourselves. I hold the name
of my country so dear to me that I exchange these thoughts
with you and submit to you that there is no reason for anarchism in India. Let us frankly and openly say whatever we
want to say to our rulers and face the consequences if what we
have to say does not please them. But let us not abuse. I was
talking the other day to a member of the much-abused civil
service. I have not very much in common with the members of
that service, but I could not help admiring the manner in which
he was speaking to me. He said: "Mr. Gandhi, do you for one
moment suppose that all we, civil servants, are a bad lot, that
we want to oppress the people whom we have come to govern?" "No," I said. "Then, if you get an opportunity, put in a
word for the much-abused civil service." And I am here to put
in that word. Yes, many members of the Indian civil service are
most decidedly overbearing, they are tyrannical, at times
thoughtless. Many other adjectives may be used. I grant all
these things and I grant also that after having lived in India for
a certain number of years, some of them become somewhat degraded. But what does that signify? They were gentlemen before they came here, and if they have lost some of the moral
fiber, it is a reflection upon ourselves. [Cries of "No."] Just
think out for yourselves, if a man who was good yesterday has
become bad after having come in contact with me, is he responsible that he has deteriorated or am I? The atmosphere of
sycophancy and falsity that surrounds them on their coming to
India demoralizes them as it would many of us. It is well to
take the blame sometimes. If we are to receive self-government,
we shall have to take it. We shall never be granted self-
government. Look at the history of the British empire and the
British nation; freedom loving as it is, it will not be a party to
give freedom to a people who will not take it themselves. Learn
your lesson if you wish to from the Boer War. Those who were
enemies of that empire only a few years ago have now become
friends. [At this point there was an interruption and there was

a movement on the platform to leave; the speech therefore
ended here abruptly.]

8.
Statement Before the Court*

[MOTIHARI,]

April 18, 1917

With the permission of the court, I would like to make a brief
statement showing why I have taken the very serious step of
seemingly disobeying the order made under Section 144 of the
Criminal Procedure Code. In my humble opinion, it is a question of difference of opinion between the local administration
and myself. I have entered the country with motives of rendering humanitarian and national service. I have done so in response to a pressing invitation to come and help the ryots, who
urge they are not being fairly treated by the indigo planters. I
could not render any help without studying the problem. I
have, therefore, come to study it with the assistance, if possible, of the administration and the planters. I have no other

---

* MKG was in Champaran area of the present-day state of Bihar in
North India. This was his first satyagraha after his return to India in
1915. He had gone to the area at the call of the peasants to inquire into
the conditions of the indigo cultivators. He was served a notice by the
district administration to leave the district. He declined to do so and appeared before the district magistrate on Wednesday, April 18, 1917. He
read the statement printed below, and being asked to plead and, finding
that the case was likely to be unnecessarily prolonged, pleaded guilty.
The magistrate would not award the penalty but postponed judgment till
3 p.m. Meanwhile he was asked to see the superintendent and then the
district magistrate. The result was that he agreed not to go out to the villages, pending instructions from the government as to their view of his
mission. The case was then postponed to Saturday, April 21. And on that
the state withdrew the proceedings against him.

motive and I cannot believe that my coming here can in any
way disturb the public peace or cause loss of life. I claim to
have considerable experience in such matters. The administration, however, have thought differently. I fully appreciate their
difficulty, and I admit too that they can only proceed upon information they receive. As a law-abiding citizen, my first in-
stinct would be, as it was, to obey the order served upon me. I
could not do so without doing violence to my sense of duty to
those for whom I have come. I feel that I could just now serve
them only by remaining in their midst. I could not, therefore,
voluntarily retire. Amid this conflict of duty, I could only
throw the responsibility of removing me from them on the administration. I am fully conscious of the fact that a person,
holding in the public life of India a position such as I do, has to
be most careful in setting examples. It is my firm belief that in
the complex constitution under which we are living, the only
safe and honorable course for a self-respecting man is, in the
circumstances such as face me, to do what I have decided to
do, that is, to submit without protest to the penalty of disobedience. I have ventured to make this statement not in any way
in extenuation of the penalty to be awarded against me, but to
show that I have disregarded the order served upon me, not for
want of respect for lawful authority, but in obedience of the
higher law of our being—the voice of conscience.*

CWMG, vol. 13, pp. 374–75

---

* A day before the trial in a letter he wrote to Esther Faering, a Danish
missionary:

> I know you will want me to tell you that I am about to be imprisoned. I
> have come here to remove some labor grievances. The authorities do not
> want me. Hence the impending imprisonment. Do ask Mr. M. at the
> Ashram to send you some papers, and you will know. I am absolutely
> joyed to think that I shall be imprisoned for the sake of conscience.

CWMG, vol. 13, p. 371.

9.
The Great Trial*

AHMEDABAD

March 18, 1922

At the Circuit House at Shahi Bag, the trial of Mr. Gandhi and Mr. Banker commenced on Saturday noon. Sir J. T. Strangman† with Rao Bahadur Girdharlal‡ conducted the prosecution while the accused were undefended. The judge§ took his seat at 12 noon and said there was a slight mistake in the charges framed, which he corrected. The charges were then read out by the registrar, the offense being in three articles published in the Young India *of September 29, December 15, of 1921, and February 23, 1922. The offending articles were then read out; first of them was "Tampering with Loyalty"; the second, "The Puzzle and Its Solution"; and the last was "Shaking the Manes." The judge said the law required that the charge should not only be read out but explained. In this case, it would not be necessary for him to say much by way of explanation. The charge in each case was that of bringing or attempting to bring into hatred or contempt or exciting or attempting to excite disaffection toward His Majesty's Government established by law in British India. Both the accused*

---

* On March 18, 1922, MKG and his associate, the publisher of the journal *Young India*, were tried for sedition and spreading disaffection against the colonial state for having written and published three essays: "Tampering with Loyalty," "The Puzzle and Its Solution," and "Shaking the Manes."
   The following is a transcript of the proceedings of the court.

† Advocate-general.

‡ Special public prosecutor.

§ Judge R. S. Broomfield.

*were charged with the three offenses under Section 124 A,
contained in the articles read out, written by Mr. Gandhi and
printed by Mr. Banker. The words "hatred and contempt"
were words the meaning of which was sufficiently obvious.
The word "disaffection" was defined under the section, where
they were told that disaffection included disloyalty and feelings of enmity and the word used in the section had also been
interpreted by the High Court of Bombay in a reported case
as meaning political alienation or discontent, a spirit of disloyalty to government or existing authority.* The charges having been read out, the judge called upon the accused to plead
to the charges. He asked Mr. Gandhi whether he pleaded guilty
or claimed to be tried.*

MR. GANDHI: I plead guilty on each count of the charge. I
merely observe that the King's name is omitted from the charge
sheet and, in my opinion, very properly.

THE JUDGE: Mr. Banker, do you plead guilty, or do you
claim to be tried?

MR. BANKER: I plead guilty.

*Sir J. Strangman then wanted the judge to proceed with the
trial fully;† but the judge said he did not agree with what had
been said by the counsel. The judge said that from the time he
knew he was going to try the case, he had thought over the
question of sentence and he was prepared to hear anything
that the counsel might have to say, or Mr. Gandhi wished to
say, on the sentence. He honestly did not believe that the mere
recording of evidence in the trial which counsel had called for
would make any difference to them, one way or the other. He,
therefore, proposed to accept the pleas.*

---

* The interpretation of the judge was: "An attempt to excite disaffection
toward government is equivalent to excite political hatred of government
as established by law, to excite political discontent and alienate the people from their allegiance."

† He urged that "the charges should be investigated as fully as possible
and also that the Court will be in a better position to pass sentence if it
has the whole of the facts."

*Mr. Gandhi smiled at this decision. The judge said nothing
further remained but to pass sentence and before doing so,
he'd liked to hear Sir J. T. Strangman. He was entitled to base
his general remarks on the charges against the accused and on
their pleas.*

SIR J. T. STRANGMAN: It will be difficult to do so. I ask
the Court that the whole matter may be properly considered. If
I stated what has happened before the committing magistrate,
then I can show that there are many things which are material
to the question of the sentence. The first point, he said, he
wanted to make out, was that the matter which formed the
subject of the present charges formed a part of the campaign to
spread disaffection openly and systematically to render government impossible and to overthrow it. The earliest article that
was put in from *Young India* was dated May 25, 1921, which
said that it was the duty of a noncooperator to create disaffection toward the government.* The counsel then read out
portions of articles written by Mr. Gandhi in the *Young India.*
Court said nevertheless it seemed to it that the Court could
accept plea on the materials of which the sentence had to be
based. Sir J. Strangman said the question of sentence was entirely for the Court to decide. The Court was always entitled to
deal in a more general manner in regard to the question of the
sentence than the particular matter resulting in the conviction.
He asked leave to refer to articles before the Court and what
result might have been produced if the trial had proceeded in
order to ascertain what the facts were. He was not going into
any matter which involved dispute. The judge said there was
not the least objection. Sir J. Strangman said he wanted to
show that these articles were not isolated. They formed part
of an organized campaign, but so far as *Young India* was

---

* Commenting that the government's charge on Sunderlal, student
leader of Central Provinces, was not for violence but for purely spreading
disaffection, MKG had written in *Young India* that "it may be stated to
be the creed of the noncooperator to give voice to the popular disaffection toward the government and to spread it. Disaffection is the very essence of noncooperation." Vide vol. 20, pp. 138–40.

concerned, they would show that from the year 1921. The counsel then read out extracts from the paper, dated June 8, on the duty of a noncooperator,* which was to preach disaffection toward the existing government and preparing the country for civil disobedience. Then in the same number there was an article on disobedience.†

Then in the same number there was an article on disaffection—a virtue or something to that effect.‡ Then there was an article on the 28th of July, 1921,§ in which it was stated that "we have to destroy the system." Again, on September 30, 1921,¶ there was an article headed "Punjab Prosecutions" where it was stated that a noncooperator worth his name should preach disaffection. That was all so far as *Young India* was concerned. They were earlier in date than the article "Tampering with Loyalty" and it was referred to the governor of Bombay. Continuing, he said, the accused was a man of high educational qualifications and evidently, from his writings, a recognized leader. The harm that was likely to be caused was considerable. They were the writings of an educated man, and not the writings of an obscure man, and the Court must consider to what the results of a campaign of the nature disclosed in the writings must inevitably lead. They had examples before them in the last few months. He referred to the occurrences in Bombay last November and Chauri Chaura, which leading to murder and destruction of property, involving many people in misery and misfortune. It was true that, in the course of those articles, they would find nonviolence was insisted upon as an item of the campaign and as an item of the creed. But what was the use of preaching nonviolence when he preached disaffection toward government or openly instigated

---

* *CWMG*, vol. 20, pp. 178–87.

† This was published in *Young India*, June 15, 1921; ibid., pp. 228–30.

‡ Vide vol. 20, pp. 220–21.

§ Ibid., p. 431.

¶ This was in fact written on September 1, 1921.

others to overthrow it? The answer to that question appeared to him to come from Chauri Chaura, Madras, and Bombay. These were circumstances which he asked the Court to take into account in sentencing the accused and it would be for the Court to consider those circumstances which involve sentences of severity. As regards the second accused, his offense was lesser. He did the publication and he did not write. His offense nevertheless was a serious one. His instructions were that he was a man of means and he asked the Court to impose a substantial fine in addition to such term of imprisonment as might be inflicted upon. He quoted Section 10 of the Press Act as bearing on the question of fine. When making a fresh declaration, he said a deposit of Rs. 1,000 to Rs. 10,000 was asked in many cases.

COURT: Mr. Gandhi, do you wish to make a statement to the Court on question of sentence?

MR. GANDHI: I would like, with the Court's permission, to read a written statement.

COURT: Could you give me the writing to put it on record?

MR. GANDHI: I shall give it as soon as I finish reading it.

Before reading his written statement, Mr. Gandhi spoke a few words as introductory remarks to the whole statement. He said: Before I read this statement I would like to state that I entirely endorse the learned advocate-general's remarks in connection with my humble self. I think that he was entirely fair to me in all the statements that he has made, because it is very true and I have no desire whatsoever to conceal from this Court the fact that to preach disaffection toward the existing system of government has become almost a passion with me, and the learned advocate-general is also entirely in the right when he says that my preaching of disaffection did not commence with my connection with *Young India,* but that it commenced much earlier and in the statement that I am about to read, it will be my painful duty to admit before this Court that it commenced much earlier than the period stated by the advocate-general. It is the most painful duty with me, but I have to discharge that duty knowing the responsibility that rests upon me, and I wish to endorse all the blame that the learned advocate-general has thrown on my shoulders in connection with the Bombay, the Madras, and the Chauri Chaura occurrences. Thinking over these deeply and sleeping over them night after night, it is impossible to dissociate myself from the diabolical crimes of Chauri Chaura or the mad outrages in Bombay and Madras. He is quite right when he says that, as a man of responsibility, a man having received a fair share of education, having had a fair share of experience of this world, I should know the consequences of every one of my acts. I knew that I was playing with fire. I ran the risk and, if I was set free, I would still do the same. I know that I was feeling it so every day and I have felt it also this morning that I would have failed in my duty if I did not say what I said here just now. I wanted to avoid violence. I want to avoid violence. Nonviolence is the first article of my faith. It is also the last article of my creed. But I had to make my choice. I had either to submit to a system which I considered had done an irreparable harm to my country, or incur the risk of the mad fury of my people bursting forth when they understood the truth from my lips. I know that my people have sometimes gone mad; I am deeply sorry for it. I am, therefore, here to submit not to a light penalty but to the highest penalty. I do not ask for mercy. I do not ask for any extenuating act of clemency. I am here to invite and cheerfully submit to the highest penalty that can be inflicted upon me for what in law is a deliberate crime and what appears to me to be the highest duty of a citizen. The only course open to you, the judge, is as I am just going to say in my statement, either to resign your post or inflict on me the severest penalty, if you believe that the system and the law you are assisting to administer are good for the people of this country and that my activity is therefore injurious to the public weal. I do not expect that kind of conversion, but by the time I have finished with my statement, you will, perhaps, have a glimpse of what is raging within my breast to run this maddest risk that a sane man can run.

The statement was then read out.

STATEMENT

I owe it perhaps to the Indian public and to the public in England, to placate which this prosecution is mainly taken up, that I should explain why, from a staunch loyalist and cooperator, I have become an uncompromising disaffectionist and noncooperator. To the Court, too, I should say why I plead guilty to the charge of promoting disaffection toward the government established by law in India. My public life began in 1893 in South Africa in troubled weather. My first contact with British authority in that country was not of a happy character. I discovered that as a man and an Indian I had no rights. More correctly, I discovered that I had no rights as a man because I was an Indian. But I was not baffled. I thought that this treatment of Indians was an excrescence upon a system that was intrinsically and mainly good. I gave the government my voluntary and hearty cooperation, criticizing it freely where I felt it was faulty, but never wishing its destruction. Consequently, when the existence of the empire was threatened in 1899 by the Boer challenge, I offered my services to it, raised a volunteer ambulance corps, and served at several actions that took place for the relief of Ladysmith. Similarly in 1906, at the time of the Zulu revolt, I raised a stretcher-bearer party and served till the end of the rebellion. On both these occasions I received medals and was even mentioned in dispatches. For my work in South Africa I was given by Lord Hardinge a Kaiser-i-Hind Gold Medal. When the war broke out in 1914 between England and Germany, I raised a volunteer ambulance corps in London consisting of the then resident Indians in London, chiefly students. Its work was acknowledged by the authorities to be valuable. Lastly, in India, when a special appeal was made at the War Conference in Delhi in 1918 by Lord Chelmsford for recruits, I struggled at the cost of my health to raise a corps in Kheda and the response was being made when the hostilities ceased and orders were received that no more recruits were wanted. In all these efforts at service, I was actuated by the belief that it was possible by such services to gain a status of full

equality in the empire for my countrymen. The first shock
came in the shape of the Rowlatt Act, a law designed to rob the
people of all real freedom. I felt called upon to lead an inten-
sive agitation against it. Then followed the Punjab horrors beginning with the massacre at Jallianwala Bagh and culminating
in crawling orders, public floggings, and other indescribable
humiliations. I discovered, too, that the plighted word of the
prime minister to the Mussalmans of India regarding the integrity of Turkey and the holy places of Islam was not likely to
be fulfilled. But, in spite of the forebodings and the grave
warnings of friends, at the Amritsar Congress in 1919, I fought
for cooperation and working the Montagu-Chelmsford reforms, hoping that the prime minister would redeem his promise to the Indian Mussalmans, that the Punjab wound would
be healed, and that the reforms, inadequate and unsatisfactory
though they were, marked a new era of hope in the life of
India. But all that hope was shattered. The Khilafat promise
was not to be redeemed. The Punjab crime was whitewashed
and most culprits went not only unpunished but remained in
service and some continued to draw pensions from the Indian
revenue, and in some cases were even rewarded. I saw, too,
that not only did the reforms not mark a change of heart, but
they were only a method of further draining India of her
wealth and of prolonging her servitude.

I came reluctantly to the conclusion that the British connection had made India more helpless than she ever was before,
politically and economically. A disarmed India has no power
of resistance against any aggressor if she wanted to engage in
an armed conflict with him. So much is this the case that some
of our best men consider that India must take generations before she can achieve the dominion status. She has become so
poor that she has little power of resisting famines. Before the
British advent, India spun and wove in her millions of cottages
just the supplement she needed for adding to her meager agri-
cultural resources. This cottage industry, so vital for India's
existence, has been ruined by incredibly heartless and inhuman processes as described by English witnesses. Little do
town dwellers know how the semistarved masses of India are

slowly sinking to lifelessness. Little do they know that their miserable comfort represents the brokerage they get for the work they do for the foreign exploiter, that the profits and the brokerage are sucked from the masses. Little do they realize that the government established by law in British India is carried on for this exploitation of the masses. No sophistry, no jugglery in figures can explain away the evidence that the skeletons in many villages present to the naked eye. I have no doubt whatsoever that both England and the town dwellers of India will have to answer, if there is a God above, for this crime against humanity which is perhaps unequaled in history. The law itself in this country has been used to serve the foreign exploiter. My unbiased examination of the Punjab Martial Law cases has led me to believe that at least 95 percent of convictions were wholly bad. My experience of political cases in India leads one to the conclusion that in nine out of every ten cases the condemned men were totally innocent. Their crime consisted in the love of their country. In ninety-nine cases out of a hundred, justice has been denied to Indians as against Europeans in the courts of India. This is not an exaggerated picture. It is the experience of almost every Indian who has had anything to do with such cases. In my opinion, the administration of the law is thus prostituted consciously or unconsciously for the benefit of the exploiter. The greatest misfortune is that Englishmen and their Indian associates in the administration of the country do not know that they are engaged in the crime I have attempted to describe. I am satisfied that many English and Indian officials honestly believe that they are administering one of the best systems devised in the world and that India is making steady though slow progress. They do not know that a subtle but effective system of terrorism and an organized display of force on the one hand, and the deprivation of all powers of retaliation or self-defense on the other, have emasculated the people and induced in them the habit of simulation. This awful habit has added to the ignorance and the self-deception of the administrators. Section 124 A under which I am happily charged is perhaps the prince among the political sections of the Indian Penal Code designed to suppress the liberty of the citizen. Affection cannot be manufactured or regulated by law. If one has no affection for a person or system, one should be free to give the fullest expression to his disaffection, so long as he does not contemplate, promote, or incite to violence. But the section under which Mr. Banker and I are charged is one under which mere promotion of disaffection is a crime. I have studied some of the cases tried under it, and I know that some of the most loved of India's patriots have been convicted under it. I consider it a privilege, therefore, to be charged under it. I have endeavored to give in their briefest outline the reasons for my disaffection. I have no personal ill will against any single administrator, much less can I have any disaffection toward the king's person. But I hold it to be a virtue to be disaffected toward a government which in its totality has done more harm to India than any previous system. India is less manly under the British rule than she ever was before. Holding such a belief, I consider it to be a sin to have affection for the system. And it has been a precious privilege for me to be able to write what I have in the various articles tendered in evidence against me. In fact, I believe that I have rendered a service to India and England by showing in noncooperation the way out of the unnatural state in which both are living. In my humble opinion, noncooperation with evil is as much a duty as is cooperation with good. But, in the past, noncooperation has been deliberately expressed in violence to the evildoer. I am endeavoring to show to my countrymen that violent noncooperation only multiplies evil and that, as evil can only be sustained by violence, withdrawal of support of evil requires complete abstention from violence. Nonviolence implies voluntary submission to the penalty for noncooperation with evil. I am here, therefore, to invite and submit cheerfully to the highest penalty that can be inflicted upon me for what in law is a deliberate crime and what appears to me to be the highest duty of a citizen. The only course open to you, the judge, is either to resign your post and thus dissociate yourself from evil, if you feel that the law you are called upon to administer is an evil and that in reality I am innocent; or to inflict on me the severest penalty if you believe that the system and the law you are assisting to administer are good for the people of this country and that my activity is, therefore, injurious to the public weal.

COURT: Mr. Banker, do you wish to say anything to the Court as regards the sentences?

MR. BANKER: I only want to say that I had the privilege of printing these articles and I plead guilty to the charge. I have got nothing to say as regards the sentence.

The following is the full text of the judgment:

Mr. Gandhi, you have made my task easy in one way by pleading guilty to the charge. Nevertheless what remains, namely, the determination of a just sentence, is perhaps as difficult a proposition as a judge in this country could have to face. The law is no respecter of persons. Nevertheless, it will be impossible to ignore the fact that you are in a different category from any person I have ever tried or am likely to have to try. It would be impossible to ignore the fact that, in the eyes of millions of your countrymen, you are a great patriot and a great leader. Even those who differ from you in politics look upon you as a man of high ideals and of noble and of even saintly life. I have to deal with you in one character only. It is not my duty and I do not presume to judge or criticize you in any other character. It is my duty to judge you as a man subject to the law, who has by his own admission broken the law and committed what to an ordinary man must appear to be grave offenses against the state. I do not forget that you have constantly preached against violence and that you have on many occasions, as I am willing to believe, done much to prevent violence, but having regard to the nature of your political teaching and the nature of many of those to whom it is addressed, how you could have continued to believe that violence would not be the inevitable consequence it passes my capacity to understand. There are probably few people in India who do not sincerely regret that you should have made it impossible for any government to leave you at liberty. But it is so. I am trying to balance what is due to you against what appears to me to be necessary in the interests of the public, and I propose, in passing sentence, to follow the precedent of a case, in many respects similar to this case, that was decided some twelve years ago, I mean the case against Mr. Bal Gangadhar Tilak under this same section. The sentence that was passed upon him as it finally stood was a sentence of simple imprisonment for six years. You will not consider it unreasonable, I think, that you should be classed with Mr. Tilak, and that is the sentence, two years' simple imprisonment on each count of the charge, i.e., six years in all, which I feel it my duty to pass upon you and I should like to say in doing so that, if the course of events in India should make it possible for the government to reduce the period and release you, no one will be better pleased than I.

THE JUDGE (to Mr. Banker): I assume that you have been to a large extent under the influence of your chief. The sentence that I propose to pass upon you is simple imprisonment for six months on each of the first two counts, that is, simple imprisonment for one year and a fine of a thousand rupees on the third count, with six months' simple imprisonment in default.

MR. GANDHI: I would say one word. Since you have done me the honor of recalling the trial of the late Lokamanya Bal Gangadhar Tilak, I just want to say that I consider it to be the proudest privilege and honor to be associated with his name. So far as the sentence itself is concerned, I certainly consider that it is as light as any judge would inflict on me, and so far as the whole proceedings are concerned, I must say that I could not have expected greater courtesy.

Then the friends of Mr. Gandhi crowded round him as the judge left the court, and fell at his feet. There was much sobbing on the part of both men and women. But all the while Mr. Gandhi was smiling and cool and giving encouragement to everybody who came to him. Mr. Banker also was smiling and taking this in a lighthearted way. After all his friends had taken leave of him, Mr. Gandhi was taken out of the court to the Sabarmati Jail. And thus the great trial finished.

CWMG, vol. 23, pp. 110–20

II.

EXEMPLAR

The idea of an exemplar was important for Gandhi. He believed that lives of great teachers had enduring value through which we could grapple with our times. From the very early period of his public life Gandhi wrote about such exemplars and translated into Gujarati the writings of philosophers and narrated parables from such lives. The story of Socrates—a story of the incessant search for truth and the willingness to die for it—held deep attraction for him.

I.
Story of a Soldier of Truth (in Six Parts)

I.

PREFACE

The heroic Socrates, an extraordinary person with a fine moral character, was born in 471 B.C. A Greek, he lived a virtuous and benevolent life. Unable to bear his moral excellence and his virtue, some envious persons made false accusations against

him. Socrates lived in fear of God* and cared little for the ob-
loquy of men. He had no fear of death. A reformer, he strove
to cleanse Athens, the capital of Greece [sic], of the evil which
had entered its [political] life and thus came in contact with a
large number of persons. He made a powerful impression on
the minds of the young who followed him about in crowds.

[Socrates' teaching] had the result of putting an end to the
unconscionable gains made by persons [with predatory tenden-
cies]. It came in the way of those who lived by exploiting others. In Athens it was an offense to disregard the traditional
religion of the polis or encourage others to do so. The offense,
if proved, was punishable with death. Socrates adhered to the
traditional religion but called upon the people to fight the corrupt elements [associated with its observance]. He himself
would have nothing to do with them. Under the law of Athens,
such offenses were tried before a popular assembly. Socrates
was charged with violating the religion of the state and teaching others to do likewise and was tried before an assembly of
elders. Many members of the assembly had suffered as a result
of Socrates's teaching. Because of this, they bore him a grudge.
They wrongfully declared him guilty and condemned him to
die by taking poison. A prisoner sentenced might be put to
death in any one of a number of ways. Socrates was condemned
to death by poisoning. This brave man took poison by his own
hand and died. On the day of his death he discoursed to his
friend and companion on the perishable nature of the human
body and the immortality of the soul. It is said that up to the
very last moment Socrates showed no fear, and that he took
the poison smilingly. As he finished the last sentence of his discourse, he drank the poison from the cup as eagerly as we
might drink sherbet from a glass. Today the world cherishes
Socrates's memory. His teaching has benefited millions. His

---

* MKG's Gujarati summaries of important works had a pedagogic function and were not intended to be historically accurate. His use of language and choice of terms were influenced by his understanding of the
linguistic universe of his readers. Here, for example, he renders the
Greek "gods" as Khuda in Gujarati. Elsewhere he refers to God as
Khuda-Ishwar.

accusers and his judges stand condemned by the world. Socrates has gained immortality and Greece stands in high esteem because of him and others like him. Socrates's speech in his own defense was committed to writing by his companion, the celebrated Plato. It has been translated into many languages. The defense is excellent and imbued with moral fervor. We, therefore, wish to translate it, but rather than render it literally, we print only a summary of it. We have much to struggle for, not only in South Africa but in India as well. Only when we succeed in these [tasks] can India be rid of its many afflictions. We must learn to live and die like Socrates. He was, moreover, a great satyagrahi. He adopted satyagraha against his own people. As a result the Greeks became a great people. If, through cowardice or fear of dishonor or death, we fail to realize or examine our shortcomings and fail to draw the people's attention to them, we shall do no good to India's cause, notwithstanding the number of external remedies we may adopt, notwithstanding the Congress sessions [we may hold], not even by becoming extremists. India's good does not lie along that direction. When the disease is diagnosed and its true nature revealed in public, and when, through suitable remedies, the body [politic] of India is cured and cleansed both within and without, it will become immune to the germs of the disease, that is, to the oppression by the British and the others. If, however, the body itself is in a state of decay, then if we destroy one kind of germs, it will be attacked by another, and this will ruin the body [politic]—India herself. We argued thus and saw in the words of a great soul like Socrates the qualities of an elixir. We wanted our readers, therefore, to imbibe a deep draught of it, so that they might be able to fight—and to help others fight—the disease. It is with this objective in mind that we summarize Socrates's speech.

CWMG, vol. 8, pp. 172–74

2.

"I cannot tell, O Athenians, how far you have been carried away by my accusers' words. For my own part, they nearly made me forget who I was, so plausible were they. But I say that their arguments are a lie. Among their falsehoods there was one which astonished me most. They asked you not to be misled by my eloquence. It is they who are rhetorical. I have no skill in the art of speaking. If by rhetoric they mean truth, I admit that I possess it. However, if they allow that I am a truthful person, I am not an orator in their sense of the word. For they have spoken with dazzling effect, but there is nothing of truth in their words. For my part, I shall place before you the whole truth and nothing but the truth. I have not come to you with a prepared speech. I am an old man. It is not for me to speak before you eloquently or in brilliant words. Do not be surprised, therefore, if I speak as simply as I am used to. I am now more than seventy years old, and this is my first experience of a law court. I am thus a stranger to the dignified ways of a court and to the manner of speech appropriate to it. Do not therefore mind my style. As judges, your duty is to consider whether or not what I say is just. My duty is to place before you nothing but the truth.

"My accusers are many in number. One of the charges is that I inquire into all things and make the worse appear the better reason, and so mislead the people. Those who accuse me thus are powerful persons. They say that I do not adhere to the religion of our forefathers. Moreover, they made these accusations when I was not there and it was therefore impossible for me to defend myself. I hope that your hearts will be freed from the bias created by their malicious or cunning reports. Nevertheless, I know that my task is a difficult one. I shall say what is needful, be the issue as God wills it.

"I mentioned a while ago the substance of their charge against me. They also lampoon me in plays and show me as trying to walk on air. I have not even thought about these things. I do not mean to suggest that it is impossible to walk on air. If anyone can do so, let him try by all means. For my part I have no knowledge of these matters, yet Meletus has made a charge against me to that effect. Many of you here in this assembly have known me for a long time. You may consult among yourselves and find out whether I have ever talked to anyone on these matters. If all of you agree that I have not, you will see that the other charges against me must be equally false.

"My accusers say, moreover, that I undertake to educate men and demand payment of money in return. This, again, is false. Even if it were true, I see nothing wrong in it. There are many teachers among us who ask to be paid for their work. If they do their teaching well and are paid for it, I see no dishonor in that. If we owned an animal, we would engage a man to train it and pay him for his work. Why, then, should we not teach our children to be good, to do their duty as citizens? And if we found a teacher who might lead them along the right path, why should we not pay him? But, speaking for myself, I have not had the opportunity to be such a teacher.

"You may well ask me, 'If you have no faults, why is it that so many accusations are brought against you? If you have done nothing to mislead the people, why are these accusations made against you and not against someone else?' This would not be an unfair question to ask. I shall endeavor to show why these charges have been brought against me. Perhaps you think that I am jesting. Be assured, however, that I speak nothing but the truth. The reason for their accusations is that I possess a certain wisdom. If you ask, 'What kind of wisdom?' I can only say that, although it be but human wisdom, even the oracle has said that I have more of it than others.

"Though these are the words of the oracle, I did not readily believe them. Accordingly, I went to one reputed to be the wisest among us. I asked him a few questions and discovered that his was only a pretense to knowledge. I make no such claim. To that extent, therefore, I must be wiser than he is. For he who knows the extent of his own ignorance is wiser than another who does not. But when I proved his ignorance to that

learned man, he came to bear me a grudge. Then I went to another person of learning. He also laid claim to knowledge,
which was only a cover for his ignorance. I proved the truth to
him and thus made an enemy of him. I approached a large
number of men in this manner, and all of them tried to shield
their ignorance. I showed to each one of them how ignorant he
was and so incurred his displeasure. I observed that the greater
the pretense to knowledge, the greater in fact the darkness. I
also came to realize that true knowledge consists in being
aware of how utterly ignorant one is.

"I went to many a poet and many an artisan. I found that a
large number of poets could not explain the meaning of their
compositions. The artisans were certainly superior [to me] in
virtue of their skill, but out of pride in their skill, they assumed
themselves to be wiser than others in other matters as well. All
of them are really steeped in ignorance without knowing it. I
learnt that I was more fully aware than any of them of the true
state of our ignorance."

CWMG, vol. 8, pp. 185–87

3.

SOCRATES'S DEFENSE

"You will now understand why I have so many accusers. I have
been so busy bringing home to the people how ignorant we are
and how very limited our knowledge is that I have taken no
part in other public affairs. I have neglected my own affairs
and have remained very poor. But I thought that I was serving
God by opening the eyes of men to their own ignorance. It is
because I chose to do this that people are enraged.

"Some young men who have little work to do follow me
about and imitate me in cross-examining half-baked persons.
The persons who are thus cross-examined and exposed as

frauds become angry with me. Being unable to bring any other charge against me, they say that I look into things far too closely, that I disbelieve in the gods and make the worse appear the better reason. Intent on covering up their own ignorance, they fill your ears with calumnies against me. Such are Meletus and a few others. Meletus says that I corrupt the youth of Athens. I shall now examine Meletus himself."

SOCRATES: Meletus, do you not think that young men should be trained to be virtuous in every possible manner?

MELETUS: I do.

S: Who is it then who makes them virtuous?

M: The laws.

S: That is not the answer to my question. What I asked was, "Which man improves them?"

M: It is the judges who do so.

S: Do you mean to say that those who occupy the seats of justice are able to teach them virtue?

M: Certainly.

S: All of them? Or only some of them?

M: All of them.

S: That is well said. Now I ask you whether the listeners here can [also] improve the young or not.

M: They can, too.

S: You mean then that all the Athenians can instruct them in virtue while I alone corrupt them.

M: Most certainly you do. Yes, that is what I mean.

S: You have made a serious charge against me. What you say probably holds good in the case of horses, too. Will you say that one man does them harm and everyone else improves them? On the contrary, is it not that only a very few are skilled in the art of training horses and the rest are ignorant? Surely you will admit that the same rule applies in the case of other animals? I think you cannot help doing so, for, of course, it does. And in saying that the case stands differently with men, you have given no thought, as far as I can see, to your charge against me. Besides, won't you admit that those who spend much time in the company of bad persons come under their evil influence?

M: I must admit that it is true.

S: Would you then say that anyone would want to injure himself intentionally?

M: That I cannot say.

S: Now tell me, do I corrupt the young intentionally or unintentionally?

M: I say you corrupt them intentionally.

S: How can you say that? You are young. I am an old man. Do you really believe that I do not realize how, by corrupting others, I would myself become the worse for it? You have yourself admitted that this is what would happen. For we saw that those who keep company with the bad themselves become bad. No one will believe it likely that I want to be hurt. If my argument is correct, your charge that I corrupt the young intentionally falls to the ground. Now let us suppose that I corrupt them unintentionally. In that case, it was your duty to show me how I did this. You have not even tried to correct my error. You would have nothing to do with me. You only brought me up [here] for punishment. It is thus clear from what Meletus has said that he has never given the slightest thought to any serious matter. Now let us consider how I corrupt the young. Meletus, you say that I corrupt them by teaching them not to believe in the gods of the city?

M: Yes, most certainly, I mean that.

S: What do you imply by that? Do I teach [them] to disbelieve in the gods of the city or to believe in some other gods?

M: I mean that you do not believe in any gods at all.

S: Bravo Meletus! You say that I believe neither the sun nor the moon to be a god, as the rest of the city does.

M: Yes, I do say that you believe the sun to be stone and the moon to be earth.

S: Who will believe you? No one will believe your charge. If I tried to teach any such thing, everyone would know that there was nothing new in that. These are others' ideas. I myself do not believe in what they say. However, since you accuse me thus about the sun and the moon, you will also say, I suppose, that I wholly disbelieve in the existence of God.

M: I do most certainly assert that you deny the existence of God.

S: You are then deliberately asserting something impossible. How can I say that there is no God? Can anyone assert the existence of man's attributes but deny the existence of man? Or assert the existence of things pertaining to horses but deny the existence of horses? Or assert the existence of things pertaining to angels but deny the existence of angels?

M: The existence of what pertains to a thing implies the existence of the thing itself.

S: You admit that I talk of things pertaining to gods; you must admit therefore that I grant the existence of gods.

CWMG, vol. 8, pp. 196–99

4.

"I have nothing more to say about Meletus's charge. I believe, moreover, that most of the people here are opposed to me. You will condemn me not on the basis of what Meletus and others say, but because of the prejudice and suspicion of the multitude. But many a good man has suffered in this way and many more will suffer thus in future.

"Someone may well ask: 'Are you not ashamed, Socrates, of pursuing studies which are likely to lead to your death?' I should answer such a man with perfect justice: 'You are wrong. Even a man of slight worth must be prepared for death. He must think only of one thing when embarking on any course of action, namely, whether he is acting rightly or wrongly, whether the action is worthy of a good man or not.' If, as you imply, an act which involves the risk of death is a bad act, all the great warriors who fell in the battle at Troy, while doing their duty, must be deemed very bad men indeed. Patroclus was warned by his mother that if he killed Hector, his own death would follow close upon Hector's. Patroclus replied that it was a thousand times to be preferred that he should die for killing Hector to that he should live on as a coward. Patroclus was not frightened of death. The right thing for a man is not to desert his post, even if he has to run the risk of being killed or any other risk, whether he has chosen the post of his own will or has been put there by a superior.

"Consider, moreover, that when I was in the service of this state, I remained at the post where my commander had placed me and ran the risk of death. How strange would it be if, when my heart bade me seek a certain wisdom, I did not follow its bidding or failed to speak out for fear of death? If I should fear death, that would be contrary to my belief that I am an ignorant man. If I think myself wise, without being wise, I would certainly deserve to be brought to trial. To fear death is to presume knowledge. For who has discovered for certain that death is a thing to be afraid of? Why should we not believe that death is the greatest good that can happen to men? Men fear it as though they knew very well that it was the greatest of evils! What greater ignorance can there be than this, of assuming that we know what we do not know? On these matters I think differently from others. If I have any wisdom, it is this: I claim to know nothing about death, and therefore make no attempt to conceal my ignorance. But I do well know that it is evil to do wrong and to disobey my superior. I will therefore never shrink in fear from what I hold to be right. If you were, therefore, to say to me without listening to my accusers' argument, 'Socrates, this time we will spare you, but on the condition that you cease this quest of yours; if you are found engaged in these pursuits again, you shall die,' I should say in reply, 'Athenians, I hold you in the highest regard and love; but I will obey God rather than you. As long as I have breath and strength, I will not give up philosophy, or exhorting everyone I meet and those who would listen to me, saying, "O excellent Athenians! You are citizens of a famous city. You are known to be men of strength and wisdom. Yet you are so keen on making money that you give little thought to the means you employ for the purpose. You are eager for positions of honor and for reputation. Are you not ashamed of these things? You show little concern for your soul, for wisdom and truth. You take no thought for the perfection of your soul."' If, in reply, someone were to say that he did care for his soul and sought truth, I would not let it go at that. I would ask him in what way he cared for all these things. I would test him before I let him go. If in the course of the inquiry I found that he had no truth in him, I would reproach him with setting the lower value on the more important things and the higher value on those that are of less account. This I should do with everyone—citizen or stranger, young or old—but more especially with you, since I am better known among you and more nearly akin to you. Be assured that it is the command of God that I should speak thus. I even go so far as to claim that the commands of God are very dear to me and that this fact is in itself conducive to the highest good of the city. I have only one interest. To all, the young and the old, I say only one thing, namely, that you should care less for wealth and more for the soul; that you should strive for its perfection. Virtue does not come from wealth, but wealth, and all other things of this world, will come to you if you have virtue. If anyone says that I corrupt the people of this city by teaching them this, it would mean that virtue is vice. But if any man says that I teach anything else, he is trying to mislead you."

CWMG, vol. 8, pp. 212–14

5.

"And therefore I say to you: whether or not you believe the accusation, whether or not you acquit me, be sure that I will not forsake the path I have chosen for myself even if I have to die for it many times.

"Please do not be angry with me for what I say. Pay heed to my words. I think you will profit by them. What I am about to say now will perhaps make you angry. But listen carefully without anger. Since I am what I am, if you put me to death, you will do more harm to yourselves than to me. Meletus and others can do me no harm for it is not in their power to do so. It is impossible that a good man can be injured by a lesser person. As a consequence of his charge against me, I may be put to death, or exiled, or deprived of my rights as a citizen. You imagine that these things will be a great punishment for me. But I do not think of them as such. Rather, a person who tries to put another to death unjustly only harms himself. Do not therefore feel that I am arguing in my defense. I stand here to tell you what is in your own interest. I want to save you from the wrong of violating the divine command. If you put me to death, you will not easily find another man to fill my place. It is, of course, not for me to say this, but I cannot help pointing it out. As a strong horse needs reins, you need reins. Since you are also strong, I think it is the will of God that I should serve as your reins, and if you take my advice, you will spare me. But it is likely that you will thoughtlessly order my death, being vexed with me as one sleeping is vexed with another who wakes him from his sleep and rushes at him ready to strike. And then you will drop off to sleep again, unless you have another man to fill my place. I strive for your good, having been sent by God for that purpose. You can see that I have neglected my own affairs, busying myself unceasingly for your good, counseling each one of you like a father or an elder brother and striving to lead you along the right path. You would have had some reason to doubt me if I had asked to be paid for what I was doing or made money thereby. But my accusers have not charged me with demanding money. And I have, in my poverty, the most convincing evidence that I have not accepted or demanded any payment of money.

"Perhaps you will ask me why, if I go on exhorting people to virtue, moving from house to house, I do not take part in the political affairs of the city and strive for its welfare. I have often given my reason for that. I think I hear a divine voice whispering into my ear, telling me not to take part in politics. And I think it well that this has been so. If I had attempted to take part in politics, I should have perished long ago, without doing either you or myself any good. Do not be angry with me for speaking the truth. No man would be free from danger to his life if he opposed the misrule prevailing in the city and tried to prevent injustice. He who would approach every question from the standpoint of justice had better stay out of the bother and bustle of politics.

"Let me give examples to prove this. You will see then that even the fear of death cannot force me to do what I consider to be wrong. But you will also see from them that, if I had busied myself in political affairs, I would have perished long ago. You may perhaps find that what I am about to tell you interests you but little. Nevertheless, it is true. I was at one time a member of our assembly. It happened once that you resolved to sentence ten generals to death. I alone of all the members opposed the proposal. All of you then cried out for my death. But I stood firm; I thought that I ought to face death or imprisonment rather than join you in your unjust proposal. This happened in the days of democracy.

"When democracy had yielded place to oligarchy in this city, a person named Lyson was ordered to be brought over so that he could be put to death as sentenced. I was among those who received this order. I knew that the sentence of death against Lyson had been passed unjustly. I ran the risk of death if I refused to go and bring him over. I did not fear death; I refused to go. If that government had not been overthrown soon afterward, I would certainly have been put to death.

"You will now see that if I had taken part in public affairs and had always upheld the cause of justice (justice being the breath of my life, I could not have done otherwise), I could not have remained alive all these years. Throughout my whole life I have done no one an injustice, in private or in public; I have never acted in violation of justice. I have never presumed to be a teacher. But I never refused to answer anyone's questions, if he sought me out to learn from me. Moreover, I pay the same attention to the questions of both the poor and the rich, answering each one to the best of my ability. If, in spite of this, anyone has failed to learn goodness from my words, I am not to be blamed. If anyone among you asserts that I taught one thing to one man and something else to another, be sure he does not speak the truth.

"It has been asked why so many persons want to spend their time in my company; you know the reason why. If there are persons who think that they are wise while they are not, other persons delight to hear them cross-examined. It is certainly very amusing to listen to that. I think it is a duty enjoined upon me by a god that I should examine people. I have done nothing wrong thereby. If it is true that I have corrupted the young by my teaching, those of them who are now grown up and are in a position to understand their true interests would have come forward to accuse me in your presence. Or even if they did not do so, their kinsmen would have come forward to do so. I see some of these young men and their kinsmen here in this assembly. Why has Meletus not called any of them as witnesses? If he and my other accusers have forgotten to summon them, I would permit them to do so even now. Let their evidence be taken. Instead of deposing against me, they will testify that their children have benefited by my company. They will have no reason, save a love of justice, to speak in my favor, and they have nothing to gain by so doing.

"I have said most of what I had to say in my defense. It generally happens that the relatives of the accused come to the court and entreat the judges for mercy, and the prisoner himself sheds tears. I have done none of these things, neither have I any intention of doing them. This again will perhaps make some of you angry. I have kinsmen, too. I have three sons—one of them is grown up and the other two are still small. But I do not want to bring any of them before you. If I refrain from doing so, it is not because I mean to slight you. Do not impute it to my arrogance either. Let us [also] put on one side the fact that I have no fear of death. But I think it would be a discredit to me, and to you, if, at this age and with my reputation, such as it is, I had my kinsmen to shed tears before you. It would be unworthy of me. Everyone admits that in some way Socrates is different from the mass of mankind. If there should be among you any persons who excel the others and if they were to be prosecuted as I am being prosecuted, it would be shameful of them, from fear of death, to make anyone cry before you. If death were a misfortune, or if it were true that having once escaped death one would become immortal, an appeal to the sentiments of pity through one's relatives could possibly be justified. When our eminent men, although virtuous, begin to entertain such fear of death, foreigners are bound to scoff at us. They will say: 'Even those Athenians who are chosen for high office because of their superior virtue behave no better than women. How poor in spirit then must the other Athenians be!' I believe therefore that no good man should enact such a farce. If anyone attempts it, you ought to disallow it for the sake of the city's reputation. Whatever your sentence, it is the duty of the persons concerned to endure it in patience. And your duty is to despise those who give way to such pitiful melodrama.

"But, leaving aside all talk of credit or discredit, I do not think it is proper for the accused to plead for mercy. His duty is to ask for justice and to do so by stating facts and arguing from them. The duty of the judge is not to show favor but to dispense justice impartially. And therefore it behooves you and us that we should none of us forswear ourselves.

"If I were to entreat you to break your oath, it would amount to proving Meletus's charge against me, namely, that I do not believe in God. If anyone who believes in God teaches someone to violate his oath, then that will amount to teaching him to disobey God. Such a person does not believe in God. But I believe in God more firmly than anyone among you is ever likely to, and therefore, trusting in Him, I leave my case in your hands without fear."

CWMG, vol. 8, pp. 217–21

6.

It was by mistake, we [the editor] announced last week that this series was concluded. Socrates ended his defense. He was then found guilty by a majority vote. Socrates spoke as follows on the question of the punishment to be awarded to him:

I am not vexed at your finding me guilty. Your decision is not an unexpected one. I am surprised rather at the large number of votes in my favor. I had thought the majority against me would be an overwhelming one. Instead, I find the margin is narrow. If three more had voted in my favor, I would have escaped [punishment]. I find, moreover, that I have been absolved of the charge of not believing in the gods. You can now sentence me to death. What can I say about it? What do I deserve to pay or suffer for having given up offices and political appointments and gone from house to house to teach virtue? If in the gymnasium someone keeps you amused and gives you the illusion of happiness, you will maintain him at public expense. I taught you the way to real happiness, not merely to the semblance of it. If, therefore, I am entitled to ask for anything, it is that in my old age you should maintain me at public expense. Perhaps you will think me arrogant for talking in this way after having been pronounced guilty, for demanding a reward instead of punishment. But it would not be true. Though you have found me guilty, I believe myself innocent. I have wronged no one. You have not been able to understand this, for my examination lasted only a day. How much can I explain to you in so short a time? If I had had more time with you, perhaps, I could have persuaded you to better effect. Since I am innocent, I do not propose any penalty for myself. Shall I propose imprisonment? That will not be right. Shall I pay a fine? I do not have the money for it. Shall I propose exile? How can I do that? I do not hold my life so dear as to want to pass the rest of my days wandering from place to place, continually haunted by fear. Someone may well suggest that I should retire into solitude and hold my peace. I cannot do that either. I believe I am commanded by the gods to discourse to people on what I hold to be virtue. I am also commanded by the gods to look unceasingly for principles of moral conduct. I do not think these are matters which you understand. But that is no reason why I should hold my peace.

Socrates was then awarded the death penalty by the court.

Unperturbed, the great Socrates immediately addressed the assembly as follows:

In any case, I have only a few years left to live. You could not be troubled to wait and you have earned an evil name for yourselves by condemning an innocent man to death. If you had waited a while, I would have died in the course of nature, for I am an old man, far advanced in years. If I had used ignoble arguments before you and adopted the course common on such occasions, I would have escaped the death penalty. But that would have been inconsistent with my duty. I am sure a free man will never do anything unworthy of himself to save himself from death or other danger. One ought not to try to save oneself from death by any and every means. In battle, a man can save himself by laying down his arms and surrendering to the enemy. But we think such a man a coward. In the same way, anyone who resorts to unscrupulous means to save himself from death is an unworthy person. I think it is more difficult to save oneself from wickedness than from death, for wickedness is swifter than death. Being impatient and rash, you have taken a step which spells wickedness—wickedness which is so swift in its advance. You have sentenced me to death. I shall now leave this world. My opponents will be looked upon as men who betrayed truth and perpetrated an injustice. I will suffer my punishment. But they will [also] suffer the penalty for their [evil] deeds. This is what always happens. Perhaps it is just as well that it should be so. And now, before I die, I wish to address a few words to you. I am sure that after I die you will come to suffer greatly. You must not believe that, by getting rid of me, you will be able to go your wicked ways undisturbed. Do not assume that there will be no one to reproach you. Before I am taken to the place of execution, I shall address a few remarks to those who trust my words. So, those who wish to hear what I have to say may please stay on. I want to explain to you the meaning of death as I see it. Believe that what has happened to me is a good thing and that those who believe that death is an evil must be mistaken. Death may mean one of two things. Either the dead man wholly ceases to be and loses all sensation or the soul

migrates to another abode. If the first belief is true and there is
an end to all sensation, death is but the highest form of sleep.
We look upon sleep as a blessing. If that is so, death, being the
highest kind of sleep, must be a still greater blessing. If, on
the other hand, we believe that death is a journey to another
place, I shall only join those who have preceded me. In their
presence, I shall get pure justice. There is no evil in this. If I
have to go where Homer has gone, and other great souls with
him, I shall deem it a great good fortune. I count it a high
honor that I should join the souls of those who were victims of
unjust punishment. Believe it as a truth that no good man can
come by evil either in life or after death. Such a man is never
forsaken by God. And you may be sure that the man of truth
is always happy. Therefore I am not unhappy that I am to die
today and be released from these mortal coils. And so I am not
angry with the judges or with my accusers. If they have wanted
to do me evil, they deserve to be censured for that, but their
intention can have no evil effect on me. Now my last request:
If, when my sons grow up, they begin to care for riches or for
any other thing before virtue, if they think they are something
when they are nothing at all, warn them, censure them, punish
them just in the same manner as I have warned you against
these things and reproached you with the love of them. If you
can do this, I shall consider that you have been kind to me and
my sons. Now the time has come, and we must go hence: I to
die, and you to live. God alone can tell which is the better
state, mine or yours. This is a historical event, that is, an event
that actually occurred. We pray to God, and want our readers
also to pray, that they, and we, too, may have the moral
strength which enabled Socrates to follow virtue to the end
and to embrace death as if it were his beloved. We advise everyone to turn his mind again and again to Socrates's words and
conduct.

CWMG, vol. 8, pp. 227–29

III.

THE FIELD

This short section deals with what Gandhi called his "Field of Labor." Gandhi was convinced that truth and nonviolence permeate every aspect of our personal and collective existence, that they are the foundations of the organizations we create, laws that we abide by, and relations of production that we are part of. The very basis of an affective community for him are in truth and nonviolence. This section provides a glimpse of the manner in which Gandhi sought to articulate his field of labor.

I.
Nonviolence

When a person claims to be nonviolent, he is expected not to be angry with one who has injured him. He will not wish him harm; he will wish him well; he will not swear at him; he will not cause him any physical hurt. He will put up with all the injury to which he is subjected by the wrongdoer. Thus nonviolence is complete innocence. Complete nonviolence is complete absence of ill will against all that lives. It therefore embraces even subhuman life not excluding noxious insects or beasts. They have not been created to feed our destructive propensities. If we only knew the mind of the Creator, we should find their proper place in His creation. Nonviolence is therefore, in its active form, goodwill toward all life. It is pure Love. I read it in the Hindu scriptures, in the Bible, in the Koran. Nonviolence is a perfect state. It is a goal toward which all mankind moves naturally though unconsciously. Man does not become divine when he personifies innocence in himself. Only then does he become truly man. In our present state, we are partly men and partly beasts and, in our ignorance and even arrogance, say that we truly fulfill the purpose of our species when we deliver blow for blow and develop the measure of anger required for the purpose. We pretend to believe that retaliation is the law of our being, whereas in every scripture we find that retaliation is nowhere obligatory but only permissible. It is restraint that is obligatory. Retaliation is indulgence requiring elaborate regulating. Restraint is the law of our being. For highest perfection is unattainable without highest restraint. Suffering is thus the badge of the human tribe. The goal ever recedes from us. The greater the progress, the greater the recognition of our unworthiness. Satisfaction lies in the effort, not in the attainment. Full effort is full victory. Therefore, though I realize more than ever how far I am from that goal, for me the law of complete Love is the law of my being. Each time I fail, my effort shall be all the more determined for my failure. But I am not preaching this final law through the Congress or the Khilafat organization. I know my own limitations only too well. I know that any such attempt is foredoomed to failure. To expect a whole mass of men and women to obey that law all at once is not to know its working. But I do preach from the Congress platform the deductions of the law. What the Congress and the Khilafat organization have accepted is but a fragment of the implications of that law. Given true workers, the limited measure of its application can be realized in respect of vast masses of people within a short time. But the little measure of it to be true must satisfy the same test as the whole. A drop of water must yield to the analyst the same results as a lakeful. The nature of my nonviolence toward my brother cannot be different from that of my nonviolence to the universe. When I extend the love for my brother to the whole universe, it must still satisfy the same test. A particular practice is a policy when its application is limited to time or space. Highest policy is therefore fullest practice. But honesty as policy while it lasts is not anything different from honesty as a creed. A merchant believing in honesty as a policy will sell the same measure and quality of cloth to the yard as a merchant with honesty as a creed. The difference between the two is that the political merchant will leave his honesty when it does not pay, the believing one will continue it even though he should lose his all. The political nonviolence of the noncooperator does not stand this test in the vast majority of cases. Hence the prolongation of the struggle. Let no one blame the unbending English nature. The hardest "fiber" must melt in the fire of love. I cannot be dislodged from the position because I know it. When British or other nature does not respond, the fire is not strong enough, if it is there at all. Our nonviolence need not be of the strong, but it has to be of the truthful. We must not intend harm to the English or to our cooperating countrymen if and whilst we claim to be nonviolent. But the majority of us have intended harm, and we have refrained from doing it because of our weakness or under the ignorant belief that mere refraining from physical hurt amounted to due fulfillment of our pledge. Our pledge of nonviolence excludes the possibility of future retaliation. Some of us seem, unfortunately, to have merely postponed the date of revenge. Let me not be misunderstood. I do not say that the policy of nonviolence excludes the possibility of revenge when the policy is abandoned. But it does most emphatically exclude the possibility of future revenge after a successful termination of the struggle. Therefore, whilst we are pursuing the policy of nonviolence, we are bound to be actively friendly to English administrators and their cooperators. I felt ashamed when I was told that in some parts of India it was not safe for Englishmen or well-known cooperators to move about safely. The disgraceful scenes that took place at a recent Madras meeting were a complete denial of nonviolence. Those who howled down the chairman, because he was supposed to have insulted me, disgraced themselves and their policy. They wounded the heart of their friend and helper, Mr. Andrews.* They injured their own cause. If the chairman believed that I

---

* Charles Freer Andrews (1871–1940); English missionary, author, educationist, and a close associate of MKG.

was a scoundrel, he had a perfect right to say so. Ignorance is no provocation. But a noncooperator is pledged to put up with the gravest provocation. Provocation there would be, when I act scoundrel-like. I grant that it will be enough to absolve every noncooperator from the pledge of nonviolence and that any noncooperator will be fully justified in taking my life for misleading him. It may be that even cultivation of such limited nonviolence is impossible in the majority of cases. It may be that we must not expect people even out of self-interest not to intend harm to the opponent whilst they are doing none. We must then, to be honest, clearly give up the use of the word "nonviolence" in connection with our struggle. The alternative need not be immediate resort to violence. But the people will not then be called upon to subject themselves to any discipline in nonviolence. A person like me will not then feel called upon to shoulder the responsibility for Chauri Chaura. The school of limited nonviolence will then still flourish in its obscurity, but without the terrible burden of responsibility it carries today. But if nonviolence is to remain the policy of the nation, for its fair name and that of humanity, we are bound to carry it out to the letter and in the spirit. And if we intend to follow out the policy, if we believe in it, we must then quickly make up with the Englishmen and the cooperators. We must get their certificate that they feel absolutely safe in our midst and that they may regard us as friends although we belong to a radically different school of thought and politics. We must welcome them to our political platforms as honored guests. We must meet them on neutral platforms as comrades. We must devise methods of such meeting. Our nonviolence must not breed violence, hatred, and ill will. We stand like the rest of fellow mortals to be judged by our works. A program of nonviolence for the attainment of swaraj necessarily means ability to conduct our affairs on nonviolent lines. That means inculcation of a spirit of obedience. Mr. Churchill,* who understands only the gospel of force, is quite right in saying that the Irish problem is different in

* Sir Winston Churchill (1874–1965): British statesman and writer, secretary of state for war, 1918–21; prime minister, 1940–45, 1951–55.

character from the Indian. He means in effect that the Irish, having fought their way to their swaraj through violence, will be well able to maintain it by violence, if need be. India, on the other hand, if she wins swaraj in reality by nonviolence, must be able to maintain it chiefly by nonviolent means. This Mr. Churchill can hardly believe to be possible unless India proves her ability by an ocular demonstration of the principle. Such a demonstration is impossible unless nonviolence has permeated society so that people in their corporate, i.e., political, life respond to nonviolence; in other words, civil instead of military authority, as at present, gains predominance. Swaraj by nonviolent means can therefore never mean an interval of chaos and anarchy. Swaraj by nonviolence must be a progressively peaceful revolution such that the transference of power from a close corporation to the people's representatives will be as natural as the dropping of a fully ripe fruit from a well-nurtured tree. I say again that such a thing may be quite impossible of attainment. But I know that nothing less is the implication of nonviolence. And if the present workers do not believe in the probability of achieving such a comparatively nonviolent atmosphere, they should drop the nonviolent program and frame another which is wholly different in character. If we approach our program with the mental reservation that, after all, we shall wrest the power from the British by force of arms, then we are untrue to our profession of nonviolence. If we believe in our program, we are bound to believe that the British people are not unamenable to the force of affection as they are undoubtedly amenable to force of arms. For the unbelievers, the councils are undoubtedly the school of learning with their heavy program of humiliations spread over a few generations or a rapid but bloody revolution probably never witnessed before in the world. I have no desire to take part in such a revolution. I will not be a willing instrument for promoting it. The choice, in my opinion, lies between honest nonviolence with noncooperation as its necessary corollary or reversion to responsive cooperation, i.e., cooperation cum obstruction.

CWMG, vol. 23, pp. 24–27

2.
To the Reader*

DELHI

Wednesday

September 24, 1924

What should I write to you? The relationship between you and me is, I think, unusual. It is not for money or fame that I have taken up the editorship of *Navajivan*. I have taken it up in order to enter your heart with my words. The editorship came my way unsought; but ever since I have been thinking of you. Every week I endeavor to put my soul into *Navajivan*. I do not write even one word there without God as witness. I have not considered it my duty to place before you only such offerings as would please you. I have often offered bitter doses. Through every dose, whether bitter or sweet, I have sought to define my ideas of plain duty and pure patriotism. The fast which I am undergoing now is for making me more fit for the editorship. I know that many readers of *Navajivan* are guided by my writings. I may perhaps have done them some harm by wrong guidance. This thought used to torture me.

I had not the least doubt regarding untouchability. There was no room for doubt regarding the spinning wheel either. The wheel is like crutches to the lame. It is the means of satisfying the hunger of the starving. To a poor woman, it is a fortress for protecting her virtue. I am convinced that it would be impossible to ward off starvation from India without a general acceptance of the spinning wheel. Therefore there is no chance of error in plying or propagating the spinning wheel.

There is also no room for doubt about the need for Hindu-Muslim unity. Swaraj is inconceivable without it.

---

* Written during the 21-day fast for Hindu-Muslim unity done by MKG from September 17, 1924, to October 8, 1924, in Delhi.

But I had always my doubts whether you were prepared to comprehend absolute nonviolence. I have repeatedly and loudly proclaimed that tolerance and nonviolence are the qualities of the brave. Those who have the strength to kill can alone refrain from killing. Might not my writings lead you to regard cowardice as nonviolence? Might it not be that you abandon the duty of defending yourself? That would stand to my discredit. I have said very often in speech and writing that cowardice can never be considered a virtue. The sword indeed has a place in this world; but not cowardice. It is likely that the coward would perish and that is but fair. What I am trying to prove is that even he who takes a sword is likely to perish. The man with a sword, whom does he protect and whom does he kill? Physical strength stands no comparison before spiritual strength. Nonviolence reveals the strength of spirit while the sword that of the body. With the use of the sword, spirit degenerates into matter. By resorting to nonviolence, the soul recovers its spiritual nature. One who does not understand this truth must protect his wards by using the sword if necessary. I cannot explain with words the priceless virtue of nonviolence. It can be taught only through practice. That is why I am practicing this virtue at the moment. I would not touch with a sword even those Muslims who destroy our temples; I would not hate them; I would win them over only with love. I have written that even if one true *premi** is born in India, he would be able to protect his religion. I wish to become such a one. I always write to persuade you, too, to do likewise. I know that I am filled with overflowing love. But is there any limit to love? I know that my love is not limitless. Can I play with a serpent? I have a firm belief that even a serpent would be at peace in the presence of an incarnation of nonviolence.

I am examining myself by fasting; I am gathering more love. While I do my duty, I wish to make you aware of yours. Nothing would be gained by your fasting with me. For fasting, too, there is a time and a title. Your duty is to fulfill the threefold program which I have placed before you in various ways. I am confident that you will draw many other corollaries from that

* A loving person.

program. Instead of doubting the propriety of my fast or lamenting over it, you should pray to God that it may proceed smoothly, that I may resume my service to you through *Navajivan* and that my words may acquire a new power.

Your servant,
MOHANDAS GANDHI

CWMG, vol. 25, pp. 207–9

3.
My Field of Labor*

I know that to many my speech will appear incomplete and even insipid. But I cannot give any practical or useful advice by going outside my province. My field of labor is clearly defined and it pleases me. I am fascinated by the law of love. It is the philosopher's stone for me. I know ahimsa alone can provide a remedy for our ills. In my view the path of nonviolence is not the path of the timid or the unmanly. Ahimsa is the height of Kshatriya dharma as it represents the climax of fearlessness. In it there is no scope for flight or for defeat. Being a quality of the soul, it is not difficult of attainment. It comes easily to a person who feels the presence of the soul within. I believe that no other path but that of nonviolence will suit India. The symbol of that dharma for India is the spinning wheel as it alone is the friend of the distressed and the giver of plenty for the poor. The law of love knows no bounds of space or time. My swaraj, therefore, takes note of *Bhangis, Dheds, Dublas,*† and the weakest of the weak, and except the spinning wheel I know no other thing

---

* Excerpt from the presidential address at the Kathiawad Political Conference, Bhavnagar, January 8, 1925.

† Marginalized and oppressed communities in the state of Gujarat.

which befriends all these. I have not discussed your local questions of which I have not sufficient knowledge. I have not dealt with the questions of the ideal constitution for the states as you alone can be its fashioners. My duty lies in discovering and employing means by which the nation may evolve the strength to enforce its will. When once the nation is conscious of its strength it will find its own way or make it. That prince is acceptable to me who becomes a prince among his people's servants. The subjects are the real masters. But what is the servant to do if the master goes to sleep? Everything, therefore, is included in trying for a true national awakening. Such being my ideal, there is room for Indian states in swaraj as conceived by me and there is full protection guaranteed to the subjects for their rights. The true source of rights is duty. I have therefore spoken only about the duties of princes as well as the peoples. If we all discharge our duties, rights will not be far to seek. If, leaving duties unperformed we run after rights, they will escape us like a will-o'-the-wisp. The more we pursue them, the farther will they fly. The same teaching has been embodied by Krishna in the immortal words: "Action alone is thine. Leave thou the fruit severely alone."* Action is duty; fruit is the right.

CWMG, vol. 25, pp. 563–64

4.
Excerpts from a Letter to Balkrishna†

New principles do not come up every day before a philosopher; but conflicts of duty do crop up every day—ponder over the difference between the two. It is when duties conflict that a soldier obeys his general and he puts his own reason aside. The

---

* *Bhagavad Gita*, discourse II: verse 47.

† Dated August 15, 1927.

intelligence of one who always indulges in its exercise obstructs his self-realization. When a leader is not deliberately immoral, it is nonviolence to submit to his intelligence. Nonviolence is humbler than even a mango tree. It is said that a mango tree bends as it grows up. When nonviolence grows fully, it acts like a cipher. Instead of attempting to prove its own point, nonviolence lets everyone else prove his. Hence it has been sung: "When nonviolence is established, in its vicinity all hatred is given up."* Who can hate a cipher and how?

CWMG, vol. 34, p. 357

5.
Ahimsa in Education†

One of the questions put to me was as follows: *The moment one begins to talk of ahimsa, a series of trifling questions are mooted, e.g., whether it is permissible to kill dogs, tigers and wolves, snakes, lice, etc., and whether one may eat brinjals or potatoes or else the questioner engages in a disputation over the question of maintaining an army or of offering armed resistance. Nobody seems to trouble to inquire how the principle of ahimsa should be worked out as part of education. Will you kindly shed some light on this question?*

This is not a new problem. It has been discussed threadbare in these columns off and on in one shape or another. But I know that I have not succeeded in making it absolutely clear to my readers. The task, I am afraid, is beyond my capacity. But I should be thankful if I could succeed in contributing somewhat to its solution.

* *Yogasutra* by Patanjali.

† This is based upon a discussion in August–September 1928 with students and teachers of Gujarat Vidyapith, a university founded by MKG and of which he was the chancellor.

The introductory part of the question shows that questions betraying a narrow outlook are often put. By unnecessarily exercising ourselves over conundrums about the justifiability of man's killing creatures and animals of a lower order, we often seem to forget our primary duties. Every one of us is not faced every day with the question of killing obnoxious animals. Most of us have not developed courage and love enough to practice ahimsa with regard to dangerous reptiles. We do not destroy the vipers of ill will and anger in our own bosom, but we dare to raise futile discussions about the propriety of killing obnoxious creatures and we thus move in a vicious circle. We fail in the primary duty and lay the unction to our souls that we are refraining from killing obnoxious life. One who desires to practice ahimsa must for the time being forget all about snakes, etc. Let him not worry if he cannot avoid killing them, but try for all he is worth to overcome the anger and ill will of men by his patient endeavor as a first step toward cultivating universal love. Abjure brinjals or potatoes by all means, if you will, but do not for heaven's sake begin to feel yourself self-righteous or flatter yourself that you are practicing ahimsa on that account. The very idea is enough to make one blush. Ahimsa is not a mere matter of dietetics, it transcends it. What a man eats or drinks matters little; it is the self-denial, the self-restraint behind it that matters. By all means practice as much restraint in the choice of the articles of your diet as you like. The restraint is commendable, even necessary, but it touches only the fringe of ahimsa. A man may allow himself a wide latitude in the matter of diet and yet may be a personification of ahimsa and compel our homage, if his heart overflows with love and melts at another's woe, and has been purged of all passions. On the other hand, a man always overscrupulous in diet is an utter stranger to ahimsa and a pitiful wretch, if he is a slave to selfishness and passions and is hard of heart. Whether India should have an army or not, whether or not one may offer armed resistance to government, these are momentous questions that we shall have to solve one day. The Congress has in its creed already furnished an answer to them in part. But important as these questions are, they do not much concern the man in the street, they do not touch the aspect of ahimsa with which an educationist or a student is concerned. Ahimsa in relation to the life of a student stands quite apart from these questions of high politics. Ahimsa in education must have an obvious bearing of the mutual relations of the students. Where the whole atmosphere is redolent with the pure fragrance of ahimsa, boys and girls studying together will live like brothers and sisters, in freedom and yet in self-imposed restraints; the students will be bound to the teachers in ties of filial love, mutual respect, and mutual trust. This pure atmosphere will of itself be a continual object lesson in ahimsa. The students brought up in such an atmosphere will always distinguish themselves by their charity and breadth of view, and a special talent for service. Social evils will cease to present any difficulty to them, the very intensity of their love being enough to burn out those evils. For instance, the very idea of child marriage will appear repugnant to them. They will not even think of penalizing the parents of brides by demanding dowries from them. And how dare they after marriages regard their wives as chattel or simply a means of gratifying their lust? How will a young man brought up in such an environment of ahimsa ever think of fighting a brother of his own or a different faith? At any rate no one will think of calling himself a votary of ahimsa and do all or any of these things. To sum up: Ahimsa is a weapon of matchless potency. It is the *summum bonum* of life. It is an attribute of the brave, in fact, it is their all. It does not come within reach of the coward. It is no wooden or lifeless dogma, but a living and a life-giving force. It is the special attribute of the soul. That is why it has been described as the highest dharma (law). In the hands of the educationist therefore it ought to take the form of the purest love ever fresh, an ever-gushing spring of life expressing itself in every act. Ill will cannot stand in its presence. The sun of ahimsa carries all the hosts of darkness such as hatred, anger, and malice before himself. Ahimsa in education shines clear and far and can no more be hidden, even as the sun cannot be hidden by any means. One may be sure that when the Vidyapith is filled with the atmosphere of this ahimsa, its students will no more be troubled by puzzling conundrums.

CWMG, vol. 37, pp. 225–27

6.
Satyagraha Ashram

The draft rules of the Ashram were published some time back in *Navajivan*. I had invited outside opinion on these; a big controversy had also begun in the Ashram itself. Suggestions were made to introduce vital changes in it. Some of these were even implemented. Despite this, a shocking, fictitious report appeared in the newspaper before the time came for publishing these rules. So I must put before the readers the changes which are being tried at present. As the name of the Satyagraha Ashram is suggestive of its qualities, it has always been our endeavor to stick to truth and to rely on its support alone. It cannot be said that we have always succeeded in our efforts. It cannot be claimed that all the inmates of the Ashram have worshipped truth. It can definitely be said that on the whole truth has been adhered to. Even in difficult situations, many in the Ashram, the young as well as the old, have adhered to it. Ashramites have found one handicap in insisting upon truth. Many difficulties were experienced in minutely observing the rules with a strictness that would do credit to the Satyagraha Ashram. We did not find ourselves capable of coping with the subtler meanings of the rules, a fact which we gradually realize. Hence we arrived at the decision to keep those very rules intact but to change the name. We could hardly find anyone with the mental attitude in which one does not even feel the desire for possessions, in order to do credit to the Satyagraha Ashram. In observing truth in a manner that would do credit to the Ashram, one should never exaggerate even in a state of swoon. In spite of holding this belief, we found it difficult to be always free from this fault. Though we realized that for the observance of brahmacharya, one should be free even from the thought of lust, we found that our control over our minds was very ineffective. In order to practice ahimsa, which would do credit to the Ashram, we should have no anger in us, we should harbor no jealousy of one another. We should have the strength to affectionately embrace a thief if he happens to come along. Let snakes, etc., kill us, but we must have the strength to refrain from killing them. We found ourselves far removed from such ahimsa. Thinking on such lines, we decided to maintain the Ashram as an ideal and run all its external activities under another name. Industry and physical work have always been the outward manifestations of the Satyagraha Ashram and we can claim that they have brought considerable credit to it. We, therefore, assumed the name of Udyoga Mandir. Satyagraha Ashram would entrust its work to this mandir and keep for itself a small ground for prayers, which are necessary for its existence. These changes are being implemented since a month or so ago. The managing committee of the mandir has the right to make whatever changes it wants. Nevertheless, after much thought, it has decided to stick to the rules of the Ashram. The only difference is that these rules will remain as ideals and every member will constantly strive toward their fulfillment. The report that those who are not prepared to observe brahmacharya will now be able to join the Ashram is baseless. The managing committee has especially deliberated over this question and decided that without brahmacharya the Udyoga Mandir cannot be maintained in the spirit of yajna. Industry of any kind whatsoever does not find a place in the Ashram but only such industries are taken in hand which can sustain the poorer classes among the people, raise them economically, and enable them to make progress. The managing committee has unanimously arrived at a firm decision that these activities could be carried on only if the men and women who take part in it observe brahmacharya. And this is indeed so. Not a single activity in the Ashram can be pursued for economic gain. These activities are developed solely from the standpoint of how best they could be pursued by the people. Those men and women who are engaged in enlarging their families or satisfying their lust can neither obtain nor impart this training. The outcome of all this is that those who are working at present in the Satyagraha Ashram in accordance with its rules will carry on the very same activities in the name of Udyoga Mandir. This change of name was necessary for the sake of humility and truth. The organizers will again accept the name Satyagraha Ashram when they gain self-confidence. Of course one vital change has been introduced which seemed to be impossible for the Satyagraha Ashram. During the last three months an experiment is being made of running a single kitchen for the entire Ashram. Control of the palate is one of the rules of the Ashram. Accordingly spices, etc., were not used. Some found this very difficult. It was felt that it would be undesirable to do away with a common kitchen. Hence while retaining it, two varieties of food, one spiced and the other unspiced, were introduced. When families cooked separately they used spices in the Ashram. According to the new rules, spices had no place, but now they have been included.

CWMG, vol. 38, pp. 22–24

7.
Ahimsa v. Compassion

There is as much difference between ahimsa and compassion as there is between gold and the shape given to it, between a root and the tree which sprouts from it. Where there is no compassion, there is no ahimsa. The test of ahimsa is compassion. The concrete form of ahimsa is compassion. Hence it is said there is as much ahimsa as there is compassion. If I refrain from beating up a man who comes to attack me, it may or may not be ahimsa. If I refrain from hitting him out of fear, it is not ahimsa. If I abstain from hitting him out of compassion and with full knowledge, it is ahimsa. That which is opposed to pure economics cannot be ahimsa. Pure *artha* is that which includes the supreme *artha*. Ahimsa is never a losing transaction. The subtraction of one side of ahimsa from the other yields zero, that is to say, the two sides are equal. He who eats to live, lives to serve and earns just enough for his food and clothing, is though acting, free from action, and nonviolent though committing violence. Ahimsa without action is an impossibility. Action does not merely mean activity of hands and feet. The mind performs greater activity than even hands and feet. Every thought is an action. There can be no ahimsa in the absence of thought. The dharma of ahimsa has been conceived only for an embodied being like man. When a person who may eat anything limits, out of compassion, the things he will eat, he observes to that extent the dharma of ahimsa. On the other hand, when an orthodox person does not eat meat, etc., he does a good thing but we cannot say that he necessarily has ahimsa in him. Where there is ahimsa, there ought to be conscious compassion. If the dharma of ahimsa is really good, insistence on following it in every way in our daily life is not a mistake but a duty. There should be no clash between worldly actions and dharma. Action which is opposed to dharma deserves to be eschewed. It is *himsa* and delusion and ignorance to say that ahimsa cannot be practiced at all times, in all places and fully and so to set it aside. True endeavor consists in seeing that one's daily conduct follows ahimsa. This requires real endeavor. Acting thus, a man will ultimately gain the supreme state because he will become fit fully to observe ahimsa. For other men perfect ahimsa will only remain in the form of a seed. There is violence at the root in the very act of living and hence arose the negative word "ahimsa" indicating of the dharma to be observed by embodied beings.

CWMG, vol. 40, pp. 191–92

8.
The Sermon on the Mount*

Q. *You often refer to the Sermon on the Mount. Do you be-*
lieve in the verse "If any man will take away thy coat, let him
have thy cloak also"? Does it not follow from the principle of
nonviolence? If so, then do you advise the weak and poor ten-
ant of a village to submit gladly to the violent encroachment
of the zamindar on his "abadi land" or tenancy rights, which
so often occurs in a village these days?

A. Yes, I would unhesitatingly advise tenants to evacuate the
land belonging to a tyrant. That would be like giving your
cloak also when only the coat is demanded. To take what is required may be profitable; to have more given to you is highly
likely to be a burden. To overload a stomach is to court slow
death. A zamindar wants his rent, he does not want his land.
It would be a burden on him when he does not want it. When
you give more to a robber than he needs, you spring a surprise
on him, you give him a shock although agreeable. He has not
been used to it. Historical instances are on record to show that
such nonviolent conduct has produced a wholesome effect
upon evildoers. These acts cannot be done mechanically; they
must come out of conviction and love or pity for the other
man. Nor need you work out all the apparent implications of
my answer. If you do, you will come across blind alleys. Suffice
it to say that in the verse quoted by you, Jesus put in a pictur-
esque and telling manner the great doctrine of nonviolent noncooperation. Your noncooperation with your opponent is violent
when you give a blow for a blow, and is ineffective in the long
run. Your noncooperation is nonviolent when you give your opponent all in the place of just what he needs. You have disarmed
him once for all by your apparent cooperation, which in effect is

* MKG often answered publicly questions that were posed to him in letters. This is from one such "Question Box" from July 1940.

complete noncooperation. A girl, who rather than give her living body to a would-be ravisher presents him with her corpse, confounds him and dies a heroine's death. Hers is a stout heart in a frail body.

9.
Problem of Nonviolence

A gentleman writes as follows:* Such questions are frequently raised. They cannot be brushed aside, either, as being trivial. These problems have been discussed both in the West and the East in books dealing with the deeper meaning of life. In my humble view, there is only one solution to these problems, since they all arise from the same cause. The actions mentioned above certainly involve violence, for every motion or action involves it and, therefore, no action is altogether innocent. The difference between one action and another lies only in the degree of violence involved in either. The very association of the atman with the body rests on violence. Every sin is a form of violence, and complete freedom from sin is possible only with the deliverance of the atman from the body. A human being, therefore, may keep perfect nonviolence as his or her ideal and strive to follow it as completely as possible. But no matter how near it he reaches, he will find some degree of violence unavoidable, in breathing or eating, for instance. There is life in each grain which we consume. When, therefore, we adopt a vegetarian diet and abstain from nonvegetarian food, we cannot claim that we completely avoid violence. But we prefer the former and regard the violence involved in it as inescapable.

---

* The question is not given in the source, but the correspondent had asked MKG about the impossibility of observing perfect nonviolence in everyday life.

This is why eating for pleasure must never be indulged in. We should eat only in order that we may live, and should live only to realize the self. If our living for this purpose involves any violence, we may be a party to it as being unable to escape it. We can now see that if, in spite of all our precautions, there are germs in the water and bugs [in the furniture], we may do whatever we find necessary to get rid of them. I do not believe that it is a divine law that everyone should act in the same way at certain times and in certain circumstances. Nonviolence is a quality of the heart. Whether there is violence or nonviolence in our actions can be judged only by reference to the spirit behind them. Everyone, therefore, who regards the observance of nonviolence as a moral duty should guide his actions by the principle stated above. I know that there is a flaw in this reply. One may commit violence as much as one chooses and then, deceiving oneself and the world, justify one's actions with the plea of their being unavoidable. This article is not meant for such persons. It is addressed only to those who believe in the principle of nonviolence and are assailed by moral doubts from time to time. Such persons will commit even unavoidable violence most hesitatingly, and limit, not expand, the scope of their activities, so much so that they will not use any of their powers for selfish ends. They will use all their energies for public service, dedicating to God everything they do. All the gifts and abilities of a good man, that is, a nonviolent, compassionate man, are for service to others. There is violence always in the attachment to one's ego. When doing anything, one must ask oneself this question: "Is my action inspired by egoistic attachment?" If there is no such attachment, then there is no violence.

Excerpts from "Some More Posers in Ahimsa"

Still another friend writes: *You say that an absolute obser-*
vance of ahimsa is incompatible with life in the body, that so
long as a man is in the flesh he cannot escape the commission
of himsa *in some form or other as the very process of our*
physical existence involves himsa. *How then can ahimsa be*
the highest virtue, the supreme duty? Would you set forth as
the highest religious ideal a code of conduct which is alto-
gether impossible of being fulfilled in its completeness by
man? And if you do, what would be the practical worth of
such an ideal?

My humble submission is that, contrary to what this writer
says, the very virtue of a religious ideal lies in the fact that it
cannot be completely realized in the flesh. For a religious ideal
must be proved by faith and how can faith have play if perfection could be attained by the spirit while it was still surrounded
by its "earthly vesture of decay"? Where would there be scope
for its infinite expansion which is its essential characteristic?
Where would be room for that constant striving, that ceaseless
quest after the ideal that is the basis of all spiritual progress, if
mortals could reach the perfect state while still in the body? If
such easy perfection in the body was possible, all we would
have to do would be simply to follow a cut-and-dry model.
Similarly if a perfect code of conduct were possible for all there
would be no room for a diversity of faiths and religions because there would be only one standard religion which everybody would have to follow. The virtue of an ideal consists in
its boundlessness. But although religious ideals must thus from
their very nature remain unattainable by imperfect human beings, although by virtue of their boundlessness they may seem
ever to recede farther away from us, the nearer we go to them,
still they are closer to us than our very hands and feet because
we are more certain of their reality and truth than even of our

own physical being. This faith in one's ideals alone constitutes true life, in fact, it is man's all in all. Blessed is the man who can perceive the law of ahimsa in the midst of the raging fire of himsa all around him. We bow in reverence before such a man; he lays the whole world under debt by his example. The more adverse the circumstances around him, the intenser grows his longing for deliverance from the bondage of flesh which is a vehicle of himsa and beckons him on to that blessed state which in the words of the poet, "Even the Great Masters saw only in a trance / Which even their tongue could not declare," a state in which the will to live is completely overcome by the ever-active desire to realize the ideal of ahimsa and all attachment to the body ceasing, man is freed from the further necessity of possessing an earthly tabernacle. But so long as that consummation is not reached, a man must go on paying the toll of himsa, for himsa is inseparable from all physical existence and it will have its due.

CWMG, vol. 38, pp. 68–69

IV.

THE PRACTICE

Nonviolence is a mode of practice. It is present in each action, each thought behind that action. It is an ideal that can be attained only in and through daily practice. How is one to train oneself to be nonviolent? How does one acquire the fitness to offer civil disobedience? This section contains instructions to volunteers, discussions within political movements on organizing for nonviolent action, and a constant reminder that nonviolence is not the weapon of the weak.

I.
The Theory and Practice of Passive Resistance*

I shall be at least far away from Phoenix, if not actually in the Motherland, when this commemoration issue is published. I would, however, leave behind me my innermost thoughts upon that which has made this special issue necessary. Without passive resistance, there would have been no richly illustrated and important special issue of *Indian Opinion*, which has, for the last eleven years, in an unpretentious and humble manner, endeavored to serve my countrymen and South Africa, a period covering the most critical stage that they will, perhaps, ever

* This was written after MKG left South Africa for India in July 1914 for the "Golden Number" of *Indian Opinion*, dealing with the Indian struggle in South Africa, and was released on December 1, 1914.

have to pass through. It marks the rise and growth of passive resistance, which has attracted worldwide attention. The term does not fit the activity of the Indian community during the past eight years. Its equivalent in the vernacular,* rendered into English, means truth force. I think Tolstoy called it also soul force or love force, and so it is. Carried out to its utmost limit, this force is independent of pecuniary or other material assistance; certainly, even in its elementary form, of physical force or violence.

Indeed, violence is the negation of this great spiritual force, which can only be cultivated or wielded by those who will entirely eschew violence. It is a force that may be used by individuals as well as by communities. It may be used as well in political as in domestic affairs. Its universal applicability is a demonstration of its permanence and invincibility. It can be used alike by men, women, and children. It is totally untrue to say that it is a force to be used only by the weak so long as they are not capable of meeting violence by violence. This superstition arises from the incompleteness of the English expression. It is impossible for those who consider themselves to be weak to apply this force. Only those who realize that there is something in man which is superior to the brute nature in him, and that the latter always yields to it, can effectively be passive resisters. This force is to violence and, therefore, to all tyranny, all injustice, what light is to darkness. In politics, its use is based upon the immutable maxim that government of the people is possible only so long as they consent either consciously or unconsciously to be governed. We did not want to be governed by the Asiatic Act of 1907 of the Transvaal, and it had to go before this mighty force. Two courses were open to us—to use violence when we were called upon to submit to the Act, or to suffer the penalties prescribed under the Act, and thus to draw out and exhibit the force of the soul within us for a period long enough to appeal to the sympathetic chord in the governors or the lawmakers. We have taken long to achieve what we set about striving for. That was because our passive

* Satyagraha.

resistance was not of the most complete type. All passive resisters do not understand the full value of the force, nor have we men who always from conviction refrain from violence. The use of this force requires the adoption of poverty, in the sense that we must be indifferent whether we have the wherewithal to feed or clothe ourselves. During the past struggle, all passive resisters, if any at all, were not prepared to go that length. Some again were only passive resisters so-called. They came without any conviction, often with mixed motives, less often with impure motives. Some even, whilst engaged in the struggle, would gladly have resorted to violence but for most vigilant supervision. Thus it was that the struggle became prolonged; for the exercise of the purest soul force, in its perfect form, brings about instantaneous relief. For this exercise, prolonged training of the individual soul is an absolute necessity, so that a perfect passive resister has to be almost, if not entirely, a perfect man. We cannot all suddenly become such men, but, if my proposition is correct—as I know it to be correct—the greater the spirit of passive resistance in us, the better men we will become. Its use, therefore, is, I think, indisputable, and it is a force which, if it became universal, would revolutionize social ideals and do away with despotism and the ever-growing militarism under which the nations of the West are groaning and are being almost crushed to death, and which fairly promises to overwhelm even the nations of the East. If the past struggle has produced even a few Indians who would dedicate themselves to the task of becoming passive resisters as nearly perfect as possible, they would not only have served themselves in the truest sense of the term, they would also have served humanity at large. Thus viewed, passive resistance is the noblest and the best education. It should come, not after the ordinary education in letters of children, but it should precede it. It will not be denied that a child, before it begins to write its alphabet and to gain worldly knowledge, should know what the soul is, what truth is, what love is, what powers are latent in the soul. It should be an essential of real education that a child should learn that, in the struggle of life, it can easily conquer hate by love, untruth by truth, violence by self-suffering. It was because I felt the force of this truth, that, during the latter part of the struggle, I endeavored, as much as I could, to train the children at Tolstoy Farm and then at Phoenix along these lines, and one of the reasons for my departure to India is still further to realize, as I already do in part, my own imperfection as a passive resister, and then to try to perfect myself, for I believe that it is in India that the nearest approach to perfection is most possible.

CWMG, vol. 12. pp. 460–61

2.
Speech on the Secret of Satyagraha in South Africa*

In brief, the significance of satyagraha consists in the quest for a principle of life. We did not say to anyone in so many words that our fight was in pursuance of this quest. If we had said so, the people there would only have laughed at us. We only made known the secondary aim of our movement, which was that the government there, thinking us lowly and mean, was making laws to oust us from the country, and that it was right for us to defy these laws and show that we were brave. Suppose the government passes a law saying that colored persons shall wear yellow caps; in fact, a law of this kind was made in Rome for the Jews. If the government intended to treat us in a similar fashion and made a law that appeared to humiliate us, it was for us to make it clear to the government that we would not obey such a law. If a child says to his father: "Please put on your turban the wrong side up for me," the father understands that the child wants to have a laugh at his expense and at once obeys the command. But when someone else, with uncharitable motives, says the same thing, he clearly answers, "Look,

* In reply to a question during a postprayer meeting at Satyagraha Ashram, Kochrab, Ahmedabad.

brother, so long as my head is on my shoulders, you cannot humiliate me in this manner. You conquer my head first and then make me wear my turban in any fashion you please." The government there in a similar way, thinking the Indians lowly, wanted to treat them as slaves and as far as possible to prevent their coming into the country. And with this end in view, it began inventing ever new laws, such as putting names of Indians in a separate register, making them give finger-prints in the manner of thieves and bandits, forcing them to live in particular areas, forbidding their movement beyond a specified boundary, making rules for them to walk on particular footpaths and board specified carriages in trains, treating their wives as concubines if they could not produce marriage certificates, levying from them an annual tax of forty-five rupees per capita, etc., etc. Often a disease manifests itself in the body in various forms. The disease in this case, as has been explained, was the evil purpose of the government of South Africa, and all the rules and regulations mentioned above were the various forms that it took. We, therefore, had to prepare ourselves to fight against these. There are two ways of countering injustice. One way is to smash the head of the man who perpetrates injustice and to get your own head smashed in the process. All strong people in the world adopt this course. Everywhere wars are fought and millions of people are killed. The consequence is not the progress of a nation but its decline. Soldiers returning from the front have become so bereft of reason that they indulge in various antisocial activities. One does not have to go far for examples. In the Boer War, when the British won a victory at Mafeking, the whole of England, and London in particular, went so mad with joy that for days on end everyone did nothing but dance night and day! They freely indulged in wickednesses and rowdyism and did not leave a single bar with a drop of liquor in it. The *Times*, commenting, said that no words could describe the way those few days were spent, that all that could be said was that "the English nation went amafficking [a-Mafeking]." Pride makes a victorious nation badtempered. It falls into luxurious ways of living. Then for a time, it may be conceded, peace prevails. But after a short while, it comes more and more to be realized that the seeds of war have not been destroyed but have become a thousand times more nourished and mighty. No country has ever become, or will ever become, happy through victory in war. A nation does not rise that way, it only falls further. In fact, what comes to it is defeat, not victory. And if, perchance, either our act or our purpose was ill-conceived, it brings disaster to both belligerents. But through the other method of combating injustice, we alone suffer the consequences of our mistakes, and the other side is wholly spared. This other method is satyagraha. One who resorts to it does not have to break another's head; he may merely have his own head broken. He has to be prepared to die himself, suffering all the pain. In opposing the atrocious laws of the government of South Africa, it was this method that we adopted. We made it clear to the said government that we would never bow to its outrageous laws. No clapping is possible without two hands to do it, and no quarrel without two persons to make it. Similarly, no state is possible without two entities [the rulers and the ruled]. You are our sovereign, our government, only so long as we consider ourselves your subjects. When we are not subjects, you are not the sovereign, either. So long as it is your endeavor to control us with justice and love, we will let you to do so. But if you wish to strike at us from behind, we cannot permit it. Whatever you do in other matters, you will have to ask our opinion about the laws that concern us. If you make laws to keep us suppressed in a wrongful manner and without taking us into confidence, these laws will merely adorn the statute books. We will never obey them. Award us for it what punishment you like, we will put up with it. Send us to prison and we will live there as in a paradise. Ask us to mount the scaffold and we will do so laughing. Shower what sufferings you like upon us, we will calmly endure all and not hurt a hair of your body. We will gladly die and will not so much as touch you. But so long as there is yet life in these our bones, we will never comply with your arbitrary laws. It all began on a Sunday evening in Johannesburg when I sat on a hillock with another gentleman called Hemchandra. The memory of that day is so vivid that it might have been yesterday. At my side lay a government gazette. It contained the several clauses of the law concerning Indians. As I read it, I shook with rage. What did the government take us for? Then and there I produced a translation of that portion of the gazette that contained the said laws and wrote under it: "I will never let these laws govern me." This was at once sent for publication to *Indian Opinion* at Phoenix. I did not dream at the time that even a single Indian would be capable of the unprecedented heroism the Indians revealed or that the satyagraha movement would gain the momentum it did. Immediately, I made my view known to fellow Indians and many of them declared their readiness for satyagraha. In the first conflict, people took part under the impression that our aim would be gained after only a few days of suffering. In the second conflict, there were only a very few people to begin with but later many more came along. Afterward when, on the visit of Mr. Gokhale, the government of South Africa pledged itself to a settlement, the fight ceased. Later, the government treacherously refused to honor its pledge; on which a third satyagraha battle became necessary. Gokhale at that time asked me how many people I thought would take part in the satyagraha. I wrote saying they would be between thirty and sixty. But I could not find even that number. Only sixteen of us took up the challenge. We were firmly decided that so long as the government did not repeal its atrocious laws or make some settlement, we would accept every penalty but would not submit. We had never hoped that we should find many fellow fighters. But the readiness of one person without self-interest to offer himself for the cause of truth and country always has its effect. Soon there were twenty thousand people in the movement. There was no room for them in the prisons, and the blood of India boiled. Many people say that if Lord Hardinge had not intervened, a compromise would have been impossible. But these people forget to ask themselves why it was that Lord Hardinge intervened. The sufferings of the Canadian Indians were far greater than those of the South African Indians. Why did he not use his good offices there? Where the spiritual might of thousands of men and women has been mustered, where innumerable men and women are eager to lay down their lives, what indeed is impossible? There was no other course open for Lord Hardinge than to offer mediation and he only showed his wisdom in adopting it. What transpired later is well known to you: the government of South Africa was compelled to come to terms with us. All of which goes to show that we can gain everything without hurting anybody and through soul force or satyagraha alone. He who fights with arms has to depend on arms and on support from others. He has to turn from the straight path and seek tortuous tracks. The course that a satyagrahi adopts in his fight is straight and he need look to no one for help. He can, if necessary, fight by himself alone. In that case, it is true, the outcome will be somewhat delayed. If I had not found as many comrades in the South African fight as I did, all that would have happened is that you would not have seen me here in your midst today. Perhaps all my life would have had to be spent in the struggle there. But what of that? The gain that has been secured would only have been a little late in coming. For the battle of satyagraha one only needs to prepare oneself. We have to have strict self-control. If it is necessary for this preparation to live in forests and caves, we should do so. The time that may be taken up in this preparation should not be considered wasted. Christ, before he went out to serve the world, spent forty days in the wilderness, preparing himself for his mission. Buddha, too, spent many years in such preparation. Had Christ and Buddha not undergone this preparation, they would not have been what they were. Similarly, if we want to put this body in the service of truth and humanity, we must first raise our soul by developing virtues like celibacy, nonviolence, and truth. Then alone may we say that we are fit to render real service to the country. In brief, the aim of the satyagraha struggle was to infuse manliness in cowards and to develop the really human virtues, and its field was the passive resistance against the government of South Africa.

CWMG, vol. 13, pp. 287–91

3.
Instructions to Volunteers*

SATYAGRAHA CAMP,

NADIAD, April 17, 1918

1. The volunteers must remember that, as this is a satyagraha campaign, they must abide by truth under all circumstances.

2. In satyagraha, there can be no room for rancor; which means that a satyagrahi should utter no harsh word about anyone, from a *ravania* to the governor himself; if someone does so, it is the volunteer's duty to stop him.

3. Rudeness has no place in satyagraha. Perfect courtesy must be shown even to those who may look upon us as their enemies and the villagers must be taught to do the same. Rudeness may harm our cause and the struggle may be unduly prolonged. The volunteers should give the most serious attention to this matter and think out in their minds as many examples as possible of the advantages accruing from courtesy and the disadvantages resulting from rudeness and explain them to the people.

4. The volunteers must remember that this is a holy war. We embarked upon it because, had we not, we would have failed in our dharma. And so all the rules which are essential for living a religious life must be observed here, too.

5. We are opposing the intoxication of power, that is, the blind application of law, and not authority as such. The difference

---

* These were issued by MKG during the no-tax campaign, popularly know as Kheda Satyagraha in 1918.

must never be lost sight of. It is, therefore, our duty to help the officers in their other work.

6. We are to apply here the same principle that we follow in a domestic quarrel. We should think of the government and the people as constituting a large family and act accordingly.

7. We are not to boycott or treat with scorn those who hold different views from ours. It must be our resolve to win them over by courteous behavior.

8. We must not try to be clever. We must always be frank and straightforward.

9. When they stay in villages, the volunteers should demand the fewest services from the village folk. Wherever it is possible to reach a place on foot, they should avoid using a vehicle. We must insist on being served the simplest food. Restraining them from preparing dainties will add grace to the service we render.

10. As they move about in villages, the volunteers should observe the economic condition of the people and the deficiencies in their education and try, in their spare time, to make them good.

11. If they can, they should create opportunities when they may teach the village children.

12. If they notice any violation of the rules of good health, they should draw the villagers' attention to the fact.

13. If, at any place, they find people engaged in quarreling among themselves, the volunteers should try to save them from their quarrels.

14. They should read out to the people, when the latter are free, books which promote satyagraha. They may read out

stories of Prahlad, Harishchandra, and others. The people should also be made familiar with instances of pure satyagraha to be found in the West and in Islamic literature. 1

15. At no time and under no circumstances is the use of arms permitted in satyagraha. It should never be forgotten that in this struggle the highest type of nonviolence is to be maintained. Satyagraha means fighting oppression through voluntary suffering. There can be no question here of making anyone else suffer. Satyagraha is always successful; it can never meet with defeat: let every volunteer understand this himself and then explain it to the people.

CWMG, vol. 14, pp. 350–51

4.
The Doctrine of the Sword

In this age of the rule of brute force, it is almost impossible for anyone to believe that anyone else could possibly reject the law of the final supremacy of brute force. And so I receive anonymous letters advising me that I must not interfere with the progress of noncooperation even though popular violence may break out. Others come to me and assuming that secretly I must be plotting violence, inquire when the happy moment for declaring open violence will arrive. They assure me that the English will never yield to anything but violence secret or open. Yet others, I am informed, believe that I am the most rascally person living in India because I never give out my real intention and that they have not a shadow of a doubt that I believe in violence just as much as most people do. Such being the hold that the doctrine of the sword has on the majority of mankind, and as success of noncooperation depends principally on absence of violence during its pendency and as my views in this matter affect the conduct of a large number of people, I am anxious to state them as clearly as possible. I do believe that where there is only a choice between cowardice and violence I would advise violence. Thus when my eldest son asked me what he should have done, had he been present when I was almost fatally assaulted in 1908, whether he should have run away and seen me killed or whether he should have used his physical force which he could and wanted to use, and defended me, I told him that it was his duty to defend me even by using violence. Hence it was that I took part in the Boer War, the so-called Zulu rebellion, and the late war. Hence also do I advocate training in arms for those who believe in the method of violence. I would rather have India resort to arms in order to defend her honor than that she should in a cowardly manner become or remain a helpless witness to her own dishonor. But I believe that nonviolence is infinitely superior to violence, forgiveness is more manly than punishment. Forgiveness adorns a soldier. But abstinence is forgiveness only when there is the power to punish; it is meaningless when it pretends to proceed from a helpless creature. A mouse hardly forgives a cat when it allows itself to be torn to pieces by her. I, therefore, appreciate the sentiment of those who cry out for the condign punishment of General Dyer and his ilk. They would tear him to pieces if they could. But I do not believe India to be helpless. I do not believe myself to be a helpless creature. Only I want to use India's and my strength for a better purpose. Let me not be misunderstood. Strength does not come from physical capacity. It comes from an indomitable will. An average Zulu is anyway more than a match for an average Englishman in bodily capacity. But he flees from an English boy because he fears the boy's revolver or those who will use it for him. He fears death and is nerveless in spite of his burly figure. We in India may in a moment realize that one hundred thousand Englishmen need not frighten three hundred million human beings. A definite forgiveness would therefore mean a definite recognition of our strength. With enlightened forgiveness must come a mighty wave of strength in us, which would make it impossible for a Dyer and a Frank Johnson to heap affront upon India's devoted head. It matters little to me that for the moment I do not drive my point home. We feel too downtrodden not to be angry and revengeful. But I must not refrain from saying that India can gain more by waiving the right of punishment. We have better work to do, a better mission to deliver to the world. I am not a visionary. I claim to be a practical idealist. The religion of nonviolence is not meant merely for the rishis and saints. It is meant for the common people as well. Nonviolence is the law of our species as violence is the law of the brute. The spirit lies dormant in the brute and he knows no law but that of physical might. The dignity of man requires obedience to a higher law—to the strength of the spirit. I have therefore ventured to place before India the ancient law of self-sacrifice. For satyagraha and its offshoots, noncooperation and civil resistance are nothing but new names for the law of suffering. The rishis, who discovered the law of nonviolence in the midst of violence, were greater geniuses than Newton. They were themselves greater warriors than Wellington. Having themselves known the use of arms, they realized their uselessness and taught a weary world that its salvation lay not through violence but through nonviolence. Nonviolence in its dynamic condition means conscious suffering. It does not mean meek submission to the will of the evildoer, but it means the putting of one's whole soul against the will of the tyrant. Working under this law of our being, it is possible for a single individual to defy the whole might of an unjust empire to save his honor, his religion, his soul, and lay the foundation for that empire's fall or its regeneration. And so I am not pleading for India to practice nonviolence because it is weak. I want her to practice nonviolence being conscious of her strength and power. No training in arms is required for realization of her strength. We seem to need it because we seem to think that we are but a lump of flesh. I want India to recognize that she has a soul that cannot perish and that can rise triumphant above every physical weakness and defy the physical combination of a whole world. What is the meaning of Rama, a mere human being, with his host of monkeys, pitting himself against the insolent strength of ten-headed Ravana surrounded in supposed safety by the raging waters on all sides of Lanka? Does it not mean the conquest of physical might by spiritual strength? However, being a practical man, I do not wait till India recognizes the practicability of the spiritual life in the political world. India considers herself to be powerless and paralyzed before the machine guns, the tanks, and the aeroplanes of the English. And she takes up noncooperation out of her weakness. It must still serve the same purpose, namely, bring her delivery from the crushing weight of British injustice if a sufficient number of people practice it. I isolate this noncooperation from Sinn Feinism, for, it is so conceived as to be incapable of being offered side by side with violence. But I invite even the school of violence to give this peaceful noncooperation a trial. It will not fail through its inherent weakness. It may fail because of poverty of response. Then will be the time for real danger. The high-souled men, who are unable to suffer national humiliation any longer, will want to vent their wrath. They will take to violence. So far as I know, they must perish without delivering themselves or their country from the wrong. If India takes up the doctrine of the sword, she may gain momentary victory. Then India will cease to be the pride of my heart. I am wedded to India because I owe my all to her. I believe absolutely that she has a mission for the world. She is not to copy Europe blindly. India's acceptance of the doctrine of the sword will be the hour of my trial. I hope I shall not be found wanting. My religion has no geographical limits. If I have a living faith in it, it will transcend my love for India herself. My life is dedicated to service of India through the religion of nonviolence, which I believe to be the root of Hinduism. Meanwhile, I urge those who distrust me not to disturb the even working of the struggle that has just commenced, by inciting to violence in the belief that I want violence. I detest secrecy as a sin. Let them give nonviolent noncooperation a trial and they will find that I had no mental reservation whatsoever.

CWMG, vol. 18, pp. 131–34

5.
Nonviolence

It is my conviction that we are in sight of the promised land, but the danger is the greatest when victory seems the nearest. No victory worth the name has ever been won without a final effort, more serious than all the preceding ones. God's last test is ever the most difficult. Satan's last temptation is ever the most seductive. We must stand God's last test and resist Satan's last temptation, if we would be free. Nonviolence is the most vital and integral part of noncooperation. We may fail in everything else and still continue our battle if we remain nonviolent. But we capitulate miserably if we fail in adhering to nonviolence. Let it be remembered that violence is the keystone of the government edifice. Since violence is its sheet anchor and its final refuge, it has rendered itself almost immune from violence on our side by having prepared itself to frustrate all violent effort by the people. We therefore cooperate with the government in the most active manner when we resort to violence. Any violence on our part must be a token of our stupidity, ignorance, and impotent rage. To exercise restraint under the gravest provocation is the truest mark of soldiership. The veriest tyro in the art of war knows that he must avoid the ambushes of his adversary. And every provocation is a dangerous ambush into which we must resolutely refuse to walk. The story of Aligarh is an illustration in point. It seems clear enough that sufficient provocation was given by the police. We have long recognized that it is their business to do so. The people of Aligarh walked into the trap laid for them. They allowed themselves to be provoked, and resorted to arson. It is not yet clear who killed the constable in mufti. The burden is on the people to show that they did not. Let us be hard on ourselves. If we wish to walk along the straight and narrow path (which is necessarily the shortest), we must not be self-indulgent. We may not throw the blame for any mishap on the budmashes.

We must be responsible for their acts. Or we declare ourselves unfit for swaraj. We must gain control even over them. Even they must realize the necessity of not interfering with the national and the religious work we are engaged in. In a movement of purification, the whole country is lifted up not excluding the wicked and the fallen. Let there be no mistake, that is our deliberate claim. If it is merely a lip claim, we shall prove ourselves guilty of having set up a system more satanic than the one we condemn as such. Therefore whilst we are following the course of nonviolent noncooperation, we are bound in honor to live up to it in thought, word, and deed. Let us make the frank confession if we are too weak or too incredulous to live up to our creed. The reader must not run away with the idea that I feel we are not standing the test. On the contrary I believe that we have obtained a marvelous hold over the people, that they have understood the necessity of nonviolence as they have never done before. But it would be wrong for us not to take due warning from the slightest deviation from the path deliberately chosen by us. I find it necessary, too, to utter the word of caution, because the provocation by the government is on the increase. It is the greatest in the U.P.* The arrest of Mr. Sherwani at five o'clock in the morning, his swift trial, conviction, sentence, and removal the same day are enough to irritate the most sober-minded. The details of the trial show that the magistrate knew little of law and cared less. The evidence before him, if all of it has been given to the press, was quite insufficient for a conviction. It almost seems that the conviction and sentence were prearranged. The production of evidence in that case was a huge farce. We are having a rehearsal of trials under the ordinary law. Where is the difference between an executive order and a judicial trial? The latter is more deadly as it is more difficult to expose. To say that a man had no trial carries greater conviction of injustice than to have to say that the trial was farcical. Repressive laws may be repealed; it does not follow therefore that repression will be done away with. The substance will be the same though the form is

* United Provinces (at present called Uttar Pradesh).

changed. What we want is a change of substance, of spirit, of heart. And if we desire that change, we must first change ourselves, i.e., be proof against repression. Just as we may not retort with violence, so may we not weaken under repression no matter how severe or trying it may be. An authentic rumor comes from the U.P. that at least three more or less noted workers found the jail life too trying, gave undertakings to refrain from certain acts, and procured their discharge. If this is true, it is sad. We must be firm as a rock. There must be no going back. We must be able cheerfully to bear any torture that may be our lot in the jails of India. We may expect no quarter from the government. We must expect it to do the worst it can whether within or without the law. Its one purpose is to bend us, since it will not mend itself. I am not passing harsh judgment on the government. Dharwar and Aligarh are the latest instances of the government's defiance of propriety. If I am to credit another rumor, in a U.P. jail a brave Mussulman prisoner was put in a dark cell and locked up in it for three days in the midst of foul stenches. My informant asked me, what a man who could not bear these stenches was to do. The harsh but deliberate answer I gave was that he was even then not to apologize, he was free to dash his head against the walls of the prison rather than submit to the wish of the tyrant. This is not an idle expression of opinion, but a tidbit from my South African experiences. The jail life in South Africa was not a bed of roses. Many a prisoner had to undergo solitary confinement. Hundreds had to do sanitary work. Several fasted. One woman was discharged a skeleton because the authorities would not allow her the only food she would eat. But she had a proud and resolute spirit. Out of the thousands who suffered imprisonment in South Africa, with one or two exceptions in the early stages I do not recall a single instance of a prisoner having weakened and apologized to purchase his freedom. Some like Parsi Rustomji, Imam Kadir Bavazir, Thambi Naidu, and many others whose names I could set down never flinched but repeatedly sought imprisonment. The Temple of Freedom is not erected without the blood of sufferers. Nonviolent method is the quickest, the surest, and the best. Let us be true to our solemn oath taken at Congress and Khilafat gatherings, and triumph is at hand.

6.
Civil Disobedience

Civil disobedience was on the lips of every one of the members of the All-India Congress Committee. Not having really ever tried it, everyone appeared to be enamored of it from a mistaken belief in it as a sovereign remedy for our present-day ills. I feel sure that it can be made such if we can produce the necessary atmosphere for it. For individuals there always is that atmosphere except when their civil disobedience is certain to lead to bloodshed. I discovered this exception during the satyagraha days. But even so, a call may come which one dare not neglect, cost what it may. I can clearly see the time coming to me when I must refuse obedience to every single state-made law, even though there may be a certainty of bloodshed. When neglect of the call means a denial of God, civil disobedience becomes a peremptory duty. Mass civil disobedience stands on a different footing. It can only be tried in a calm atmosphere. It must be the calmness of strength, not weakness, of knowledge, not ignorance. Individual civil disobedience may be and often is vicarious. Mass civil disobedience may be and often is selfish in the sense that individuals expect personal gain from their disobedience. Thus, in South Africa, Kallenbach and Polak offered vicarious civil disobedience. They had nothing to gain. Thousands offered it because they expected personal gain also in the shape, say, of the removal of the annual poll tax levied upon ex-indentured men and their wives and grown-up children. It is sufficient in mass civil disobedience if the resisters understand the working of the doctrine. It was in a practically uninhabited tract of country that I was arrested in

South Africa when I was marching into prohibited area with over two to three thousand men and some women.* The company included several Pathans and others who were able-bodied men. It was the greatest testimony of merit the government of South Africa gave to the movement. They knew that we were as harmless as we were determined. It was easy enough for that body of men to cut to pieces those who arrested me. It would have not only been a most cowardly thing to do, but it would have been a treacherous breach of their own pledge, and it would have meant ruin to the struggle for freedom and the forcible deportation of every Indian from South Africa. But the men were no rabble. They were disciplined soldiers and all the better for being unarmed. Though I was torn from them, they did not disperse, nor did they turn back. They marched on to their destination till they were, every one of them, arrested and imprisoned. So far as I am aware, this was an instance of discipline and nonviolence for which there is no parallel in history. Without such restraint I see no hope of successful mass civil disobedience here. We must dismiss the idea of overawing the government by huge demonstrations every time someone is arrested. On the contrary we must treat arrest as the normal condition of the life of a noncooperator. For we must seek arrest and imprisonment, as a soldier who goes to battle seeks death. We expect to bear down the opposition of the government by courting and not by avoiding imprisonment, even though it be by showing our supposed readiness to be arrested and imprisoned en masse. Civil disobedience then emphatically means our desire to surrender to a single unarmed policeman. Our triumph consists in thousands being led to the prisons like lambs to the slaughterhouse. If the lambs of the world had been willingly led, they would have long ago saved themselves from the butcher's knife. Our triumph consists again in being imprisoned for no wrong whatsoever. The greater our innocence, the greater our strength and the swifter our victory. As it is, this government is cowardly, we are afraid

---

* MKG was arrested near Palmford on November 6, 1913, while leading men, women, and children into the Transvaal on their "Great March."

of imprisonment. The government takes advantage of our fear of jails. If only our men and women welcome jails as health resorts, we will cease to worry about the dear ones put in jails, which our countrymen in South Africa used to nickname His Majesty's Hotels. We have too long been mentally disobedient to the laws of the state and have too often surreptitiously evaded them to be fit all of a sudden for civil disobedience. Disobedience to be civil has to be open and nonviolent. Complete civil disobedience is a state of peaceful rebellion—a refusal to obey every single state-made law. It is certainly more dangerous than an armed rebellion. For it can never be put down if the civil resisters are prepared to face extreme hardships. It is based upon an implicit belief in the absolute efficiency of innocent suffering. By noiselessly going to prison a civil resister ensures a calm atmosphere. The wrongdoer wearies of wrongdoing in the absence of resistance. All pleasure is lost when the victim betrays no resistance. A full grasp of the conditions of successful civil resistance is necessary at least on the part of the representatives of the people before we can launch out on an enterprise of such magnitude. The quickest remedies are always fraught with the greatest danger and require the utmost skill in handling them. It is my firm conviction that, if we bring about a successful boycott of foreign cloth, we shall have produced an atmosphere that would enable us to inaugurate civil disobedience on a scale that no government can resist. I would therefore urge patience and determined concentration on swadeshi upon those who are impatient to embark on mass civil disobedience.

CWMG, vol. 20, pp. 464–66

7.
Excerpt from a Letter to Konda Venkatapaayya*

Your first question is whether the requisite nonviolent atmosphere can at all be attained and if so when. This is really a question as old as noncooperation. It puzzles me to find some of the closest and most esteemed of coworkers putting the question as if the requirement was a new thing. I have not the shadow of a doubt that, if we can secure workers with an abiding faith in nonviolence and in themselves, we can ensure the nonviolent atmosphere required for the working of civil disobedience. The discovery I have made during these few days is that very few understand the nature of nonviolence. The meaning of the adjective "civil" before "disobedience" is of course "nonviolent." Why should the people not be trained to refrain from participating in activities which are likely to throw them off their balance? I agree that it will be difficult to get thirty crores of people to be nonviolent, but I refuse to believe that it is difficult, if we can get intelligent and honest workers, to make people who are not actively participating in the movement remain indoors.

CWMG, vol. 23, p. 1

8.
Was It a Failure?

Repeatedly does one read in the papers that noncooperation was a perfect failure. Several courteous critics often apologetically broach the question in conversations, and gently tell me

* Letter dated March 4, 1922.

that the country would have made great progress if I had not led it astray by my ill-conceived noncooperation. I should not refer to this subject, which may be said to have no bearing on the politics of the day, but for my belief that noncooperation has come to us as an active force that may assume a universal form any moment, and but for the purpose of reassuring those who are bravely holding on in the face of criticism and skepticism. Let me, however, admit the dangerous half-truth that noncooperation entirely failed the moment it became violent. Indeed, noncooperation and violence are here contradictory terms. It is a living belief that violence lived on itself and it required counterviolence for its daily maintenance that gave rise to nonviolent noncooperation. The fact, therefore, is that the moment noncooperation became violent, it lost its vitality and nation-building character. But insofar as it was and remained nonviolent, it was a demonstrably complete success. The mass awakening that took place in 1920 all of a sudden was perhaps the greatest demonstration of the efficacy of nonviolence. The government has lost prestige never to be regained. Titles, law courts, educational institutions no longer inspire the awe they did in 1920. Some of the best lawyers in the country have given up law forever as a profession and are happy for having accepted comparative poverty as their lot. The few national schools and colleges that remain are giving a good account of themselves, as witness the great organization that came into being in Gujarat when the floods turned into a waste what was once a rich garden. But for the students and teachers of national institutions and other noncooperators the timely help that the afflicted peasantry of Gujarat received and so much needed would never have been at its disposal. It is possible to multiply illustrations of this character and prove that wherever there is real national life, a bond between the classes and the masses in India, noncooperation is the cause of it. Take again the three constructive items of the program. Khadi is a growing factor in national regeneration and is serving over fifteen hundred villages through an army of nearly two thousand workers and is giving tangible productive relief to over fifty thousand spinners and at least ten thousand weavers, printers, dyers, dhobis, and other artisans. Untouchability is a waning thing just struggling for existence. Hindu-Muslim unity of 1920–21 showed its vast possibilities. The violence, deceit, falsehood, and the like that mark the rupture between the two great communities today are no doubt ugly signs, but they are a demonstration of crude self-consciousness. The process of churning that the movement of noncooperation was and is has brought the dirt to the surface. And if nonviolent noncooperation is a living and purifying force, it will presently bring to view the pure unity that is invisibly forming itself under the very visible dirt that obtrudes itself on our gaze today. It is therefore clear to me as daylight that real swaraj, whenever it comes to us, will have to be not a donation rained on us from London but a prize earned by hard and health-giving noncooperation with organized forces of evil.

CWMG, vol. 35, pp. 224–25

9.
Democracy and Nonviolence*

Q. Why do you say "Democracy can only be saved through nonviolence"?

A. Because democracy, so long as it is sustained by violence, cannot provide for or protect the weak. My notion of democracy is that under it the weakest should have the same opportunity as the strongest. That can never happen except through nonviolence. No country in the world today shows any but patronizing regard for the weak. The weakest, you say, go to the wall. Take your own case. Your land is owned by a few capitalist owners. The same is true of South Africa. These large holdings cannot be sustained except by violence, veiled if not open.

---

* Excerpted from "A Question Box" wherein posers on varied subjects were answered.

Western democracy, as it functions today, is diluted Nazism or Fascism. At best it is merely a cloak to hide the Nazi and the Fascist tendencies of imperialism. Why is there the war today, if it is not for the satisfaction of the desire to share the spoils? It was not through democratic methods that Britain bagged India. What is the meaning of South African democracy? Its very constitution has been drawn to protect the white man against the colored man, the natural occupant. Your own history is perhaps blacker still, in spite of what the northern states did for the abolition of slavery. The way you have treated the Negro presents a discreditable record. And it is to save such democracies that the war is being fought! There is something very hypocritical about it. I am thinking just now in terms of nonviolence and trying to expose violence in its nakedness. India is trying to evolve true democracy, i.e., without violence. Our weapons are those of satyagraha expressed through the charkha, the village industries, primary education through handicrafts, removal of untouchability, communal harmony, prohibition, and nonviolent organization of labor as in Ahmedabad. These mean mass effort and mass education. We have big agencies for conducting these activities. They are purely voluntary, and their only sanction is service of the lowliest. This is the permanent part of the nonviolent effort. From this effort is created the capacity to offer nonviolent resistance called noncooperation and civil disobedience, which may culminate in mass refusal to pay rent and taxes. As you know, we have tried noncooperation and civil disobedience on a fairly large scale and fairly successfully. The experiment has in it promise of a brilliant future. As yet our resistance has been that of the weak. The aim is to develop the resistance of the strong. Your wars will never ensure safety for democracy. India's experiment can and will, if the people come up to the mark or, to put it another way, if God gives me the necessary wisdom and strength to bring the experiment to fruition.

10.
Excerpt from a Speech[*]

Hence I ask you, is our nonviolence the nonviolence of the coward, the weak, the helpless, the timid? In that case, it is of no value. A weakling is a born saint. A weak person is obliged to become a saint. But we are soldiers of nonviolence, who, if the occasion demands, will lay down their lives for it. Our nonviolence is not a mere policy of the coward. But I doubt this. I am afraid that the nonviolence we boast of might really be only a policy. It is true that, to some extent, nonviolence works even in the hands of the weak. And, in this manner, this weapon has been useful to us. But, if one makes use of nonviolence in order to disguise one's weakness or through helplessness, it makes a coward of one. Such a person is defeated on both the fronts. Such a one cannot live like a man and the devil he surely cannot become. It is a thousand times better that we die trying to acquire the strength of the arm. Using physical force with courage is far superior to cowardice. At least we would have attempted to act like men. That was the way of our forefathers. That is because some people hold the view that the ancestors of the human race were animals. I do not wish to enter into the controversy whether Darwin's theory is tenable or not. However, from one standpoint we must all have originally been animals. And I am ready to believe that we are evolved from the animal into the human state. That is why physical strength is called brute force. We are born with such strength, hence if we used it we could be, to say the least, courageous. But we are born as human beings in order that we may realize God who dwells within our hearts. This is the basic distinction between us and the beasts. It is not that the serpent crawls on its belly, whereas we walk on our legs. The bullock has four legs, I have two. We have attained the human form. We are evolved gradually from such species as the serpent, etc.,

[*] At Gandhi Seva Sangh Meeting on March 25, 1938.

to the human state. Along with the human form, we also have human power—that is, the power of nonviolence. We can have an insight into the mystery of soul force. In that consists our humanity. Man is by nature nonviolent. But he does not owe his origin to nonviolence. We fulfil our human life when we see the atman, and when we do so we pass the test. Now is the time for our test. God-realization means seeing Him in all beings. Or, in other words, we should learn to become one with every creature. This is man's privilege and that distinguishes him from the beasts. This can happen only when we voluntarily give up the use of physical force and when we develop the nonviolence which lies dormant in our hearts. It can be awakened only through real strength. Do we really have this nonviolence of the strong?

CWMG, vol. 66, pp. 420–21

II.
Interview to Dr. John Mott*

[DR. MOTT:] *What do you consider to be the most valuable contribution that India can make to the progress of the world?*

[GANDHIJI:] Nonviolence, which the country is exhibiting at the present day on a scale unprecedented in history. But for it, there might have been a blaze, for provocation of the gravest kind has not been wanting on the side of the government. There is no doubt a school in the country that believes in violence, but it is a mere excrescence on the surface and its ideals are not likely to find a congenial soil in the country. What causes you solicitude for the future of the country? Our apathy and hardness of heart, if I may use that biblical phrase, as typified in the attitude toward the masses and their poverty. Our youth are full of noble feelings and impulses but these have not yet taken any definite practical shape. If our youth had a living and active faith

---

* The interview was conducted in February 1929.

in truth and nonviolence, for instance, we should have made much greater headway by now. All our young men, however, are not apathetic. In fact, without the closest cooperation of some of our educated young men and women, I should not have been able to establish contact with the masses and to serve them on a nationwide scale; and I am sustained by the hope that they will act as the leaven, and in time transform the entire mass.

CWMG, vol. 40, pp. 57–58

12.
Talk with a Pacifist*

[GANDHIJI:] For nonviolence to permeate us we should have a living faith in God. Nonviolence comes to us through doing good continually without the slightest expectation of return. It simply spends itself and it is its own reward, and done in that spirit it is done not merely for friends but certainly for adversaries. That is the indispensable lesson in nonviolence. It was thrown my way by God in South Africa in an atmosphere which was as adverse as it well could be. I was in a country where I knew no European or Indian. I had gone there to make a career as a lawyer. But I succeeded in learning the eternal law of suffering as the only remedy for undoing wrong and injustice. It means positively the law of nonviolence. You have to be prepared to suffer cheerfully at the hands of all and sundry, and you will wish ill to no one, not even to those who may have wronged you. Just now a good many people are talking of world peace, promoting peace societies and passing resolutions. This is good as far as it goes. But it may not be nonviolence. An army of nonviolence exposes itself to all the risks that an army of violence does. Only the latter expects to retaliate even when it is not the aggressor. An army of nonviolence runs risks without the wish to retaliate.

* In March 1938.

[THE PACIFIST:] *But the war spirit is creeping slowly over us. How are we to combat it?*

[G.] I know how difficult it is for you to combat it in England. You have to approach the problem with faith and determination even though you may be very few. I would recommend the study of Richard Gregg's book* on the practice of nonviolence. A true pacifist refuses to use the fruit of arms-peace and order. So long as we eat a single grain of wheat grown under the protection of arms, we participate in violence. When one realizes this, one has to be an exile in one's own country and a rebel. But everything has to be done according to the measure of one's strength. A few people with the courage of their convictions can become perfect nuisances to the whole state. How far it is possible to reduce the whole thing to practice is for each individual to judge. Our English movement for peace is growing. But shall we simply go on enrolling more and more members? I am not enamored of numbers. A peace army does not rely upon numbers unless they understand the implications of nonviolence. I would, therefore, concentrate on a few becoming saturated with the spirit of nonviolence and disciplining themselves for the utmost suffering. How exactly to act in particular situations is a matter of waiting on God. The answer comes straight in response to prayer from the heart. Such prayer carries with it the anguish of the soul.

CWMG, vol. 66, pp. 397–98

13.
Interview to Tingfang Lew, Y. T. Wu, and P. C. Hsu[†]

The Chinese delegates put searching questions . . . One of them asked: *"Is it not necessary that individuals should practice*

---

* *The Power of Non-violence.*

[†] This interview with a Chinese delegation took place on January 1, 1939.

nonviolence first in their own person, in their relations with other individuals?"

GANDHIJI: It would be a delusion to think otherwise. If one does not practice nonviolence in one's personal relations with others and hopes to use it in bigger affairs, one is vastly mistaken. Nonviolence like charity must begin at home. But if it is necessary for the individual to be trained in nonviolence, it is even more necessary for the nation to be trained likewise. One cannot be nonviolent in one's own circle and violent outside it. Or else one is not truly nonviolent even in one's own circle; often the nonviolence is only in appearance. It is only when you meet with resistance, as for instance when a thief or murderer appears, that your nonviolence is put on its trial. You either try or should try to oppose the thief with his own weapons or you try to disarm him by love. Living among decent people, your conduct may not be described as nonviolent. Mutual forbearance is not nonviolence. Immediately, therefore, you get the conviction that nonviolence is the law of life, you have to practice it toward those who act violently toward you, and the law must apply to nations as to individuals. Training is no doubt necessary. And beginnings are always small. But if the conviction is there, the rest will follow.

Q. *In the practice of nonviolence, is there not danger of developing a "martyrdom complex" or pride creeping in?*

A. If one has that pride and egoism, there is no nonviolence. Nonviolence is impossible without humility. My own experience is that whenever I have acted nonviolently I have been led to it and sustained in it by the higher promptings of an unseen power. Through my own will I should have miserably failed. When I first went to jail, I quailed at the prospect. I had heard terrible things about jail life. But I had faith in God's protection. Our experience was that those who went to jail in a prayerful spirit came out victorious, those who had gone in their own strength failed. There is no room for self-pitying in it, either, when you say God is giving you the strength. Self-pity comes when you do a thing for which you expect recognition from others. But here there is no question of recognition.

Another friend thus placed his dilemma: *"I am a firm*

believer in nonviolence. Eight years ago, I read your Experiments with Truth *and . . . translated the book into Chinese. And then came the Japanese invasion. My faith in nonviolence was put to a severe test. . . . On the one hand, I felt I could not preach nonviolence to my people who . . . believed that resistance with force was the only way out. . . . But on the other hand, when I try to take a sympathetic attitude and try to do something helpful in such a situation, I find I am giving moral and material support directly and indirectly to something which is against the highest that I know. . . ."*

G. Yours is a difficult situation. Such difficulties have confronted me more than once. I took part on the British side in the Boer War by forming an ambulance corps. I did likewise at the time of what has been described as the Zulu revolt. The third time was during the great war. I believed in nonviolence then. My motive was wholly nonviolent. That seemingly inconsistent conduct gave me strength. My example cannot be used as a precedent for others to follow. Looking back upon my conduct on those three occasions, I have no sense of remorse. I know this, too, that my nonviolent strength did not suffer diminution because of those experiences. The actual work I was called upon to do was purely humanitarian, especially during the Zulu revolt. I and my companions were privileged to nurse the wounded Zulus back to life. It is reasonable to suggest that but for our services some of them would have died. I cite this experience not to justify my participation however indirect it was. I cite it to show that I came through that experience with greater nonviolence and with richer love for the great Zulu race. And I had an insight into what war by white men against colored races meant. The lesson to be learnt from it by you is that, placed as you are in a position of hopeless minority, you may not ask your people to lay down their arms unless their hearts are changed and by laying down their arms they feel the more courageous and brave. But whilst you may not try to wean people from war, you will in your person live nonviolence in all its completeness and refuse all participation in war. You will develop love for the Japanese in your hearts. You will examine yourself whether you can really love them, whether you have not some ill will toward them for all the harm they are doing. It is not enough to love them by re-membering their virtues. You must be able to love them in spite of all their misdeeds. If you have that love for the Japanese in your hearts, you will proceed to exhibit in your conduct that higher form of courage which is the hallmark of true nonvio-lence and which your Chinese friends will not fail to detect and recognize as such. You will not wish success to Japanese arms because you "love" the Japanese. At the same time you will not pray for the success of Chinese arms. It is very difficult to judge, when both sides are employing weapons of violence, which side "deserves" to succeed. You will therefore pray only that the right should prevail. Whilst you will keep yourself aloof from all violence you will not shirk danger. You will serve friend and foe alike with a reckless disregard for your life. You will rush forth if there is an outbreak of an epidemic or a fire to be combated and distinguish yourself by your sur-passing courage and nonviolent heroism. But you will refuse to call the curses of heaven upon the Japanese. If by chance some Japanese soldiers or airmen fall into the hands of the Chinese and are in danger of being lynched by an infuriated Chinese mob or otherwise ill-treated, you will plead for them with your own people and if necessary even protect them with your life. You know the story of Emily Hobhouse. Though an English-woman, she courageously went to the Boer concentration camps. She exhorted the Boers never to lose heart, and it is said that if she had not steeled the hearts of the Boer women as she did, the war might have taken a different turn. She was full of wrath against her own people for whom she had not a good word to say. You would not copy her unmeasured wrath which somewhat vitiated her nonviolence, but you will copy her love for the "enemy" that made her denounce the misdeeds of her own countrymen. Your example will affect the Chinese and might even shame some Japanese who will become bearers of your message among the Japanese. A very slow process, you will perhaps say. Yes, possibly, under the existing adverse cir-cumstances to begin with. But it will gather momentum and speed in an incalculable manner as you proceed. I am an irrepressible optimist. My optimism rests on my belief in the infinite possibilities of the individual to develop nonviolence. The more you develop it in your own being, the more infectious it becomes, till it overwhelms your surroundings and by and by might oversweep the world.

Q. *I, a believer in nonviolence, often find that I am actuated by mixed motives. So does a war general have mixed motives. Is it not possible to fight with love for the enemy in one's heart? May we not shoot out of love?*

A. We do often have mixed motives. But that would not be nonviolence. There can be degrees in violence, not in nonviolence. The constant effort of the votary of nonviolence is to purge himself of hatred toward the so-called enemy. There is no such thing as shooting out of love in the way you suggest.

The last to place before Gandhiji his problem was Mr. P. C. Hsu.

P. C. HSU: *I can say honestly, I have no feeling of hatred toward the Japanese people but I feel their military system is an evil. . . . I had hoped that at Tambaram, at any rate, an international link between the two countries on the basis of mutual goodwill and peace would be forged. But I was disillusioned. . . . Our difficulty is this: While sincerely believing in nonviolence, we have not found a way of making it effective.*

G. Should that present a difficulty? A person who realizes a particular evil of his time and finds it overwhelms him dives deep in his own heart for inspiration, and when he gets it, he presents it to others. Meetings and group organizations are all right. They are of some help, but very little. They are like the scaffolding that an architect erects—a temporary and makeshift expedient. The thing that really matters is an invincible faith that cannot be quenched. Faith can be developed. Only the way it can be developed and in which it works differs from that in the case of violence. You cannot develop violence through prayer. Faith, on the other hand, cannot be developed except through prayer. Nonviolence succeeds only when we have a living faith in God. Buddha, Jesus, Muhammad—they were all warriors of peace in their own style. We have to enrich the heritage left by these world teachers. God has His own wonderful way of executing His plans and choosing His instruments. The Prophet and Abu Bakr trapped in a cave were saved from their persecutors by a spider which had woven its web across the mouth of that cave. All the world teachers, you should know, began with a zero!!

Q. *Whilst we have isolated individuals who have the mind of Jesus, because they are not united, not organized, theirs remains a mere cry in the wilderness. The question that arises in my mind is: Can love be organized, and if so, how?*

A. Organization in the orthodox sense may not be possible. But there is no bar to united nonviolent action. I am trying to show by a series of experiments that it is possible. It has its own technique.

Q. *If China wins the war, will she be worse off or better off for her victory?*

A. If China wins and copies Japanese methods, she will beat Japan hollow at her own game. But the victory of China will not mean a new hope for the world. For China will then be a multiple edition of Japan. But whether China wins or goes down, your line of action is clear. If China is defeated on the battlefield, your nonviolence will remain undaunted and will have done its work. If China wins, you will go to the gallows in the attempt to wean China from copying Japan's methods.

CWMG, vol. 68, pp. 267–71

14.
An Excerpt from a Discussion with Agatha Harrison*

The nonviolence that we have offered hitherto has not been the nonviolence of the brave. As a weapon of the weak, as an expedient, it was good enough. It did answer its purpose for a while. But how long can the nonviolence of the weak last? I

* This discussion took place on March 29–30, 1939.

have not been able to answer for Europe because I have not worked it out in India. And yet I would not rewrite those chapters in our history. God fulfills Himself even through the weakness of His instruments sometimes. But if we now do not overhaul the basis of our nonviolence and if we continue to drift in the old style, it would be nothing short of a catastrophe. We shall not have evolved the nonviolent strength and courage, and, faced with a crisis, might behave like cowards.

CWMG, vol. 69, p. 89.

15.
Congress and Nonviolence:
Discussion at Congress Working Committee Meeting*

GANDHIJI: I have been oppressed all the time by the fact that I now represent a totally different mentality from that of the Working Committee. When I asked for absolution it was not a formal thing. My article in the *Harijan*† is a true picture of my mind. I put the same thing to the viceroy. I told him that this was the last interview. He should send for the president of the Congress if he must have an offer on behalf of the Congress. I think in the course of days he will invite the president. It is the most difficult job for me to give a decisive opinion on these matters. I would much rather that you left me alone. Granting the implications that I have drawn from the last resolution, you cannot possibly escape its logical conclusion. You will want to seize power. You will have to surrender certain things in order to get it. You will have to be like other parties. You will be driven into their ways. Maybe you will be an advanced party. This picture repels me. I don't believe in the expression "seizure

* This meeting was held in July 1940 to discuss MKG's request that he be absolved from the activities of the Indian National Congress.

† "Both Happy and Unhappy," *CWMG*, vol. 72, pp. 194–97.

of power." There is no such thing as "seizure of power." I have no power save what resides in the people. I am a mere representative of the power in the people. While Rajaji was developing his theme I felt that a wide gulf separated me from him. He thinks he will be best able to serve his country by taking advantage of every opportunity to serve the country. He takes office in that light. I differ fundamentally from him. He may satisfy himself with the illusion that he is serving nonviolence. I am not afraid of power. Someday or the other we will have to take it. The viceroy is here to serve his country, its interests, and therefore he must use all resources that India has mercilessly. If we participate in war effort, we shall have learnt some lesson in the art of violence, even if the Britishers are defeated. This will give us some experience, some power such as a soldier has, but all this at the cost of independence. This seems to me the logical consequence of your resolution. This does not appeal to me. If we are nonviolent I know how to deal with the situation. The vast majority of our people had violence in them, but they were taught the power of nonviolence. Now you must teach them the power of violence. There is confusion in the people now. It is not my interpretation which has caused it but the resolution itself. I cannot guide you in this atmosphere. Whatever I say will embarrass you. I told the viceroy that the British, if they succeed, will not be better than Mussolini or Hitler. If there is peace with Hitler, India will be exploited by all powers. But if we are nonviolent and Japan comes, we will see that they do not get anything without our consent. Nonviolence has worked wonders in twenty years. We cannot do any such thing with violence. . . .

JAWAHARLAL NEHRU: The question was brought forward by Gandhiji in the world context. He wanted to place the message of nonviolence before the world.

GANDHIJI: Not exactly world context. I thought of the immediate problem. I did not have the world picture before me but India, and India alone. In the position they have taken, the Working Committee is free to render help and to prepare an army. It is free to take office. The viceroy thought the resolution favored him. He said: "You want to defend India, you want aeroplanes, battleships, tanks, etc. We will give you all these. This will serve our purpose and also yours. This is the golden opportunity. You should come and get equipped. Under pressure we will go forward double speed." I regret the Congress took what I considered as a backward step, but it is a perfectly honorable step. It has taken the only step that it could. I will still try to wean it and the rank and file from this mistake. If the rank and file feel with me, the Working Committee will retract the step. A larger issue of internal anarchy was before us. What contribution shall we make if anarchy overtakes us? Will the masses cooperate in the nonviolent effort? I will test the masses and if I find that they will desert me I will shape my policy accordingly, but I won't collapse before they collapse. The terrible things that are going on in Europe fill me with anguish. I do not know where I could come in there. I feel I can do something and hence the statement. Private armies never appeal to me. The masses will be exploited by us. We will go and tell them you must give us your last penny to defend your hearths and homes. I cannot do this. This is not for me. I want to proclaim to the country that India will defend itself nonviolently so far as the Congress is concerned.

C. RAJAGOPALACHARI: I cannot go with Gandhiji in his conception of the state. Ours is a political organization not working for nonviolence but for the political ideal. We are working in competition with other political parties.

JAWAHARLAL NEHRU: I agree with Rajaji in his understanding of violence and nonviolence; else we cannot function on the political plane.

GANDHIJI: Very difficult questions have arisen in the course of the discussion. Rajaji has summarily rejected the idea that we can retain power by nonviolent means. This was illustrated even when we attained it by nonviolent means while the Congress was in office. To the extent they used violence the ministries failed. Their action showed bankruptcy of our nonviolence. Perhaps we could not have done otherwise. I advised giving up of office. Rajaji, however, does not accept what I have said, that it is possible to hold office without the use of more than police violence. I again want to emphasize two things. I do not [sic] believe that declaration of independence is necessary. The legal declaration may come afterward. If the government expects any help from us our help will be moral. It will be infinitely superior to what they can get by manipulation, coaxing, or coercion. I do feel if they have courage to do the right thing, the scales will be turned in their favor. Independence in action must be declared. Very lightly it was said by some members that we must dismiss from our minds civil resistance. I have never dismissed it. A time may come when we shall resort to civil disobedience. I cannot conceive the idea of our sitting silently when people are made to cooperate under compulsion. This process is going on now. The process was gentle and not much felt till the French capitulation. I cannot conceive my remaining silent or sitting at ease with this coercion going on unhampered. But can our people show nonviolence through and through? The nonviolence of the weak will bring us some relief but not real joy and power—it will end in our being exhausted. If we begin with nonviolence of the weak and end also with that, we are finished. Therefore now, when the testing time has come, you say it is not possible. All honor to your integrity and courage of conviction. But I cannot help feeling that our nonviolence has ended in disaster, I say again with experience and conviction that it is possible to touch power through nonviolence, but we may not take it. A nonviolent organization may not accept office but it can get things done its way. Thus alone can we have power if we have not nonviolent control over people. Jawaharlal has done less than justice to those who believe in nonviolence. He means that they want to be superior men leaving the dirty work of violence to be done by others. I hold, on the other hand, that we don't take power at all. It involves emoluments, glory, and things which people prize. Those in power consider that they are superior and others subordinate. When a nonviolent man refuses to take over power he says, "I decline because if I accept I shall make a mess of it. I am not built that way. Let credit go to others." I never felt that I was superior to those who took power nor did they feel that they were inferior or called upon to do a dirty job. Now suppose you at this critical moment hold fast to nonviolence in the midst of other parties who swear by violence, you will be in a minority. Why should a small nonviolent group immediately expect to win power before they convert others? Let others hold power. A group of nonviolent men wishing to convert the country to nonviolence will not bother about power. In holding fast to the creed you will have converted a majority of the people. A man who has self-confidence will convert the country. But you say millions will never arrive at that stage. I feel practically certain they can. Do not lay down this proposition. I became nonviolent after laborious processes. It is the essence of nonviolence that we give the same credit to the whole of mankind that we claim for ourselves. I have never felt that I alone can practice nonviolence. Quite the contrary, I consider myself mediocre. I belong purely to the rank and file and yet I can lead the masses. I can produce heroes from the illiterates of Gujarat. Time was when these illiterates said, "What can we do?" Today these very people are wielding power. If we can convert a few thousands, we can convert millions. Both masses of Hindus and Muslims acted nonviolently in 1920. Could it not be a great thing for us to have acquired such an influence upon public opinion and upon those who wield power that we do not have to compel obedience? Nonviolence cannot suddenly mount to power. I am not satisfied with swaraj for the few. It is for millions. They must feel it. By violent means they cannot feel it. This opportunity has come into our hands. We have got to decide. I do not leave out even lepers from my nonviolent calculation. I am not talking through my hat. I have a leper in my Ashram. He feels now that he can play his part though he cannot wield arms. Logically I have endeavored to show that there is nothing to prevent you from taking power if certain conditions are fulfilled. Many Indian villages and institutions are behaving nonviolently. We are trying to produce a homogeneous nation. We must allow time for it. What has violence accomplished in the world? I think impatience has seized us. If we do not take office, others will take office. If you think that you can serve the people by entering into competition with others, you are mistaken. We are democrats. We would be presumed to be ruling by the will of the people. We must dismount if people rebel. We have not given that trial to nonviolence which we might have. All of us did our best. Let us do better. If we do better, if we have got the proper courage, we shall have left something for India to be proud of. I would like you to feel with me that it is perfectly possible to hold the state without an army. If anybody comes I will square accounts with him along nonviolent lines. Why should we fear that they will swallow us? Violent people fight violent people. They do not touch nonviolent people. We build up huge armaments in order to ward off an attack in some distant future. The divisions in the country also provide us with reason for our keeping to nonviolence. We can hold our people peacefully against the whole world. Our nonviolence is of the weak. It is not nonviolence of the brave. If we have affection for our neighbor, there will be no Hindu-Muslim riots. These riots can be prevented. If they can be prevented, other anarchy can also be prevented.

CWMG, vol. 72, pp. 235–40

16.
Draft Resolution for the Working Committee

The Working Committee have noted that confusion prevails amongst congressmen as to the interpretation of their last statement made in Wardha on 21 June. They observe that several newspapers and others in common with many congressmen have believed that the committee had given up nonviolence as an integral part of the Congress policy. Certain paragraphs of the statement do lend themselves to such interpretation in spite of the following emphatic and unequivocal declaration therein of the Congress policy: "The war in Europe, resulting from a desire for imperialist domination over other peoples and countries, and a suicidal race in armaments, has led to human sorrow and misery on a scale hitherto unknown. It has demonstrated the inefficacy of organized violence, on however vast a scale, for the defense of national freedom and the liberties of peoples. It has shown beyond a doubt that warfare cannot lead to peace and freedom and the choice before the world is uttermost degradation and destruction through warfare or the way of peace and nonviolence on a basis of freedom for all peoples. . . . The committee wish to make it clear that the methods and basic policy of nonviolence in the national struggle for freedom continue with full force and are not affected in the least by the inability to extend it to the region of national defense." The Working Committee have come to the conclusion that they should exclusively rely upon Congress volunteers pledged to nonviolence and the Congress discipline to deal with internal disorders to the extent it is possible. The volunteers will cooperate in a nonviolent way with other similar organizations in their nonviolent activities. The Working Committee advises all Congress committees to form volunteer corps provided that they are sure that the candidates know the implications of nonviolence and the value of strict discipline. The Congress nonviolence has been hitherto confined to the fight with the British government. If success achieved so far has made nonviolence, to the extent mentioned, the settled policy of the Congress beyond assail, it must be admitted that success cannot be claimed for nonviolent effort in the case of communal riots. The Working Committee are of opinion that the fault must be laid at the door of volunteer organizations. The Working Committee hope that at this the critical hour in the history of India volunteer organizations would be able effectively to deal with riots and the like in a nonviolent manner. The Working Committee never had occasion to determine whether India can be defended nonviolently, nor is it even now called upon to do so, though the proved futility of violence to defend the nations of Europe is sufficient indication for the Working Committee for coming to a decision. But till the hour for taking a final decision arrives, the Working Committee must keep an open mind. But so far as the present is concerned, the Working Committee are firmly of opinion that in pursuance of their nonviolent policy congressmen must not have anything to do with military training or activities calculated to make India military-minded. Therefore the Working Committee cannot but view with grave alarm the attempt made in an organized manner to prepare India for military defense. In the opinion of the Working Committee, if India were free and independent without an army she would have no fear of external aggression. The best defense that free India can put up if the people accepted the Congress policy would be to cultivate friendliness with the whole world. To invest crores of rupees in armaments, fortresses, and the like would be to invite foreign attack. The Working Committee believes that India is too poor to invest money in costly defense forces and modern equipment. The Working Committee therefore warn the British government against the feverish preparations that they are making for the professed defense of India. They are of opinion that they are intended merely to help Britain. These preparations cannot help India in any real sense. The Working Committee draw the attention of the British government and people that although India is claimed by them to have provincial autonomy and every province has elected assemblies, and there is also a partially popularly elected Central Legislative Assembly, the huge expense is being incurred without any reference to these legislatures. The Working Committee believes that it is wrong and immoral to arm one man, however honest and distinguished, with unlimited powers to utilize the resources of a great country like India and to impress her people in any manner he chooses without any control or check on the part of her people. It is a procedure in no way in keeping with the British government's declarations, however unsatisfactory from the Congress standpoint, about the freedom of India. The Working Committee wishes to declare that the Congress claims to be wholly friendly to the British people. Its nonviolent policy demands nothing but goodwill toward them. But the friendliness and goodwill can have no play and no meaning, so long as India remains in helpless bondage and her resources in men and money are utilized without ascertaining the wishes of the representatives of the people elected under a system established by Great Britain. The Working Committee asks the British

government to revise their suicidal policy and take the popular
assemblies into their confidence. The Working Committee associate themselves with the appeal recently made by Gandhiji
to every Briton and hope that Great Britain will accept the
policy of nonviolence whose potency has been proved beyond
doubt even though its application was admittedly imperfect.
British government may rely upon the fullest and friendliest
cooperation of the Congress in the direction of peace effort in
the nonviolent way commended by Gandhiji. In spite of the re-
peated and firm declaration of the Congress to the contrary,
there seems to be a belief among the public, including even
some congressmen, that the Congress will be satisfied with dominion status. The Working Committee warn all concerned
that they will accept no status lower than complete independence and that declaration should be made now and given effect to, immediately so far as may be. The legal formality may
await a suitable future period. Only India free and independent in action can decide upon the part she should play in the
present war. There is talk among some congressmen that the
Congress may countenance resumption of ministerial offices.
The Working Committee wish to make it clear that there is no
prospect of the Congress countenancing such a step without a
satisfactory settlement with the government and in no case of
promoting a war effort in which they have no faith. In view of
the foregoing it is superfluous to say that the Working Committee cannot associate themselves with any government pro-
posals to expand the Central executive. In view of the recent
developments the Working Committee decides to remove the
ban upon Congress members of the Central Legislative Assembly attending its sessions.

Inasmuch as it is necessary still further to enforce strict discipline, the Working Committee asks all those who do not strictly
believe in nonviolence to resign from the Congress. It is against
the Congress constitution for anyone to become a four-anna
member unless he, believing in it, signs the Congress pledge.

GANDHIJI: I have placed this draft before you only to know
your reactions. I have no doubt that you took in Wardha the

wisest decision that you could take. The discussions today have more than confirmed my opinion. I am more than fully repaid for the labor I spent on the draft. I reduced my idea to writing only to find your reactions. I have listened to every word of the discussion. I see that there is a definite, wide gulf between us, such that it cannot be bridged. To attempt to do so would be doing a disservice to the country. I have no impatience, no irritation in me. If I find that my hold has weakened I must withdraw in the interest of the Congress itself. I have always derived my politics from ethics or religion and my strength is also derived by my deriving my politics from ethics. It is because I swear by ethics and religion that I find myself in politics. A person who is a lover of his country is bound to take lively interest in politics, otherwise he will not be able to carry on his avocation with peace. I came into the Congress with my religion. The time has arrived when I should watch you and see whether I can take you as far as necessary. I had not in the past the slightest difficulty in carrying Rajaji with me, his intelligence as well as his heart, but since this office question cropped up, I saw that our thoughts were running in different directions. I see that I cannot carry him now along with me. It is vital for me therefore to ask for absolution. Internal dissensions are a small thing. We have now concentrated sufficiently on them. If you cannot come to a decision about external aggression, you cannot come to a decision about internal dissensions. My mind does not make a vital distinction between the two. I have deliberately put in the resolution the expression "open mind." You have said that we can mount to power by nonviolent means, but you doubt the ability to retain and consolidate it except through an army. The little police force that I have in mind will not be sufficient to cope with big disorders unless we have, as a nation, sufficient nonviolence in us, or in other words we apply nonviolence to politics. The technique of nonviolence is different from that of violence. We shut our eyes to the fact that our control on the masses, over even our registered congressmen, is ineffective. The negative response is there. In positive response both fail. It is not our fault exactly. Millions are concerned. Even a military program could not have been complete in twenty years. We must therefore be patient. If the masses have won independence by nonviolence, they can also retain it by nonviolence. Twenty years is nothing for the country. Our nonviolence was restricted to capturing power. We are successful as against the British, but we failed against our own people. At several places we have had violent demonstrations by congressmen and Congress committees. Hence our difficulties and my insistence that we must develop nonviolence. This is the time; otherwise we will cut a sorry figure. Rajaji is right that if I believe that the Congress is with me I am living in a fool's paradise. I have plunged with my eyes open. I played with fire when I entered into partnership with Muslims. Hindus said the Muslims would organize themselves. They did. I have one measure for the whole of mankind. I have been thinking seriously about the weaknesses that have crept into the Congress, but always in the hope that I will carry you further when the time comes. When Bhulabhai said we are committing ourselves he is right and not right. A document is to be read together with commas and semicolons. Today we have the choice between weapons of destruction and nonviolence for internal and external purposes. We have got to make the choice. Let us say good-bye to nonviolence if we must. Today nonviolence, tomorrow violence—this is our attitude. We don't know what we shall do in future. Let alone tomorrow, let us ask ourselves: shall we shoulder the rifle now? Bhulabhai spoke of eleven hundred officers. This does not move a single muscle of mine. My horizon extends to the submerged millions. The eleven hundred are lost in that ocean. I will never be able to forgive myself if I take a false step. If you don't come to Rajaji's position today, you will come to it tomorrow. If you have imbibed nonviolence in practice, well and good; for myself I go on with it in my pocket, in my heart and mind. I shall try to convert my people and see what is in store for me; in the alternative we must give our people military training but that for ourselves and not for the empire. The empire is tottering. The sun on it is fast setting. If we lack faith in nonviolence, let us organize for violence. I hold we will fail. I agree with Maulana Saheb that those who start with violence for self-defense end with aggression. He has quoted his own coreligionist. I have got this precious thing for which I want to live. I don't want to be instrumental in militarizing the masses. A nonviolent soldier will not be despised. He may be a consumptive, but he will give a better account of himself than the tallest Pathan. I want you to seriously examine Rajaji's position and see if you can adopt it; otherwise he should be allowed to go away. Our readings on nonviolence differ at this moment. Let him carve out a position for himself. He must agitate even if he is in a hopeless minority. I started alone, but soon I enjoyed a vast majority. He should strain every nerve to persuade the Working Committee or reconstitute the committee of those who are not saturated with nonviolence up to the point I have stated. You should allow me to carry the message as I know it. The country will not lose by this twofold division if we are honest. We must all act according to our views. It fills me with intense pleasure that everyone has spoken frankly. Visualizing the position as it changes from moment to moment, we have to find out what part we can each of us play in the drama. Let Jawaharlal take the lead. He will express himself forcibly. I shall be in his pocket.

CWMG, vol. 72, pp. 240–45

17.
Excerpts from a Discussion with B. G. Kher and Others*

You see that I am answering every one of your questions straightaway without the slightest hesitation. That is because the great question underlying your questions possesses me and I have rehearsed to myself every one of the situations arising out of the various implications of ahimsa.

---

* The discussion took place on August 15, 1940.

Q. Should one stop with the human species or extend ahimsa to all creation?

GANDHIJI: I was not prepared for this question. For the Congress, ahimsa is naturally confined to the political field and therefore only to the human species. Hence out-and-out nonviolence means for our purpose every variety of nonviolence in the political field. In concrete terms it covers family relations, relations with constituted authority, internal disorders, and external aggression. Put in another way, it covers all human relations.

Q. Then what about meat-eating and egg-eating? Are they consistent with nonviolence?

G. They are. Otherwise we should have to exclude Mussalmans and Christians and a vast number of Hindus as possible coworkers in ahimsa. I have known many meat-eaters to be far more nonviolent than vegetarians.

Q. But what if we had to give them up for the sake of a principle?

G. Oh yes, we would, if we had to compromise our principle. Our principle is defined as I have shown already.

Q. If, as you have said, Polish resistance to the German invasion was almost nonviolent, and you would thus seem to reconcile yourself with it, why do you object to the Wardha resolution of the Working Committee?

G. Surely there is no analogy between the two cases. If a man fights with his sword single-handed against a horde of dacoits armed to the teeth, I should say he is fighting almost nonviolently. Haven't I said to our women that, if in defense of their honor they used their nails and teeth and even a dagger, I should regard their conduct nonviolent? She does know the distinction between himsa and ahimsa. She acts spontaneously. Supposing a mouse in fighting a cat tried to resist the cat with his sharp teeth, would you call that mouse violent? In the same way, for the Poles to stand valiantly against the German hordes vastly superior in numbers, military equipment, and strength, was almost nonviolence. I should not mind repeating that statement over and over again. You must give its full value to the word "almost." But we are four hundred million here. If we were to organize a big army and prepare ourselves to fight foreign aggression, how could we by any stretch of imagination call ourselves almost nonviolent, let alone nonviolent? The Poles were unprepared for the way in which the enemy swooped down upon them. When we talk of armed preparation, we contemplate preparation to meet any violent combination with our superior violence. If India ever prepared herself that way, she would constitute the greatest menace to world peace. For if we take that path, we will also have to choose the path of exploitation like the European nations. That is why I still regret the moment when my words lacked the power of convincing the Sardar and Rajaji. By having passed that resolution, we proclaimed to the world that the ahimsa we had subscribed to all these years was not really ahimsa but a form of himsa.

Q. How will you run your administration nonviolently?

G. If you assume that we would have won independence by nonviolent means, it means that the bulk of the country had been organized nonviolently. Without the vast majority of people having become nonviolent, we could not attain nonviolent swaraj. If, therefore, we attain swaraj by purely nonviolent means, it should not be difficult for us to carry on the administration without the military. The goondas, too, will then have come under our control. If, for instance, in Sevagram we have five or seven goondas in a population of seven hundred who are nonviolently organized, the five or seven will either live under the discipline of the rest or leave the village. But you will see that I am answering the question with the utmost caution, and my truth makes me admit that we might have to maintain a police force. But the police will be after our pattern, and not the British pattern. As we shall have adult suffrage, the voice of even the youngest of us will count. That is why I have said that the ideally nonviolent state will be an ordered anarchy. That state will be the best governed which is governed the least. The pity is that no one trusts me with the reins of government! Otherwise I would show how to govern nonviolently. If I maintain a police force, it will be a body of reformers.

Q. But you had the power in the Congress?

G. That was a paper boat. And then you must not forget that I never spared the Congress ministries. Munshi and Pantji came in for a lot of strictures from me. As I have said in another connection, even the dirty water from the gutter, when it mixes with the water of the Ganges, becomes as pure as the Ganges water; even so I had expected even the goondas would work under Congress discipline. But evidently our ministers had not attained the purifying potency of the fabled Ganges.

B. G. KHER: But the Congress ministers had no nonviolent power with them. Even if five hundred goondas had run amok and had been allowed to go unchecked, they would have dealt untold havoc. I do not know how even you would have dealt with them.

G. Surely, surely, I had rehearsed such situations. The ministers could on such occasions have gone out and allowed themselves to be done to death by the goondas. But let us face the fact that we had not the requisite ahimsa. We went in with our half-baked ahimsa. I do not mind it, inasmuch as we gave up power the moment we felt we should give it up. I am sure that, if we had adhered to strictest nonviolence during these two or three years, the Congress would have made a tremendous advance in the direction of ahimsa and also independence.

B. G. K. But four or five years ago when there was a riot, and I appealed to the leaders to go and throw themselves into the conflagration, no one was ready.

G. So you are supporting my argument. You agree that our loyalty to ahimsa was lip loyalty and not heart loyalty. And if even the half-baked ahimsa carried us a long way, does it not follow that ahimsa would have carried us very far indeed, even if it had not already brought us to the goal?

Q. But we cannot visualize how you will stand nonviolently against a foreign invasion.

G. I cannot draw the whole picture to you because we have no past experience to fall back upon and there is no reality facing us today. We have got the government army manned by the Sikhs, Pathans, and Gurkhas. What I can conceive is this that with my nonviolent army of, say, two thousand people I should put myself between two contending armies. But this, I know, is no answer. I can only say that we shall be able to reduce the invaders' violence to a minimum. The general of a nonviolent army has got to have greater presence of mind than that of a violent army, and God would bless him with the necessary resourcefulness to meet situations as they arise.

B. G. K. The world is made up of pairs of opposites. Where there is fear, there is courage, too. When we walk on the edge of a precipice we walk warily, for we have fear. Fear is not a thing to despise. Will your nonviolent army be above these pairs of opposites?

G. No. No, for the simple reason that my army will represent one of the pair—ahimsa—out of the pair of himsa and ahimsa. Neither I nor my army is above the pair of opposites. The state of *gunatita*, in the language of the Gita, rises above himsa and ahimsa both. Fear has its use, but cowardice has none. I may not put my finger into the jaws of a snake, but the very sight of the snake need not strike terror into me. The trouble is that we often die many times before death overtakes us. But let me explain what my army will be like. They need not and will not have the resourcefulness or understanding of the general, but they will have a perfect sense of discipline to carry out faithfully his order. The general should have the quality which commands the unquestioning obedience of his army, and he will expect of them nothing more than this obedience. The Dandi March was entirely my conception. Pandit Motilalji first laughed at it, he thought it to be a quixotic adventure, and Jamnalalji suggested instead a march on the viceroy's house! But I could not think of anything but the salt march as I had to think in terms of millions of our countrymen. It was a conception that God gave me. Pandit Motilalji argued for some time, and then he said he must not argue as after all I was the general, and he must have faith in me. Later when he saw me in Jambusar, he was completely converted, for he saw with his own eyes the awakening that had come over the masses. And it was an almost magical awakening. Where in history shall we find parallels of the cool courage that our women displayed in such large numbers? And yet none of the thousands who took part in the movement were above the average. They were erring, sinning mortals. God has a way of making use of the most fragile instruments and remaining Himself untouched by everything. Only He is *gunatita*.

And then what after all is the army that wins? You know Rama's reply to Vibhishana when the latter wondered how Rama would be able to conquer a foe like Ravana, when he had no chariot, no armor, nor any shoes to his feet? Rama says: *The chariot, my dear Vibhishana, that wins the victory for Rama is of a different sort from the usual one. Manliness and courage are its wheels; unflinching truth and character its banners and standards; strength, discrimination, self-restraint, and benevolence its horses, with forgiveness, mercy, equanimity their reins; prayer to God is that conqueror's unerring charioteer, dispassion his shield, contentment his sword, charity his axe, intellect his spear, and perfect science his stout bow. His pure and unwavering mind stands for a quiver, his mental quietude and his practice of yama and niyama stand for the sheaf of arrows, and the homage he pays to Brahmins and his guru is his impenetrable armor. There is no other equipment for victory comparable to this; and, my dear friend, there is no enemy who can conquer the man who takes his stand on the chariot of dharma. He who has a powerful chariot like this is a warrior who can conquer even that great and invincible enemy—the world. Hearken unto me and fear not.**

That is the equipment that can lead us to victory. I have not retired from the world, nor do I mean to. I am no recluse. I am content to do what little work I can in Sevagram and give what guidance I can to those that come to me. What we need is faith. And what is there to be lost in following the right path? The worst that can happen to us is that we shall be crushed. Better to be crushed than to be vanquished. But if we had to equip ourselves violently, I should be at my wit's end. I cannot even think out an armament plan, much less work it. On the

---

* Mahadev Desai says: "Gandhiji only made a reference to these verses from Tulsidas's *Ramayana*. I translate them here fully for the benefit of the reader."

other hand my nonviolent plan is incredibly simpler and easier, and with God as our Commander and Infallible Guide where is there cause for any fear?

Q. May a nonviolent man possess wealth, and if he may, how can he keep it nonviolently?

G. He may not own any wealth, though he may possess millions. Let him hold it in trust. If he lives among dacoits and thieves, he may possess very little, indeed little beyond a loincloth. And if he does this, he will convert them. But you must not generalize. In a nonviolent state there will be very few dacoits. For the individual the golden rule is that he will own nothing. If I decided to settle and work among the so-called criminal tribes, I should go to them without any belongings and depend on them for my food and shelter. The moment they feel that I am in their midst in order to serve them, they will be my friends. In that attitude is true ahimsa. But I have discussed this question at length in a recent article in *Harijan*. . . .

CWMG, vol. 72, pp. 387–95

V.

THE POLITICS

One large domain of nonviolent action is the realm of the political. A public sphere, in order to be truly equal, requires it to be a nonviolent space. Gandhi's endeavor was to help foster such spaces, create and nurture public discourse wherein nonviolence was not only nonnegotiable but an article of faith. Gandhi as a leader of mass movements saw it as a duty to explicate the relationship of the political with other domains of collective life.

I.
Religious Authority for Noncooperation

It is not without the greatest reluctance that I engage in a controversy with so learned a leader like Sir Narayan Chandavarkar. But in view of the fact that I am the author of the movement of noncooperation, it becomes my painful duty to state my views even though they are opposed to those of the leaders whom I look upon with respect. I have just read during my travels in Malabar Sir Narayan's rejoinder to my answer to the Bombay Manifesto against noncooperation. I regret to have to say that the rejoinder leaves me unconvinced. He and I seem to read the teachings of the Bible, the Gita, and the Koran from different standpoints or we put different interpretations on them. We seem to understand the words "ahimsa," "politics," and "religion" differently. I shall try my best to make

clear my meaning of the common terms and my reading of the
different religions. At the outset let me assure Sir Narayan that
I have not changed my views on ahimsa. I still believe that man
not having been given the power of creation does not possess
the right of destroying the meanest creature that lives. The pre-
rogative of destruction belongs solely to the Creator of all that
lives. I accept the interpretation of ahimsa, namely, that it is
not merely a negative state of harmlessness but it is a positive
state of love, of doing good even to the evildoer. But it does not
mean helping the evildoer to continue the wrong or tolerating
it by passive acquiescence—on the contrary, love, the active
state of ahimsa, requires you to resist the wrongdoer by disso-
ciating yourself from him even though it may offend him or
injure him physically. Thus if my son lives a life of shame, I
may not help him to do so by continuing to support him; on
the contrary, my love for him requires me to withdraw all support from him although it may mean even his death. And the
same love imposes on me the obligation of welcoming him to
my bosom when he repents. But I may not by physical force
compel my son to become good—that in my opinion is the
moral of the story of the Prodigal Son. Noncooperation is not
a passive state, it is an intensely active state—more active than
physical resistance or violence. Passive resistance is a misnomer. Noncooperation in the sense used by me must be nonviolent and therefore neither punitive nor vindictive nor based on
malice, ill will, or hatred. It follows therefore that it would be
sin for me to serve General Dyer and cooperate with him to
shoot innocent men. But it will be an exercise of forgiveness or
love for me to nurse him back to life, if he was suffering from
a physical malady. I cannot use in this context the word "cooperation" as Sir Narayan would perhaps use it. I would cooperate a thousand times with this government to wean it from its
career of crime, but I will not for a single moment cooperate
with it to continue that career. And I would be guilty of wrongdoing if I retained a title from it or "as service under it or supported its law courts or schools." Better for me a beggar's bowl
than the richest possession from hands stained with the blood
of the innocents of Jallianwala. Better by far a warrant of

imprisonment than honeyed words from those who have wantonly wounded the religious sentiment of my seventy million brothers. My reading of the Gita is diametrically opposed to Sir Narayan's. I do not believe that the Gita teaches violence for doing good. It is preeminently a description of the duel that goes on in our own hearts. The divine author has used a historical incident for inculcating the lesson of doing one's duty even at the peril of one's life. It inculcates performance of duty irrespective of the consequences, for, we mortals, limited by our physical frames, are incapable of controlling actions save our own. The Gita distinguishes between the powers of light and darkness and demonstrates their incompatibility. Jesus, in my humble opinion, was a prince among politicians. He did render unto Caesar that which was Caesar's. He gave the devil his due. He ever shunned him and is reported never once to have yielded to his incantations. The politics of his time consisted in securing the welfare of the people by teaching them not to be seduced by the trinkets of the priests and the pharisees. The latter then controlled and molded the life of the people. Today the system of government is so devised as to affect every department of our life. It threatens our very existence. If therefore we want to conserve the welfare of the nation, we must religiously interest ourselves in the doings of the governors and exert a moral influence on them by insisting on their obeying the laws of morality. General Dyer did produce a "moral effect" by an act of butchery. Those who are engaged in forwarding the movement of noncooperation hope to produce a moral effect by a process of self-denial, self-sacrifice, and self-purification. It surprises me that Sir Narayan should speak of General Dyer's massacre in the same breath as acts of noncooperation. I have done my best to understand his meaning, but I am sorry to confess that I have failed.

CWMG, vol. 18, pp. 194–96

2.
Interview to Professor Mays*

GANDHIJI: Passive resistance is a misnomer for nonviolent resistance. It is much more active than violent resistance. It is direct, ceaseless, but three-fourths invisible and only one-fourth visible. In its visibility it seems to be ineffective, e.g., the spinning wheel which I have called the symbol of nonviolence. In its visibility it appears ineffective, but it is really intensely active and most effective in ultimate result. This knowledge enables me to detect flaws in the way in which the votaries of nonviolence are doing their spinning. I ask for more vigilance and more untiredness. Nonviolence is an intensely active force when properly understood and used. A violent man's activity is most visible while it lasts. But it is always transitory. What can be more visible than the Abyssinians done to death by Italians? There it was lesser violence pitted against much greater. But if the Abyssinians had retired from the field and allowed themselves to be slaughtered, their seeming inactivity would have been much more effective though not for the moment visible. Hitler and Mussolini on the one hand and Stalin on the other are able to show the immediate effectiveness of violence. But it will be as transitory as that of Jhenghis's slaughter. But the effects of Buddha's nonviolent action persist and are likely to grow with age. And the more it is practiced, the more effective and inexhaustible it becomes, and ultimately the whole world stands agape and exclaims, "A miracle has happened." All miracles are due to the silent and effective working of invisible forces. Nonviolence is the most invisible and the most effective.

PROF. MAYS: *I have no doubt in my mind about the*

---

* Professor Mays, an African American, had come to India along with his colleague Dr. Tobias to attend the world's meeting of the Committees of the YMCA. This interview took place in early January 1937. Dr. Tobias met MKG on the January 10.

superiority of nonviolence, but the thing that bothers me is about its exercise on a large scale, the difficulty of so disciplining the mass mind on the point of love. It is easier to discipline individuals. What should be the strategy when they break out? Do we retreat or do we go on?

GANDHIJI: I have had that experience in the course of our movement here. People do not gain the training by preaching. Nonviolence cannot be preached. It has to be practiced. The practice of violence can be taught to people by outward symbols. You shoot at boards, then at targets, then at beasts. Then you are passed as an expert in the art of destruction. The nonviolent man has no outward weapon and, therefore, not only his speech but his action also seems ineffective. I may say all kinds of sweet words to you without meaning them. On the other hand, I may have real love in me and yet my outward expression may be forbidding. Then outwardly my action in both cases may be the same and yet the effect may be different. For the effect of our action is often more potent when it is not patently known. Thus the unconscious effect you are making on me I may never know. It is, nevertheless, infinitely greater than the conscious effect. In violence there is nothing invisible. Nonviolence, on the other hand, is three-fourths invisible, so the effect is in the inverse ratio to its invisibility. Nonviolence, when it becomes active, travels with extraordinary velocity, and then it becomes a miracle. So the mass mind is affected first unconsciously, then consciously. When it becomes consciously affected, there is demonstrable victory. In my own experience, when people seemed to be weakening, there was no consciousness of defeat in me. Thus I was fuller of hope in the efficacy of nonviolence after the renunciation of civil disobedience in 1922, and today I continue to be in the same hopeful mood. It is not a mere emotional thing. Supposing I saw no signs of dawn coming, I should not lose faith. Everything has to come in its proper time. I have discussions here with my coworkers about the scavenging work we are doing. "Why can't we do it after swaraj?" they say. "We may do it better after swaraj." I say to them, "No. The reform has to come today, it must not wait for swaraj; in fact, the right type of swaraj will come only out of such work." Now I cannot show

you, as perhaps I cannot show some of my coworkers, the connection between swaraj and scavenging. If I have to win swaraj
nonviolently, I must discipline my people. The maimed and the
blind and the leprous cannot join the army of violence. There is
also an age limit for serving in the army. For a nonviolent struggle there is no age limit; the blind and the maimed and the bed-
ridden may serve, and not only men but women also. When the
spirit of nonviolence pervades the people and actually begins to
work, its effect is visible to all. But now comes your poser. There
are people, you say, who do not believe in nonviolence as you
do. Are you to sit quiet? The friends ask: "If not now, when will
you act?" I say in reply: "I may not succeed in my lifetime, but
my faith that victory can only come through nonviolence is
stronger than ever." When I spoke on the cult of the spinning
wheel at Faizpur, a newspaper correspondent imputed astute-
ness to me. Nothing could be further from my mind. When I
came to Segaon I was told the people might not cooperate and
might even boycott me. I said: "That may be. But this is the way
nonviolence works." If I go to a village which is still farther off,
the experiment may work better. This thing has come in my
search after the technique of nonviolence. And each day that
passes makes my faith brighter. I have come here to bring that
faith to fruition and to die in the process if that is God's will.
Nonviolence to be worth anything has to work in the face of
hostile forces. But there may be action in inaction. And action
may be worse than inaction.

PROF. MAYS: *Is it ever possible to administer violence in a
spirit of love?*

G. No. Never. I shall give you an illustration from my own
experiment. A calf was lame and had developed terrible sores;
he could not eat and breathed with difficulty. After three days'
argument with myself and my coworkers I put an end to its life.
Now that action was nonviolent because it was wholly unselfish, inasmuch as the sole purpose was to achieve the calf's relief
from pain. Some people have called this an act of violence. I
have called it a surgical operation. I should do exactly the same
thing with my child, if he were in the same predicament. My

point is that nonviolence as the supreme law of our being ceases to be such the moment you talk of exceptions.

PROF. MAYS: *How is a minority to act against an overwhelming majority?*

G. I would say that a minority can do much more in the way of nonviolence than a majority. I had an English friend called Symonds. He used to say: "I am with you so long as you are in a minority. After you are in a majority we are quits." I had less diffidence in handling my minority in South Africa than I had here in handling a majority. But it would be wholly wrong therefore to say that nonviolence is a weapon of the weak. The use of nonviolence requires greater bravery than that of violence. When Daniel defied the laws of the Meads and Persians, his action was nonviolent.

PROF. MAYS: *Should the thought of consequences that might accrue to the enemy as a result of your nonviolence at all constrain you?*

G. Certainly. You may have to suspend your movement as I did in South Africa when the government was faced with the revolt of European labor. The latter asked me to make common cause with them. I said no.

PROF. MAYS: *And nonviolence will never rebound on you, whereas violence will be self-destroyed?*

G. Yes. Violence must beget violence. But let me tell you that here, too, my argument has been countered by a great man who said: "Look at the history of nonviolence. Jesus died on the Cross, but his followers shed blood." This proves nothing. We have no data before us to pass judgment. We do not know the whole of the life of Jesus. The followers perhaps had not imbibed fully the message of nonviolence. But I must warn you against carrying the impression with you that mine is the final word on nonviolence. I know my own limitations. I am but a humble seeker after truth. And all I claim is that every experiment of mine has deepened my faith in nonviolence as the greatest force at the disposal of mankind. Its use is not restricted to individuals merely but it can be practiced on a mass scale.

3.
A Discussion with Christian Missionaries*

In my opinion nonviolence is not passivity in any shape or form. Nonviolence, as I understand it, is the activest force in the world. Therefore, whether it is materialism or anything else, if nonviolence does not provide an effective antidote, it is not the active force of my conception. Or, to put it conversely, if you bring me some conundrums that I cannot answer, I would say my nonviolence is still defective. Nonviolence is the supreme law. During my half a century of experience I have not yet come across a situation when I had to say that I was helpless, that I had no remedy in terms of nonviolence.

CWMG, vol. 68, p. 202

4.
My Attitude Towards War

Rev. B. de Ligt has written in a French journal called *Evolution* a long open letter to me. He has favored me with a translation of it. The open letter strongly criticizes my participation in the Boer War and then the Great War of 1914 and invites me to explain my conduct in the light of ahimsa. Other friends, too, have put the same question. I have attempted to give the explanation more than once in these columns. There is no defense for my conduct weighed only on the scales of ahimsa. I draw no distinction between those who wield the weapons of destruction and those who do Red Cross work. Both participate in war

---

* An excerpt. The missionaries included William Paton, secretary of the International Missionary Council, and Leslie B. Moss, secretary.

and advance its cause. Both are guilty of the crime of war. But even after introspection during all these years, I feel that in the circumstances in which I found myself I was bound to adopt the course I did both during the Boer War and the Great European War and for that matter the so-called Zulu rebellion of Natal in 1906. Life is governed by a multitude of forces. It would be smooth sailing, if one could determine the course of one's actions only by one general principle whose application at a given moment was too obvious to need even a moment's reflection. But I cannot recall a single act which could be so easily determined. Being a confirmed war resister I have never given myself training in the use of destructive weapons in spite of opportunities to take such training. It was perhaps thus that I escaped direct destruction of human life. But so long as I lived under a system of government based on force and voluntarily partook of the many facilities and privileges it created for me, I was bound to help that government to the extent of my ability when it was engaged in a war unless I noncooperated with that government and renounced to the utmost of my capacity the privileges it offered me. Let me take an illustration. I am a member of an institution which holds a few acres of land whose crops are in imminent peril from monkeys. I believe in the sacredness of all life and hence I regard it as a breach of ahimsa to inflict any injury on the monkeys. But I do not hesitate to instigate and direct an attack on the monkeys in order to save the crops. I would like to avoid this evil. I can avoid it by leaving or breaking up the institution. I do not do so because I do not expect to be able to find a society where there will be no agriculture and therefore no destruction of some life. In fear and trembling, in humility and penance, I therefore participate in the injury inflicted on the monkeys, hoping someday to find a way out. Even so did I participate in the three acts of war. I could not, it would be madness for me to, sever my connection with the society to which I belong. And on those three occasions I had no thought of noncooperating with the British government. My position regarding that government is totally different today and hence I should not voluntarily participate in its wars and I should risk imprisonment and even the gallows if

I was forced to take up arms or otherwise take part in its military operations. But that still does not solve the riddle. If there was a national government, whilst I should not take any direct part in any war, I can conceive occasions when it would be my duty to vote for the military training of those who wish to take it. For I know that all its members do not believe in nonviolence to the extent I do. It is not possible to make a person or a society nonviolent by compulsion. Nonviolence works in a most mysterious manner. Often a man's actions defy analysis in terms of nonviolence; equally often his actions may wear the appearance of violence when he is absolutely nonviolent in the highest sense of the term and is subsequently found so to be. All I can then claim for my conduct is that it was, in the instances cited, actuated in the interests of nonviolence. There was no thought of sordid national or other interest. I do not believe in the promotion of national or any other interest at the sacrifice of some other interest. I may not carry my argument any further. Language at best is but a poor vehicle for expressing one's thoughts in full. For me, nonviolence is not a mere philosophical principle. It is the rule and the breath of my life. I know I fail often, sometimes consciously, more often unconsciously. It is a matter not of the intellect but of the heart. True guidance comes by constant waiting upon God, by utmost humility, by self-abnegation, by being ever ready to sacrifice one's self. Its practice requires fearlessness and courage of the highest order. I am painfully aware of my failings. But the light within me is steady and clear. There is no escape for any of us save through truth and nonviolence. I know that war is wrong, is an unmitigated evil. I know, too, that it has got to go. I firmly believe that freedom won through bloodshed or fraud is no freedom. Would that all the acts alleged against me were found to be wholly indefensible rather than that by any act of mine nonviolence was held to be compromised or that I was ever thought to be in favor of violence or untruth in any shape or form. Not violence, not untruth, but nonviolence, Truth is the law of our being.

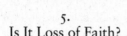

5.
Is It Loss of Faith?

A coworker writes:

Some of us feel that your "fasting unto death" may mean a conscious or unconscious loss of faith in the efficacy of nonviolence. Can you enlighten us, who have derived our faith in nonviolence from you?

It is a flattering thought that some people have derived their faith in nonviolence from me. But I would warn them that I may prove a broken reed at a critical juncture, if they have not assimilated the spirit of nonviolence and if it has not become an integral part of their life. Faith in a man is a perishable quantity, for it vanishes like smoke when their idol does not come up to their expectations; but what gives us hope and courage in the nick of time is an undying faith in a cause or a principle, irrespective of persons from whom it is derived. Having uttered this warning, let me say that my "fast unto death" was not due to loss of faith in nonviolence, but it was, as I have already said on more than one occasion, the last seal upon that faith. Sacrifice of self even unto death is the final weapon in the hands of a nonviolent person. It is not given to man to do more. I, therefore, suggest to this coworker and all the others that in this religious battle against untouchability they must be prepared joyously even to "fast unto death," if such an urgent call comes to them. If they feel that they are party to the September pledge given unsolicited to the Harijans and if they cannot make good the pledge in spite of ordinary effort, how else, being nonviolent, will they propose to deliver the goods except by laying down their lives? The Shastras tell us that, when people in distress prayed to God for relief and He seemed to have hardened His heart, they declared a "fast unto death" till God had listened to their prayer. Religious history tells us of those who survived their fast because God listened to them, but it tells us nothing of those who silently and heroically perished in the attempt to win the answer from a deaf God. I am certain that many have died in that heroic manner, but without their faith in God and nonviolence being in the slightest degree diminished. God does not always answer prayers in the manner we want Him to. For Him life and death are one, and who is able to deny that all that is pure and good in the world persists because of the silent death of thousands of unknown heroes and heroines!

CWMG, vol. 53, pp. 460–61

6.
Fasting in Nonviolent Action

If the struggle which we are seeking to avoid with all our might has to come, and if it is to remain nonviolent as it must in order to succeed, fasting is likely to play an important part in it. It has its place in the tussle with authority and with our own people in the event of wanton acts of violence and obstinate riots, for instance. There is a natural prejudice against it as part of a political struggle. It has a recognized place in religious practice. But it is considered a vulgar interpolation in politics by the ordinary politician though it has always been resorted to by prisoners in a haphazard way with more or less success. By fasting, however, they have always succeeded in drawing public attention and disturbing the peace of jail authorities. My own fasts have always, as I hold, been strictly according to the law of satyagraha. Fellow satyagrahis, too, in South Africa fasted partially or wholly. My fasts have been varied. There was the Hindu-Muslim unity fast of twenty-one days in 1924 started under the late Maulana Mahomed Ali's roof in Delhi. The indeterminate fast against the Mac-Donald Award was taken in the Yeravda Prison in 1932. The twenty-one days' purificatory fast was begun in the Yeravda Prison and was finished at Lady Thakersey's, as the government would not take the burden of my being in the prison in that condition. Then followed another fast in the Yeravda Prison in 1933 against the government refusal to let me carry on anti-untouchability work through *Harijan* (issued from prison) on the same basis as facilities had been allowed me four months before. They would not yield, but they discharged me when their medical advisers thought I could not live many days if the fast was not given up. Then followed the ill-fated Rajkot fast in 1939. A false step taken by me thoughtlessly during that fast thwarted the brilliant result that would otherwise certainly have been achieved. In spite of all these fasts, fasting has not been accepted as a recognized part of satyagraha. It has only been tolerated by the politicians. I have, however, been driven to the conclusion that fasting unto death is an integral part of satyagraha program, and it is the greatest and most effective weapon in its armory under given circumstances. Not everyone is qualified for undertaking it without a proper course of training. I may not burden this note with an examination of the circumstances under which fasting may be resorted to and the training required for it. Nonviolence in its positive aspect as benevolence (I do not use the word "love" as it has fallen into disrepute) is the greatest force because of the limitless scope it affords for self-suffering without causing or intending any physical or material injury to the wrongdoer. The object always is to evoke the best in him. Self-suffering is an appeal to his better nature, as retaliation is to his baser. Fasting under proper circumstances is such an appeal par excellence. If the politician does not perceive its propriety in political matters, it is because it is a novel use of this very fine weapon. To practice nonviolence in mundane matters is to know its true value. It is to bring heaven upon earth. There is no such thing as the other world. All worlds are one. There is no "here" and no "there." As Jeans has demonstrated, the whole universe including the most distant stars, invisible even through the most powerful telescope in the world, is compressed in an atom. I hold it therefore to be wrong to limit the use of nonviolence to cave dwellers and for acquiring merit for a favored position in the other world. All virtue ceases to have a use if it serves no purpose in every walk of life. I would therefore plead with the purely political-minded people to study nonviolence and fasting as its extreme manifestation with sympathy and understanding.

CWMG, vol. 76, pp. 317–19

7.
Question Box

Q. *Why does Gandhiji resort to a fast when he faces extreme difficulties? What is the effect of this action on the life of the public of India?*

A. Such a question has been put to me before, but never, perhaps, precisely in the same terms. The answer, however, is easy. It is the last weapon in the armory of the votary of ahimsa. When human ingenuity fails, the votary fasts. This fasting quickens the spirit of prayer, that is to say, the fasting is a spiritual act and, therefore, addressed to God. The effect of such action on the life of the people is that when the person fasting is at all known to them, their sleeping conscience is awakened. But there is the danger that the people through mistaken sympathy may act against their will in order to save the life of the loved one. This danger has got to be faced. One ought not to be deterred from right action when one is sure of the rightness. It can but promote circumspection. Such a fast is undertaken in obedience to the dictates of the inner voice and, therefore, prevents haste.

CWMG, vol. 90, p. 202

8.
Letter to Lord Irwin

SATYAGRAHA ASHRAM,
SABARMATI.

March 2, 1930

DEAR FRIEND,

Before embarking on civil disobedience and taking the risk I
have dreaded to take all these years, I would fain approach you
and find a way out. My personal faith is absolutely clear. I cannot intentionally hurt anything that lives, much less fellow
human beings, even though they may do the greatest wrong to
me and mine. Whilst, therefore, I hold the British rule to be a
curse, I do not intend harm to a single Englishman or to any
legitimate interest he may have in India. I must not be misunderstood. Though I hold the British rule in India to be a curse,
I do not, therefore, consider Englishmen in general to be worse
than any other people on earth. I have the privilege of claiming
many Englishmen as dearest friends. Indeed, much that I have
learnt of the evil of British rule is due to the writings of frank
and courageous Englishmen who have not hesitated to tell the
unpalatable truth about that rule. And why do I regard the
British rule as a curse? It has impoverished the dumb millions
by a system of progressive exploitation and by a ruinously expensive military and civil administration which the country
can never afford. It has reduced us politically to serfdom. It has
sapped the foundations of our culture. And, by the policy of
cruel disarmament, it has degraded us spiritually. Lacking the
inward strength, we have been reduced, by all but universal
disarmament, to a state bordering on cowardly helplessness. In
common with many of my countrymen, I had hugged the fond
hope that the proposed Round Table Conference might furnish
a solution. But when you said plainly that you could not give

any assurance that you or the British cabinet would pledge yourselves to support a scheme of full dominion status, the Round Table Conference could not possibly furnish the solution for which vocal India is consciously, and the dumb millions are unconsciously, thirsting. Needless to say there never was any question of Parliament's verdict being anticipated. Instances are not wanting of the British cabinet, in anticipation of the parliamentary verdict, having pledged itself to a particular policy. The Delhi interview* having miscarried, there was no option for Pandit Motilal Nehru and me but to take steps to carry out the solemn resolution of the Congress arrived at in Calcutta at its session in 1928. But the Resolution of Independence† should cause no alarm, if the word dominion status mentioned in your announcement had been used in its accepted sense. For, has it not been admitted by responsible British statesmen that dominion status is virtual independence? What, however, I fear is that there never has been any intention of granting such dominion status to India in the immediate future.

But this is all past history. Since the announcement, many events have happened which show unmistakably the trend of British policy.

It seems as clear as daylight that responsible British statesmen do not contemplate any alteration in British policy that might adversely affect Britain's commerce with India or require an impartial and close scrutiny of Britain's transactions with India. If nothing is done to end the process of exploitation, India must be bled with an ever-increasing speed. The finance member regards as a settled fact the 1/6 ratio which by a stroke of the pen drains India of a few crores. And when a serious attempt is being made through a civil form of direct action to unsettle this fact, among many others, even you cannot help appealing to the wealthy landed classes to help you to

* Which took place on December 23, 1929.

† The resolution referred to is the Congress resolution passed at Lahore in 1929. Vide *CWMG*, vol. 42, pp. 324–26.

crush that attempt in the name of an order that grinds India to atoms.

Unless those who work in the name of the nation understand and keep before all concerned the motive that lies behind the craving for independence, there is every danger of independence coming to us so changed as to be of no value to those toiling voiceless millions for whom it is sought and for whom it is worth taking. It is for that reason that I have been recently telling the public what independence should really mean.

Let me put before you some of the salient points. The terrific pressure of land revenue, which furnishes a large part of the total, must undergo considerable modification in an independent India. Even the much vaunted permanent settlement benefits the few rich zamindars, not the ryots. The ryot has remained as helpless as ever. He is a mere tenant at will. Not only, then, has the land revenue to be considerably reduced, but the whole revenue system has to be so revised as to make the ryot's good its primary concern. But the British system seems to be designed to crush the very life out of him. Even the salt he must use to live is so taxed as to make the burden fall heaviest on him, if only because of the heartless impartiality of its incidence. The tax shows itself still more burdensome on the poor man when it is remembered that salt is the one thing he must eat more than the rich man both individually and collectively. The drink and drug revenue, too, is derived from the poor. It saps the foundations both of their health and morals. It is defended under the false plea of individual freedom, but, in reality, is maintained for its own sake. The ingenuity of the authors of the reforms of 1919 transferred this revenue to the so-called responsible part of dyarchy, so as to throw the burden of prohibition on it, thus, from the very beginning, rendering it powerless for good. If the unhappy minister wipes out this revenue, he must starve education, since in the existing circumstances he has no new source of replacing that revenue. If the weight of taxation has crushed the poor from above, the destruction of the central supplementary industry, i.e., handspinning, has undermined their capacity for producing wealth. The tale of India's ruination is not complete without reference to the liabilities incurred in her name. Sufficient has been recently said about these in the public press. It must be the duty of a free India to subject all the liabilities to the strictest investigation, and repudiate those that may be adjudged by an impartial tribunal to be unjust and unfair.

The iniquities sampled above are maintained in order to carry on a foreign administration, demonstrably the most expensive in the world. Take your own salary. It is over Rs. 21,000 per month, besides many other indirect additions. The British prime minister gets £5,000 per year, i.e., over Rs. 5,400 per month at the present rate of exchange. You are getting over Rs. 700 per day against India's average income of less than annas 2 per day. The prime minister gets Rs. 180 per day against Great Britain's average income of nearly Rs. 2 per day. Thus you are getting much over five thousand times India's average income. The British prime minister is getting only ninety times Britain's average income. On bended knees I ask you to ponder over this phenomenon. I have taken a personal illustration to drive home a painful truth. I have too great a regard for you as a man to wish to hurt your feelings. I know that you do not need the salary you get. Probably the whole of your salary goes for charity. But a system that provides for such an arrangement deserves to be summarily scrapped. What is true of the viceregal salary is true generally of the whole administration.

A radical cutting down of the revenue, therefore, depends upon an equally radical reduction in the expenses of the administration. This means a transformation of the scheme of government. This transformation is impossible without independence. Hence, in my opinion, the spontaneous demonstration of 26th January, in which hundreds of thousands of villagers instinctively participated. To them independence means deliverance from the killing weight.

Not one of the great British political parties, it seems to me, is prepared to give up the Indian spoils to which Great Britain helps herself from day to day, often, in spite of the unanimous opposition of Indian opinion.

Nevertheless, if India is to live as a nation, if the slow death by starvation of her people is to stop, some remedy must be found for immediate relief. The proposed conference is certainly not the remedy. It is not a matter of carrying conviction by argument. The matter resolves itself into one of matching forces. Conviction or no conviction, Great Britain would defend her Indian commerce and interests by all the forces at her command. India must consequently evolve force enough to free herself from that embrace of death.

It is common cause that, however disorganized and, for the time being, insignificant it may be, the party of violence is gaining ground and making itself felt. Its end is the same as mine. But I am convinced that it cannot bring the desired relief to the dumb millions. And the conviction is growing deeper and deeper in me that nothing but unadulterated nonviolence can check the organized violence of the British government. Many think that nonviolence is not an active force. My experience, limited though it undoubtedly is, shows that nonviolence can be an intensely active force. It is my purpose to set in motion that force as well against the organized violent force of the British rule as [against] the unorganized violent force of the growing party of violence. To sit still would be to give rein to both the forces abovementioned. Having an unquestioning and immovable faith in the efficacy of nonviolence as I know it, it would be sinful on my part to wait any longer.

This nonviolence will be expressed through civil disobedience, for the moment confined to the inmates of the Satyagraha Ashram, but ultimately designed to cover all those who choose to join the movement with its obvious limitations.

I know that in embarking on nonviolence I shall be running what might fairly be termed a mad risk. But the victories of truth have never been won without risks, often of the gravest character. Conversion of a nation that has consciously or unconsciously preyed upon another, far more numerous, far more ancient, and no less cultured than itself, is worth any amount of risk.

I have deliberately used the word "conversion." For my ambition is no less than to convert the British people through nonviolence, and thus make them see the wrong they have done to India. I do not seek to harm your people. I want to serve them even as I want to serve my own. I believe that I have always served them. I served them up to 1919 blindly. But when my eyes were opened and I conceived noncooperation, the object still was to serve them. I employed the same weapon that I have in all humility successfully used against the dearest members of my family. If I have equal love for your people with mine, it will not long remain hidden. It will be acknowledged by them even as the members of my family acknowledged it after they had tried me for several years. If the people join me as I expect they will, the sufferings they will undergo, unless the British nation sooner retraces its steps, will be enough to melt the stoniest hearts.

The plan through civil disobedience will be to combat such evils as I have sampled out. If we want to sever the British connection, it is because of such evils. When they are removed, the path becomes easy. Then the way to friendly negotiation will be open. If the British commerce with India is purified of greed, you will have no difficulty in recognizing our independence. I respectfully invite you then to pave the way for immediate removal of those evils, and thus open a way for a real conference between equals, interested only in promoting the common good of mankind through voluntary fellowship and in arranging terms of mutual help and commerce equally suited to both. You have unnecessarily laid stress upon the communal problems that unhappily affect this land. Important though they undoubtedly are for the consideration of any scheme of government, they have little bearing on the greater problems which are above communities and which affect them all equally. But if you cannot see your way to deal with these evils and my letter makes no appeal to your heart, on the eleventh day of this month,* I shall proceed with such coworkers of the Ashram as I can take, to disregard the provisions of the salt laws. I regard this tax to be the most iniquitous of all from the poor man's standpoint. As the independence movement is essentially for the poorest in the land, the beginning will be made with this evil. The wonder is that we have submitted to

* The Salt March, or the Dandi March, commenced on March 12, 1930.

the cruel monopoly for so long. It is, I know, open to you to frustrate my design by arresting me. I hope that there will be tens of thousands ready, in a disciplined manner, to take up the work after me, and, in the act of disobeying the Salt Act to lay themselves open to the penalties of a law that should never have disfigured the statute book.

I have no desire to cause you unnecessary embarrassment, or any at all, so far as I can help. If you think that there is any substance in my letter, and if you will care to discuss matters with me, and if to that end you would like me to postpone publication of this letter, I shall gladly refrain on receipt of a telegram to that effect soon after this reaches you.* You will, however, do me the favor not to deflect me from my course unless you can see your way to conform to the substance of this letter. This letter is not in any way intended as a threat but is a simple and sacred duty peremptory on a civil resister. Therefore I am having it specially delivered by a young English friend who believes in the Indian cause and is a full believer in non-violence and whom providence seems to have sent to me, as it were, for the very purpose.†

I remain,

Your sincere friend,
M. K. GANDHI

H. E. LORD IRWIN
VICEROY'S HOUSE
NEW DELHI-3

* The viceroy's reply was simply an expression of regret that MKG should be "contemplating a course of action that is clearly bound to involve violation of the law and danger to the public peace."

† The letter was carried by hand to the viceroy by a young Englishman, Reginald Reynolds. He later recalled; "Before I went, Gandhi insisted that I read the letter carefully, as he did not wish me to associate myself with it unless I was in complete agreement with its contents. My taking of this letter was, in fact, intended to be symbolic of the fact that this was not merely a struggle between the Indians and the British." CWMG, vol. 43, p. 8, footnote 1.

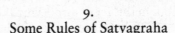

9.
Some Rules of Satyagraha

Satyagraha literally means insistence on truth. This insistence arms the votary with matchless power. This power or force is connoted by the word "satyagraha." Satyagraha, to be genuine, may be offered against parents, against one's wife or one's children, against rulers, against fellow citizens, even against the whole world.

Such a universal force necessarily makes no distinction between kinsmen and strangers, young and old, man and woman, friend and foe. The force to be so applied can never be physical. There is in it no room for violence. The only force of universal application can, therefore, be that of ahimsa or love. In other words, it is soul force.

Love does not burn others, it burns itself. Therefore, a satyagrahi, i.e., a civil resister, will joyfully suffer even unto death.

It follows, therefore, that a civil resister, whilst he will strain every nerve to compass the end of the existing rule, will do no intentional injury in thought, word, or deed to the person of a single Englishman. This necessarily brief explanation of satyagraha will perhaps enable the reader to understand and appreciate the following rules:

AS AN INDIVIDUAL

1. A satyagrahi, i.e., a civil resister, will harbor no anger.

2. He will suffer the anger of the opponent.

3. In so doing he will put up with assaults from the opponent, never retaliate; but he will not submit, out of fear of punishment or the like, to any order given in anger.

4. When any person in authority seeks to arrest a civil resister, he will voluntarily submit to the arrest, and he will not resist the attachment or removal of his own property, if any, when it is sought to be confiscated by authorities.

5. If a civil resister has any property in his possession as a trustee, he will refuse to surrender it, even though in defending it he might lose his life. He will, however, never retaliate.

6. Nonretaliation excludes swearing and cursing.

7. Therefore a civil resister will never insult his opponent, and therefore also not take part in many of the newly coined cries which are contrary to the spirit of ahimsa.

8. A civil resister will not salute the Union Jack, nor will he insult it or officials, English or Indian.

9. In the course of the struggle, if anyone insults an official or commits an assault upon him, a civil resister will protect such official or officials from the insult or attack even at the risk of his life.

AS A PRISONER

10. As a prisoner, a civil resister will behave courteously toward prison officials and will observe all such discipline of the prison as is not contrary to self-respect; as for instance, whilst he will salaam officials in the usual manner, he will not perform any humiliating gyrations and refuse to shout "Victory to Sarkar" or the like. He will take cleanly cooked and cleanly served food, which is not contrary to his religion, and will refuse to take food insultingly served or served in unclean vessels.

11. A civil resister will make no distinction between an ordinary prisoner and himself, will in no way regard himself as

superior to the rest, nor will he ask for any conveniences that may not be necessary for keeping his body in good health and condition. He is entitled to ask for such conveniences as may be required for his physical or spiritual well-being.

12. A civil resister may not fast for want of conveniences whose deprivation does not involve any injury to one's self-respect.

AS A UNIT

13. A civil resister will joyfully obey all the orders issued by the leader of the corps, whether they please him or not.

14. He will carry out orders in the first instance even though they appear to him insulting, inimical, or foolish, and then appeal to a higher authority. He is free before joining to determine the fitness of the corps to satisfy him, but after he has joined it, it becomes a duty to submit to its discipline irksome or otherwise. If the sum total of the energy of the corps appears to a member to be improper or immoral, he has a right to sever his connection, but being within it, he has no right to commit a breach of its discipline.

15. No civil resister is to expect maintenance for his dependents. It would be an accident if any such provision is made. A civil resister entrusts his dependents to the care of God. Even in ordinary warfare wherein hundreds of thousands give themselves up to it, they are able to make no previous provision. How much more, then, should such be the case in satyagraha? It is the universal experience that in such times hardly anybody is left to starve.

IN COMMUNAL FIGHTS

16. No civil resister will intentionally become a cause of communal quarrels.

17. In the event of any such outbreak, he will not take sides, but he will assist only that party which is demonstrably in the right. Being a Hindu, he will be generous toward Mussalmans and others, and will sacrifice himself in the attempt to save non-Hindus from a Hindu attack. And if the attack is from the other side, he will not participate in any retaliation but will give his life in protecting Hindus.

18. He will, to the best of his ability, avoid every occasion that may give rise to communal quarrels.

19. If there is a procession of satyagrahis, they will do nothing that would wound the religious susceptibilities of any community, and they will not take part in any other processions that are likely to wound such susceptibilities.

CWMG, vol. 42, pp. 491–93

10.
When I Am Arrested

It must be taken for granted that, when civil disobedience is started, my arrest is a certainty. It is, therefore, necessary to consider what should be done when the event takes place.

On the eve of my arrest in 1922, I had warned coworkers against any demonstration of any kind save that of mute, complete nonviolence, and had insisted that constructive work which alone could organize the country for civil disobedience should be prosecuted with the utmost zeal. The first part of the instructions was, thanks be to God, literally and completely carried out—so completely that it has enabled an English noble contemptuously to say, "Not a dog barked." For me when I learnt in the jail that the country had remained absolutely nonviolent, it was a demonstration that the preaching of nonviolence had had its effect and that the Bardoli decision was the wisest thing to do. It would be foolish to speculate what might have happened if "dogs" had barked and violence had been let loose on my arrest. One thing, however, I can say, that in that event there would have been no independence resolution at Lahore, and no Gandhi with his confidence in the power of nonviolence left to contemplate taking the boldest risks imaginable.

Let us, however, think of the immediate future. This time on my arrest there is to be no mute, passive nonviolence, but nonviolence of the activest type should be set in motion, so that not a single believer in nonviolence as an article of faith for the purpose of achieving India's goal should find himself free or alive at the end of the effort to submit any longer to the existing slavery. It would be, therefore, the duty of everyone to take up such civil disobedience or civil resistance as may be advised and conducted by my successor, or as might be taken up by the Congress. I must confess, that at the present moment, I have no all-India successor in view. But I have sufficient faith in the coworkers and in the mission itself to know that circumstances will give the successor. This peremptory condition must be patent to all that he must be an out-and-out believer in the efficacy of nonviolence for the purpose intended. For without that living faith in it he will not be able at the crucial moment to discover a nonviolent method.

It must be parenthetically understood that what is being said here in no way fetters the discretion and full authority of the Congress. The Congress will adopt only such things said here that may commend themselves to congressmen in general. If the nature of these instructions is to be properly understood, the organic value of the charter of full liberty given to me by the Working Committee should be adequately appreciated. Nonviolence, if it does not submit to any restrictions upon its liberty, subjects no one and no institution to any restriction whatsoever, save what may be self-imposed or voluntarily adopted. So long as the vast body of congressmen continue to believe in nonviolence as the only policy in the existing circumstances and have confidence not only in the bona fides of my successor and those who claim to believe in nonviolence as an article of faith to the extent indicated but also in the ability of the successor wisely to guide the movement, the Congress will give him and them its blessings and even give effect to these instructions and his.

So far as I am concerned, my intention is to start the movement only through the inmates of the Ashram and those who have submitted to its discipline and assimilated the spirit of its methods. Those, therefore, who will offer battle at the very commencement will be unknown to fame. Hitherto the Ashram has been deliberately kept in reserve in order that by a fairly long course of discipline it might acquire stability. I feel that if the Satyagraha Ashram is to deserve the great confidence that has been reposed in it and the affection lavished upon it by friends, the time has arrived for it to demonstrate the qualities implied in the word "satyagraha." I feel that our self-imposed restraints have become subtle indulgences, and the prestige acquired has provided us with privileges and conveniences of which we may be utterly unworthy. These have been thankfully accepted in the hope that someday we would be able to give a good account of ourselves in terms of satyagraha. And if at the end of nearly fifteen years of its existence, the Ashram cannot give such a demonstration, it and I should disappear, and it would be well for the nation, the Ashram and me.

When the beginning is well and truly made, I expect the response from all over the country. It will be the duty then of everyone who wants to make the movement a success to keep it nonviolent and under discipline. Everyone will be expected to stand at his post except when called by his chief. If there is spontaneous mass response, as I hope there will be, and if previous experience is any guide, it will largely be self-regulated. But everyone who accepts nonviolence whether as an article of faith or policy would assist the mass movement. Mass movements have, all over the world, thrown up unexpected leaders. This should be no exception to the rule. Whilst, therefore, every effort imaginable and possible should be made to restrain the forces of violence, civil disobedience once begun this time cannot be stopped and must not be stopped so long as there is a single civil resister left free or alive. A votary of satyagraha should find himself in one of the following states:

1. In prison or in an analogous state; or

2. Engaged in civil disobedience; or

3. Under orders at the spinning wheel, or at some constructive work advancing swaraj.

CWMG, vol. 42, pp. 496–98

11. Satyagrahis' March

Our party is likely to consist of about a hundred men. I have not been able to finalize the list yet, as, besides the present inmates of the Ashram, I am selecting for inclusion some others who observe the rules of ashram life and are eager to join, and who have to be included. The march will begin at 6:30 on the twelfth morning. I give below the program tentatively fixed:

Wednesday, the 12th	Aslali
Thursday, the 13th	Morning Bareja Evening Navagam
Friday, the 14th	Morning Vasana Evening Matar
Saturday, the 15th	Morning Dabhan Evening Nadiad
Sunday, the 16th	Morning Boriavi Evening Anand
Monday, the 17th	Morning Napa Evening Borsad
Tuesday, the 18th	Morning Raas Evening Badalpur

I request the *mahajans* and the workers of the respective places to bear in mind the following: The satyagrahi party is expected to reach each place by 8 o'clock in the morning and to sit down for lunch between 10:00 and 10:30 a.m. It may be half past nine by the time the party reaches Aslali on the first day. No rooms will be needed for rest at noon or night, but a clean, shaded place will be enough. In the absence of such a shaded place, it will be enough to have a bamboo-and-grass covering. Both bamboo and grass can be put to use again.

It is assumed that the village people will provide us food. If provisions are supplied, the party will cook its own meal. The food supplied, whether cooked or uncooked, should be the simplest possible. Nothing more than rotli or rotla or kedgeree with vegetables and milk or curds will be required. Sweets, even if prepared, will be declined. Vegetables should be merely boiled, and no oil, spices, and chilies, whether green or dry, whole or crushed, should be added or used in the cooking. This is my advice for preparing a meal:

> Morning, before departure: Rab and dhebra; the rab should be left to the party itself to prepare.

> Midday: Bhakhri, vegetable, and milk or buttermilk.

> Evening, before the march is resumed: Roasted gram, rice.

> Night: Kedgeree with vegetable and buttermilk or milk. The ghee for all the meals together should not exceed three tolas per head: One tola in the rab, one served separately to be smeared on the bhakhri, and one to be put into the kedgeree.

For me, goat's milk, if available, in the morning, at noon, and at night, and raisins or dates, and three lemons will do.

I hope that the village people will incur no expenses whatever, except for the simple food items named above. I look forward to meeting the people of each village and its neighborhood. Everyone in the party will be carrying his own bedding so that the village people will have to provide nothing except a clean place for resting in. The people should incur no expense on account of betel leaves, betel nuts, or tea for the party. I shall be happy if every village maintains complete cleanliness and fixes beforehand an enclosed place for the satyagrahis to answer calls of nature. If the villagers do not already use khadi, it is clear that they should now start using it. It is desirable that information under the following heads should be kept ready for each village:

1. Population: Number of women, men, Hindus, Muslims, Christians, Parsis, etc.

2. Number of untouchables.

3. If there is a school in the village, the number of boys and girls attending it.

4. Number of spinning wheels.

5. The monthly sale of khadi.

6. Number of people wearing khadi exclusively.

7. Salt consumed per head; salt used for cattle, etc.

8. Number of cows and buffaloes in the village.

9. The amount of land revenue paid; at what rate per acre.

10. The area of the common grazing ground if any.

11. Do the people drink? How far is the liquor shop from the village?

12. Educational and other special facilities, if any, for the untouchables. It will be good if this information is written out on a sheet of paper neatly and handed to me immediately on our arrival.

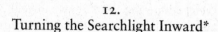

12.
Turning the Searchlight Inward*

I have been asked to deliver a sermon. I have little fitness for the task. But tonight I propose to make a confession and turn the searchlight inward. You may call this introspection a sermon if you like.

India in general and you in particular are acquainted with one part of my nature. Moreover, more than in any other part of Gujarat, in this district are concentrated workers who have come in closest touch with me. They know this habit of mine from personal experience.

I am plainspoken. I have not hesitated to describe the mountain-high faults of the government in appropriate language. And I have not hesitated often to picture as mountain high our faults appearing to us as trifling. You know, the common rule is to see our own big lapses as tiny nothings. And when we do realize our blemishes somewhat, we at once pass them on to the broad shoulders of God and say He will take care of them; and then with safety thus assured we proceed from lapse to lapse. But as you know, I have disregarded this rule for years. So doing, I have hurt the feelings of many friends and even lost some of them. Tonight I have to repeat the painful operation.

I have already told the group of people who are accompanying me that this is the last week of our march. As we shall reach our destination next Saturday, we shall not have to march any further. But we shall be faced with another task. During this last week we shall have to go through Surat district. Only this morning at prayer time I was telling my companions that as we had entered the district in which we were to offer civil disobedience, we should insist on greater purification and intenser

---

* The speech given at a village called Bhatgam on March 29, 1930, during the Salt March.

dedication. I warned them that as the district was more organized and contained many intimate coworkers, there was every
likelihood of our being pampered. I warned them against succumbing to their pampering. We are not angels. We are very
weak, easily tempted. There are many lapses to our debit. God
is great. Even today some were discovered. One defaulter confessed his lapse himself whilst I was brooding over the lapses
of the pilgrims. I discovered that my warning was given none
too soon. The local workers had ordered milk from Surat to be
brought in a motor lorry and they had incurred other expenses
which I could not justify. I therefore spoke strongly about
them. But that did not allay my grief. On the contrary, it increased with the contemplation of the wrongs done.

In the light of these discoveries, what right had I to write to
the viceroy the letter in which I have severely criticized his salary, which is more than five thousand times our average income? How could he possibly do justice to that salary? And
how can we tolerate his getting a salary out of all proportion
to our income? But he is individually not to be blamed for it.
He has no need for it. God has made him a wealthy man. I
have suggested in my letter that probably the whole of his salary is spent in charity. I have since learnt that my guess is
largely likely to be true. Even so, of course, I should resist the
giving of such a large salary. I could not vote Rs. 21,000 per
month, not perhaps even Rs. 2,100 per month. But when could
I offer such resistance? Certainly not if I was myself taking
from the people an unconscionable toll. I could resist it only if
my living bore some correspondence with the average income
of the people. We are marching in the name of God. We profess to act on behalf of the hungry, the naked, and the unemployed. I have no right to criticize the viceregal salary if we are
costing the country, say, fifty times seven pice, the average
daily income of our people. I have asked the workers to furnish
me with an account of the expenses. And the way things are
going, I should not be surprised if each of us is costing something near fifty times seven pice. What else can be the result if
they will fetch for me, from whatever source possible, the
choicest oranges and grapes, if they will bring one hundred

and twenty when I should want twelve oranges, if when I need one pound of milk, they will produce three? What else can be the result if we would take all the dainties you may place before us under the excuse that we would hurt your feeling if we did not take them? You give us guavas and grapes and we eat them because they are a free gift from a princely farmer. And then imagine me with an easy conscience writing the viceregal letter on costly glazed paper with a fountain pen, a free gift from some accommodating friend! Will this behoove you and me? Can a letter so written produce the slightest effect?

To live thus would be to illustrate the immortal verse of Akho Bhagat, who says that "stolen food is like eating unprocessed mercury." And to live above the means befitting a poor country is to live on stolen food. This battle can never be won by living on stolen food. Nor did I bargain to set out on this march for living above our means. We expect thousands of volunteers to respond to the call. It will be impossible to keep them on extravagant terms. My life has become so busy that I get little time to come in close touch even with the eighty companions so as to be able to identify them individually. There was, therefore, no course open to me but to unburden my soul in public. I expect you to understand the central point of my message. If you have not, there is no hope of swaraj through the present effort. We must become real trustees of the dumb millions. I have exposed our weaknesses to the public gaze. I have not yet given you all the details, but I have told you enough to enable you to realize our unworthiness to write the letter to the viceroy. Now the local coworkers will understand my agony. Weak, ever exposed to temptations, ever failing, why will you tempt us and pamper us? We may not introduce these incandescent burners in our villages. It is enough that one hundred thousand men prey upon three hundred million. But how will it be when we begin to prey upon one another? In that event, dogs will lick our corpses. These lights are merely a sample of the extravagance I have in mind. My purpose is to wake you up from torpor. Let the volunteers account for every pice spent. I am more capable of offering satyagraha against ourselves than against the government. I have taken many years before embarking upon civil resistance against the government. But I should not take as many days for offering it against ourselves. The risk to be incurred is nothing compared to what has to be incurred in the present satyagraha. Therefore in your hospitality toward servants like us, I would have you to be miserly rather than lavish. I shall not complain of unavoidable absence of things. In order to procure goat's milk for me, you may not deprive poor women of milk for their children. It would be like poison if you did. Nor may milk and vegetables be brought from Surat. We can do without them if necessary. Do not resort to motorcars on the slightest pretext. The rule is, do not ride if you can walk. This is not a battle to be conducted with money. It will be impossible to sustain a mass movement with money.

Anyway, it is beyond me to conduct the campaign with a lavish display of money. Extravagance has no room in this campaign. If we cannot gather crowds unless we carry on a hurricane-expensive propaganda, I would be satisfied to address half a dozen men and women. It will be said that in that case reports will not appear in newspapers. I wish to tell you once and for all that this campaign will not succeed through newspaper reports, but with the assistance of Shri Rama. And no light is necessary when we are near Him; neither are pen and ink and such other accessories required, nor even speech. An appeal can be made to Him even if one has lost one's limbs.

We may not consider anybody low. I observed that you had provided for the night journey a heavy kerosene burner mounted on a stool, which a poor laborer carried on his head. This was a humiliating sight. This man was being goaded to walk fast. I could not bear the sight. I therefore put on speed and outraced the whole company. But it was no use. The man was made to run after me. The humiliation was complete. If the weight had to be carried, I should have loved to see someone among ourselves carrying it. We would then soon dispense both with the stool and the burner. No laborer would carry such a load on his head. We rightly object to begar [forced labor]. But what was this if it was not begar? Remember that in swaraj we would expect one drawn from the so-called lower class to preside over India's destiny. If then we do not quickly mend our ways, there is no swaraj such as you and I have put before the people.

From my outpouring you may not infer that I shall weaken in my resolve to carry on the struggle. It will continue no matter how coworkers or others act. For me there is no turning back, whether I am alone or joined by thousands. I would rather die a dog's death and have my bones licked by dogs than that I should return to the Ashram a broken man. I admit that I have not well used the money you have given out of the abundance of your love. You are entitled to regard me as one of those wretches described in the verses sung in the beginning. Shun me.

CWMG, vol. 43, pp. 146–49

13.
President in Prison House

Pandit Jawaharlal is in jail. This means that the government has thrown the whole of India into prison. If we understand this, then our duty becomes clear at once. If we wish to force the jail doors open, we must do these things.

1. We should make salt everywhere and distribute it.

2. Women should picket liquor shops, that is, they should humbly plead with the sellers and consumers of liquor to desist from selling and drinking it.

3. Women should similarly dissuade those that sell and those that wear foreign cloth.

4. Spinning should be started in every home.

5. Students should leave schools and dedicate themselves to national work.

6. Lawyers should give up their practice and devote all their time to this national yajna.

7. Those in other occupations should also give for these activities as much time as they can.

8. People should leave government jobs.

9. Under no circumstances should people become disorderly or commit violence.

10. They should not look down upon anyone. They should live at peace with all. If we did this much, our strength would certainly increase and no one would dare deflect us from our path.

CWMG, vol. 43, pp. 275–76

14.
Excerpts from Talk at Oxford*

Sir Gilbert Murray . . . seemed to be very much perturbed over what he thought were most dangerous manifestations of nonviolent revolution and nationalism. "I find myself today in greater disagreement with you than even Mr. Winston Churchill," he said.

Gandhiji said: You want cooperation between nations for

* The talk was on October 24, 1931. Dr. Gilbert Murray, Dr. Gilbert Slater, and Professor Reginald Coupland were among those who attended.

the salvaging of civilization. I want it, too, but cooperation presupposes free nations worthy of cooperation. If I am to help in creating or restoring peace and goodwill and resist disturbances thereof, I must have ability to do so and I cannot do so unless my country has come into its own. At the present moment, the very movement for freedom in India is India's contribution to peace. For so long as India is a subject nation, not only she is a danger to peace, but also England, which exploits India. Other nations may tolerate today England's imperialist policy and her exploitation of other nations, but they certainly do not appreciate it; and they would gladly help in the prevention of England becoming a greater and greater menace every day. Of course you will say that India free can become a menace herself. But let us assume that she will behave herself with her doctrine of nonviolence, if she achieves her freedom through it, and for all her bitter experience of being a victim to exploitation. The objection about my talking in terms of revolution is largely answered by what I have already said about nationalism. But my movement is conditioned by one great and disturbing factor. You might, of course, say that there can be no nonviolent rebellion and there has been none known to history. Well, it is my ambition to provide an instance, and it is my dream that my country may win its freedom through nonviolence. And I would like to repeat to the whole world times without number that I will not purchase my country's freedom at the cost of nonviolence. My marriage with nonviolence is such an absolute thing that I would rather commit suicide than be deflected from my position. I have not mentioned truth in this connection, simply because truth cannot be expressed except by nonviolence. So, if you accept the conception, my position is sound. . . . You may be justified in saying that I must go more warily, but if you attack the fundamentals, you have to convince me. And I must tell you that the boycott may have nothing to do with nationalism even. It may be a question of pure reform, as without being intensely nationalistic, we can refuse to purchase your cloth and make our own. A reformer cannot always afford to wait. If he does not put into force his belief, he is no reformer. Either he is too hasty or too afraid or

too lazy. Who is to advise him or provide him with a barome-
ter? You can only guide yourself with a disciplined conscience
and then run all risks with the protecting armor of truth and
nonviolence. A reformer could not do otherwise.

CWMG, vol. 48, pp. 226–27

15.
Duty of Disloyalty

There is no halfway house between active loyalty and active
disloyalty. There is much truth in the late Justice Stephen's re-
mark that a man to prove himself not guilty of disaffection
must prove himself to be actively affectionate. In these days of
democracy there is no such thing as active loyalty to a person.
You are therefore loyal or disloyal to institutions. When therefore you are disloyal, you seek not to destroy persons but institutions. The present state is an institution which, if one knows
it, can never evoke loyalty. It is corrupt. Many of its laws governing the conduct of persons are positively inhuman. Their
administration is worse. Often the will of one person is the
law. It may safely be said that there are as many rulers as there
are districts in this country. These, called collectors, combine
in their own persons the executive as well as the judicial functions. Though their acts are supposed to be governed by laws
in themselves highly defective, these rulers are often capricious
and regulated by nothing but their own whims and fancies.
They represent not the interests of the people but those of their
foreign masters or principals. These (nearly three hundred)
men form an almost secret corporation, the most powerful in
the world. They are required to find a fixed minimum of revenue; they have therefore often been found to be most unscrupulous in their dealings with the people. This system of
government is confessedly based upon a merciless exploitation

of unnumbered millions of the inhabitants of India. From the village headmen to their personal assistants, these satraps have created a class of subordinates who, whilst they cringe before their foreign masters, in their constant dealings with the people act so irresponsibly and so harshly as to demoralize them and by a system of terrorism render them incapable of resisting corruption.

It is then the duty of those who have realized the awful evil of the system of Indian government to be disloyal to it and actively and openly to preach disloyalty. Indeed, loyalty to a state so corrupt is a sin, disloyalty a virtue.

The spectacle of three hundred million people being cowed down by living in the dread of three hundred men is demoralizing alike for the despots as for the victims. It is the duty of those who have realized the evil nature of the system, however attractive some of its features may, torn from their context, appear to be, to destroy it without delay. It is their clear duty to run any risk to achieve the end.

But it must be equally clear that it would be cowardly for three hundred million people to seek to destroy the three hundred authors or administrators of the system. It is a sign of gross ignorance to devise means of destroying these administrators or their hirelings. Moreover, they are but creatures of circumstances. The purest man entering the system will be affected by it and will be instrumental in propagating the evil. The remedy, therefore, naturally is not being enraged against the administrators and therefore hurting them, but to noncooperate with the system by withdrawing all the voluntary assistance possible and refusing all its so-called benefits. A little reflection will show that civil disobedience is a necessary part of noncooperation. You assist an administration most effectively by obeying its orders and decrees. An evil administration never deserves such allegiance. Allegiance to it means partaking of the evil. A good man will therefore resist an evil system or administration with his whole soul. Disobedience of the law of an evil state is therefore a duty. Violent disobedience deals with men who can be replaced. It leaves the evil itself untouched and often accentuates it. Nonviolent, i.e., civil, disobedience is the only and the most successful remedy and is obligatory upon him who would dissociate himself from evil.

There is danger in civil disobedience only because it is still only a partially tried remedy and has always to be tried in an atmosphere surcharged with violence. For when tyranny is rampant, much rage is generated among the victims. It remains latent because of their weakness and bursts in all its fury on the slightest pretext. Civil disobedience is a sovereign method of transmuting this undisciplined life-destroying latent energy into disciplined life-saving energy whose use ensures absolute success. The attendant risk is nothing compared to the result promised. When the world has become familiar with its use and when it has had a series of demonstrations of its successful working, there will be less risk in civil disobedience than there is in aviation, in spite of that science having reached a high stage of development.

CWMG, vol. 43, pp. 132–34

16.
Why Against Violence?

A correspondent argues: *Why are you against violence? Do you think that every act of violence is an expression of himsa? Is it not strange that we should feel a kind of horror, pity, and disgust when we see a murder or an assassination, and silently witness the slow sucking of blood going on every day in the world? If one believes that a successful bloody revolution would ameliorate a good deal of misery in the world, why should he not resort to arms? . . . Don't you realize that the rulers of the world have become so callous that, to understand you or humanity, they must again become children. I don't mean to say they are born bad. But their badness is a physical fact and, in spite of themselves, they cannot alter it.*

It is because the rulers, if they are bad, are so, not necessarily or wholly by reason of birth, but largely because of their environment, that I have hopes of their altering their course. It is perfectly true, as the writer says, that the rulers cannot alter their course themselves. If they are dominated by their environment, they do not surely deserve to be killed but should be changed by a change of environment. But the environment are we—the people who make the rulers what they are. They are thus an exaggerated edition of what we are in the aggregate. If my argument is sound, any violence done to the rulers would be violence done to ourselves. It would be suicide. And since I do not want to commit suicide, nor encourage my neighbors to do so, I become nonviolent myself and invite my neighbors to do likewise. Moreover, violence may destroy one or more bad rulers, but, like Ravana's heads, others will pop up in their places, for, the root lies elsewhere. It lies in us. If we will reform ourselves, the rulers will automatically do so. The correspondent seems to imagine that a nonviolent person has no feelings and that he is a silent witness to the "slow sucking of blood going on every day in the world." Nonviolence is not a passive force or so helpless as the correspondent will make it out to be. Barring truth, if truth is to be considered apart from nonviolence, the latter is the activest force in the world. It never fails. Violence only seemingly succeeds, and nobody has ever claimed uniform success for violence. Nonviolence never promises immediate and tangible results. It is not a mango trick. Its failures are, therefore, all-seeming. A believer in violence will kill the murderer and boast of his act. But he never killed murder. By murdering the murderer, he added to it and probably invited more. The law of retaliation is the law of multiplying evil. A nonviolent man will act upon the murderer through his love. He cannot, by punishing the murderer, undo the murder already committed. But he hopes by gentleness to get the murderer to repent of his deed and change the whole course of his life. A nonviolent man always and automatically turns the searchlight selfward and discovers that the best course of conduct is to do unto others as he would have others do unto him. If he was the murderer, he would not like to be killed for his madness but would like the opportunity of mending himself. He knows, too, that he must not destroy what he can-not create. God is the sole judge between man and man.

17.
The Greatest Force

Nonviolence is at the root of every one of my activities and therefore also of the three public activities on which I am just now visibly concentrating all my energy. These are untouch-ability, khadi, and village regeneration in general. Hindu-Muslim unity is my fourth love. But so far as any visible manifestation is concerned, I have owned defeat on that score. Let the public, however, not assume therefrom that I am inac-tive. If not during my lifetime, I know that after my death both Hindus and Mussalmans will bear witness that I had never ceased to yearn after communal peace. Nonviolence to be a creed has to be all-pervasive. I cannot be nonviolent about one activity of mine and violent about others. That would be a pol-icy, not a life force. That being so, I cannot be indifferent about the war that Italy is now waging against Abyssinia. But I have resisted most pressing invitation to express my opinion and give a lead to the country. Self-suppression is often necessary in the interest of truth and nonviolence. If India had as a na-tion imbibed the creed of nonviolence, corporate or national, I should have had no hesitation in giving a lead. But in spite of a certain hold I have on the millions of this country, I know the very grave and glaring limitation of that hold. India had an un-broken tradition of nonviolence from times immemorial. But at no time in her ancient history, as far as I know it, has it had complete nonviolence in action pervading the whole land. Nev-ertheless, it is my unshakable belief that her destiny is to de-liver the message of nonviolence to mankind. It may take ages to come to fruition. But so far as I can judge, no other country will precede her in the fulfillment of that mission.

Be that as it may, it is reasonable to contemplate the implications of that matchless force. Three concrete questions were, the other day, incidentally asked by friends:

1. *What could ill-armed Abyssinia do against well-armed Italy, if she were nonviolent?*

2. *What could England, the greatest and the most powerful member of the league, do against determined Italy, if she (England) were nonviolent in your sense of the term?*

3. *What could India do, if she suddenly became nonviolent in your sense of the term?*

Before I answer the questions, let me lay down five simple axioms of nonviolence as I know it:

1. Nonviolence implies as complete self-purification as is humanly possible.

2. Man for man, the strength of nonviolence is in exact proportion to the ability, not the will, of the nonviolent person to inflict violence.

3. Nonviolence is without exception superior to violence, i.e., the power at the disposal of a nonviolent person is always greater than he would have if he was violent.

4. There is no such thing as defeat in nonviolence. The end of violence is surest defeat.

5. The ultimate end of nonviolence is surest victory—if such a term may be used of nonviolence. In reality, where there is no sense of defeat, there is no sense of victory. The foregoing questions may be answered in the light of these axioms.

1. If Abyssinia were nonviolent, she would have no arms, would want none. She would make no appeal to the league or any other power for armed intervention. She would never give any cause for complaint. And Italy would find nothing to conquer if Abyssinians would not offer armed resistance, nor would they give cooperation willing or forced. Italian occupation in that case would mean that of the land without its people. That, however, is not Italy's exact object. She seeks submission of the people of the beautiful land.

2. If Englishmen were as a nation to become nonviolent at heart, they would shed imperialism; they would give up the use of arms. The moral force generated by such an act of renunciation would stagger Italy into willing surrender of her designs. England would then be a living embodiment of the axioms I have laid down. The effect of such a conversion would mean the greatest miracle of all ages. And yet if nonviolence is not an idle dream, some such thing has someday to come to pass somewhere. I live in that faith.

3. The last question may be answered thus. As I have said, India as a nation is not nonviolent in the full sense of the term. Neither has she any capacity for offering violence—not because she has no arms. Physical possession of arms is the least necessity of the brave. Her nonviolence is that of the weak. She betrays her weakness in many of her daily acts. She appears before the world today as a decaying nation. I mean here not in the mere political sense but essentially in the nonviolent, moral sense. She lacks the ability to offer physical resistance. She has no consciousness of strength. She is conscious only of her weakness. If she were otherwise, there would be no communal problems, nor political. If she were nonviolent in the consciousness of her strength, Englishmen would lose their role of distrustful conquerors. We may talk politically as we like and often legitimately blame the English rulers. But if we, as Indians, could but for a moment visualize ourselves as a strong people disdaining to strike, we should cease to fear Englishmen whether as soldiers, traders, or administrators, and they

to distrust us. Therefore, if we became truly nonviolent, we should carry Englishmen with us in all we might do. In other words, we being millions would be the greatest moral force in the world, and Italy would listen to our friendly word.

The reader has, I hope, by now perceived that my argument is but a feeble and clumsy attempt to prove my axioms, which to be such must be self-proved. Till my eyes of geometrical understanding had been opened, my brain was swimming, as I read and reread the twelve axioms of Euclid. After the opening of my eyes, geometry seemed to be the easiest science to learn. Much more so is the case with nonviolence. It is a matter of faith and experience, not of argument beyond a point. So long as the world refuses to believe, she must await a miracle, i.e., an ocular demonstration of nonviolence on a mass scale. They say this is against human nature—nonviolence is only for the individual. If so, where is the difference in kind between man and beast?

CWMG, vol. 62, pp. 28–30

18.
Talk to Members of Spinning Club*

QUESTION: *Why should we spin now that there is no definite civil disobedience in the offing? Some satyagrahis have actually given up spinning since civil disobedience has receded into the background.*

GANDHIJI: That to me shows that they would have made but poor satyagrahis and it is for the best that they have dropped out. I doubt if these fair-weather customers could be good for anything. For good or for ill, we have adopted the spinning wheel as the weapon for our nonviolent struggle. A soldier who will practice his weapons only when action is in

---

* The conversation took place in Delhi on June 30, 1940.

sight will surely come a cropper at the time of the test. A satyagrahi soldier always looks and plans far ahead of him. If we
have faith in the efficacy of the weapon we have chosen, we
shall never give it up or lay it down but keep it always refur-
bished and ready. Today our nonviolence is on its trial. The
Working Committee's resolution is based on the assumption
that the country is today not ready for the practice of pure
ahimsa. They would be but too glad to discover that their assumption was wrong and revise their decision accordingly. It is
for those who have a living faith in nonviolence to prove the
same and convert the Working Committee to their view instead of catching at the first excuse to resile from their faith. If
the fifty-two members who are on the register of your club
have the right faith in them, they will soon multiply into fifty-
two hundred. But mere shilly-shallying won't do. "If the salt
loseth its savor, wherewith shall it be salted?" I have not a
shadow of doubt that through the spinning wheel we can develop the nonviolence of the strong which recks no odds, however overwhelming, and knows no defeat. Weapons forged
out of iron and steel do not interest me. They might enable
you to scatter death over the enemy and to capture a measure
of the power he today wields over you. But that will not leave
the masses any the better. They will continue to groan under
the yoke of the powerful and the mighty. I am not interested in
an order which leaves out the weakest—the blind, the halt, and
the maimed. My swaraj is even for the least in the land. This
can come only through nonviolence. Nonviolence of the weak
is bad. But violence of the impotent—impotent violence—is
worse. That is what is today vitiating the atmosphere. Mere spinning à la mode will not purge the atmosphere of this poison.

Another member of the club remarked that they could not
pretend to have a faith in the spinning wheel which Gandhiji
had, but they were prepared to spin for discipline, which was
quite honest a stand to take up.

Gandhiji, while admitting that spinning for discipline had
value at one time, contended that it was altogether inadequate
to the need of the hour today. To create a truly nonviolent atmosphere in the country, spinning with faith was necessary.

Supposing there were riots imperiling the lives of thousands of innocent women and children and the conflagration threatened to spread over the whole country, it would be up to those who had true faith in nonviolence to interpose themselves between the lust-maddened rioters and quell their fury by their self-immolation. Spinning for discipline will not give them that faith.

He continued: Discipline has a place in nonviolent strategy, but much more is required. In a satyagraha army, everybody is a soldier and a servant. But at a pinch every satyagrahi soldier has also to be his own general and leader. Mere discipline cannot make for leadership. The latter calls for faith and vision. That is why I have said that spinning for discipline, whatever else it might be capable of achieving, cannot help us to win the satyagraha fight, which requires the nonviolence of the strong.

CWMG, vol. 72, pp. 216–17

19.
Whither Ahimsa, Whither Khadi?

A correspondent from Kathiawar writes:

As in many other districts or provinces, so in Kathiawar people are fast losing their faith in khadi and ahimsa. Many congressmen and Gandhians have begun to ask how nonviolence can work in matters political.

The writer of the letter adduces a number of arguments giving illustrations. I have, however, satisfied myself with quoting the salient part of the letter. It contains three errors: I have been explaining of late that neither in Kathiawar nor in other parts of India have people real faith in nonviolence or khadi. It is true that I had deceived myself into believing that people were wedded to nonviolence with khadi as its symbol. As a matter of fact, in the name of nonviolence, people manifested only the outward peaceableness of the impotent. They never even attempted to drive violence from their hearts. He who runs can see for himself the verification of this fact. It had become patent to everyone, when I went to Rajkot in connection with the Rajkot imbroglio, that there was no Rama in Rajkot and, therefore, Kathiawar. Hence it is hardly correct to say that their faith is only now beginning to wane. It is equally improper to question now the efficacy of nonviolence in matters political. What was the people's fight against the foreign power if it was not a political matter? Indeed, the disgraceful fight between brother and brother that we are witnessing today is much less political. Today, irreligion is stalking the country in the name of religion. Even the outward peace that we were able to observe in the fight against the foreign power is conspicuous by its absence today. The third error consists in the distinction the correspondent makes between congressmen and Gandhians. The distinction is baseless. If there is any Gandhian, it must be I. I am not so arrogant as to make any such claim. A Gandhian means a worshipper of Gandhi. Only God has worshippers. I have never claimed to be God. How then can I have worshippers? Moreover, how can it be said that those who call themselves Gandhians are not congressmen? There are innumerable servants of the Congress although they are not four-anna members registered in the Congress register. The reader should know that I myself belong to that category. Hence the distinction made is false. I have repeatedly said that I have neither any part nor any say in many things that are going on in the country today. It is no secret that the Congress willingly said good-bye to nonviolence when it accepted power. Again I believe that the method of rationing of food and clothing is highly injurious to the country. If I had my way, I would not buy a grain of foodstuff from outside India. It is my firm belief that even today there is enough food in the country. It has been hidden because of the rationing. Again, if people followed me, there would be no deadly quarrel between Hindus, Sikhs, and Muslims. It is clear that my writ does not run any longer. Mine is a voice in the wilderness. As for khadi, it has some kind of a place, if we separate it from ahimsa. But it does not have the pride of place it would have had as a symbol of ahimsa. Those who are in the political field wear khadi as a matter of convention. Today we see the triumph not of khadi but of mill cloth, for we have assumed that but for the manufactures from our mills, millions would have to go naked. Can there be a greater delusion than this? We grow enough cotton in the country. We have any number of handlooms and spinning wheels. India is not unused to the art of hand spinning and hand weaving, but somehow or other the fear has seized us that the millions will not take to hand spinning and weaving hand-spun yarn for their own needs. A haunted man sees fear even when there is no cause for it. And many more die of fright than of the actual disease.

CWMG, vol. 89, pp. 395–97

20.
To Every Briton

In 1896 I addressed an appeal to every Briton in South Africa on behalf of my countrymen who had gone there as laborers or traders and their assistants. It had its effect. However important it was from my viewpoint, the cause which I pleaded then was insignificant compared with the cause which prompts this appeal. I appeal to every Briton, wherever he may be now, to accept the method of nonviolence instead of that of war for the adjustment of relations between nations and other matters. Your statesmen have declared that this is a war on behalf of democracy. There are many other reasons given in justification. You know them all by heart. I suggest that at the end of the war, whichever way it ends, there will be no democracy left to represent democracy. This war has descended upon mankind as a curse and a warning. It is a curse inasmuch as it is brutalizing man on a scale hitherto unknown. All distinctions between combatants and noncombatants have been abolished.

No one and nothing is to be spared. Lying has been reduced to an art. Britain was to defend small nationalities. One by one they have vanished, at least for the time being. It is also a warning. It is a warning that, if nobody reads the writing on the wall, man will be reduced to the state of the beast, whom he is shaming by his manners. I read the writing when the hostilities broke out. But I had not the courage to say the word. God has given me the courage to say it before it is too late.

I appeal for cessation of hostilities, not because you are too exhausted to fight, but because war is bad in essence. You want to kill Nazism. You will never kill it by its indifferent adoption. Your soldiers are doing the same work of destruction as the Germans. The only difference is that perhaps yours are not as thorough as the Germans. If that be so, yours will soon acquire the same thoroughness as theirs, if not much greater. On no other condition can you win the war. In other words, you will have to be more ruthless than the Nazis. No cause, however just, can warrant the indiscriminate slaughter that is going on minute by minute. I suggest that a cause that demands the inhumanities that are being perpetrated today cannot be called just.

I do not want Britain to be defeated, nor do I want her to be victorious in a trial of brute strength, whether expressed through the muscle or the brain. Your muscular bravery is an established fact. Need you demonstrate that your brain is also as unrivaled in destructive power as your muscle? I hope you do not wish to enter into such an undignified competition with the Nazis. I venture to present you with a nobler and a braver way, worthy of the bravest soldier. I want you to fight Nazism without arms, or, if I am to retain the military terminology, with nonviolent arms. I would like you to lay down the arms you have as being useless for saving you or humanity. You will invite Herr Hitler and Signor Mussolini to take what they want of the countries you call your possessions. Let them take possession of your beautiful island, with your many beautiful buildings. You will give all these, but neither your souls nor your minds. If these gentlemen choose to occupy your homes, you will vacate them. If they do not give you free passage out, you will allow yourself, man, woman, and child, to be slaughtered, but you will refuse to owe allegiance to them. This process or method, which I have called nonviolent noncooperation, is not without considerable success in its use in India. Your representatives in India may deny my claim. If they do, I shall feel sorry for them. They may tell you that our noncooperation was not wholly nonviolent, that it was born of hatred. If they give that testimony, I won't deny it. Had it been wholly nonviolent, if all the noncooperators had been filled with goodwill toward you, I make bold to say that you who are India's masters would have become her pupils and, with much greater skill than we have, perfected this matchless weapon and met the German and Italian friends' menace with it. Indeed the history of Europe during the past few months would then have been written differently. Europe would have been spared seas of innocent blood, the rape of so many small nations, and the orgy of hatred. This is no appeal made by a man who does not know his business. I have been practicing with scientific precision nonviolence and its possibilities for an unbroken period of over fifty years. I have applied it in every walk of life, domestic, institutional, economic, and political. I know of no single case in which it has failed. Where it has seemed sometimes to have failed, I have ascribed it to my imperfections. I claim no perfection for myself. But I do claim to be a passionate seeker after Truth, which is but another name for God. In the course of that search, the discovery of nonviolence came to me. Its spread is my life mission. I have no interest in living except for the prosecution of that mission. I claim to have been a lifelong and wholly disinterested friend of the British people. At one time I used to be also a lover of your empire. I thought that it was doing good to India. When I saw that in the nature of things it could do no good, I used, and am still using, the nonviolent method to fight imperialism. Whatever the ultimate fate of my country, my love for you remains, and will remain, undiminished. My nonviolence demands universal love, and you are not a small part of it. It is that love which has prompted my appeal to you. May God give power to every word of mine. In His name I began to write this, and in His name I close it. May your statesmen have the wisdom and courage to

respond to my appeal. I am telling His Excellency the Viceroy
that my services are at the disposal of His Majesty's government, should they consider them of any practical use in advancing the object of my appeal.

NEW DELHI, July 2, 1940

CWMG, vol. 72, pp. 229–31

21.

"A Cry in the Wilderness"?

> *With hands upraised I cry:*
> *(But none listens to me)*
> *Dharma yields both artha and kama;*
> *Why is that dharma not observed?*

Bapuji Aney [on his way back from Simla] paid a flying visit
to me at Delhi on Saturday. Whether we work together or seem
to be working in opposite directions, his love for me endures,
and so he never misses an opportunity to look in wherever I
may be. He expresses himself freely before me, and often
shares with me a verse or two from his inexhaustible store.
During his Delhi visit he sympathized with me for my having
had to sever my connection with the Congress, but he really
congratulated me.

> *They should, I think, leave you in peace, and let you go your
> way. I read your appeal to every Briton. It will fall on deaf ears.
> But that does not matter to you. You cannot help telling them
> what you feel to be their dharma (duty). But it is not strange
> that they will not listen to you—seeing that the Congress itself
> did not listen to you at the critical moment. When even sage*

Vyasa failed to make himself heard, how should others fare bet-
ter? He had to conclude his great epic—Mahabharata—with a
verse which reveals the cry of his soul.

With this he cited the verse I have quoted at the head of this
article. He thereby strengthened my faith and also showed how
difficult was the way I had chosen. And yet it has never seemed
to me so difficult as it is imagined to be. Though the Sardar's
way and mine seem to diverge today, it does not mean that our
hearts also diverge. It was in my power to stop him from seced-
ing from me. But it did not seem to be proper to do so. And it
would have been morally wrong to strive with Rajaji in what he
firmly regarded as his clear duty. Instead, therefore, of dissuad-
ing Rajaji, I encouraged him to follow his course. It was my clear
duty to do so. If I have the power to carry my experiment of
ahimsa to success in an apparently new field, if my faith endures, and if I am right in thinking that the masses are fundamentally nonviolent, Rajaji and the Sardar will again be with me
as before. What are these apparently new fields for the operation
of nonviolence? Those who have followed the Working Committee's resolutions and writings in *Harijan* are now familiar
with these. Nonviolence in its operation against constituted authority is one field. We have exercised this up to now with a fair
amount of success, and I have always described it as the nonviolence of the weak. This nonviolence may be said to have come to
stay with congressmen. The other field is the exercise of ahimsa
in internal disturbances—Hindu-Muslim riots and the like. We
have not been able to show visible success in the exercise of
ahimsa in this field. What then should the congressmen do when
internal chaos is so imminent? Will they return blow for blow,
or will they cheerfully bend their heads to receive violent blows?
The answer to this is not so easy as we might think. Instead of
going into the intricacies, I should say that congressmen should
try to save the situation by laying down their lives, not by taking
any. He who meets death without striking a blow fulfills his
duty cent per cent. The result is in God's hands. But it is clear
that this nonviolence is not the nonviolence of the weak. It does
not give one the joy of jail going. One can have that joy and also

cover thereby the ill will one harbors in his breast against the government. One can also noncooperate with the government. But where swords, knives, *lathis*, and stones are freely used, what is a man to do single-handed? Is it possible for one to receive these deadly blows with ill will in one's heart? It is clear that it is impossible to do so, unless one is saturated with charity. It is only he who feels one with his opponent that can receive his blows as though they were so many flowers. Even one such man, if God favors him, can do the work of a thousand. It requires soul force—moral courage—of the highest type. The man or woman who can display this nonviolence of the brave can easily stand against external invasion. This is the third field for the exercise of nonviolence. The Congress Working Committee were of opinion that, while it might be possible for us to exercise ahimsa in internal disturbances, India has not the strength to exercise ahimsa against the invasion of a foreign foe. This their want of faith has distressed me. I do not believe that the unarmed millions of India cannot exercise ahimsa with success in this wide field. It is for congressmen to reassure the Sardar, whose faith in ahimsa of the strong has for the moment been shaken, that ahimsa is the only weapon that can suit India in the fields mentioned. Let no one ask, "But what about the martial races in India?" For me that is all the more reason why congressmen should train themselves to defend their country with a nonviolent army. This is an entirely new experiment. But who, save the Congress, is to try it—the Congress which has tried it successfully in one field? It is my unshakable faith that, if we have a sufficient number of nonviolent soldiers, we are sure to succeed even in this new field, apart from the saving of the needless waste of crores of rupees. I am therefore hoping that every Gujarati congressite—man and woman—will declare their adherence to ahimsa and reassure the Sardar that they will never resort to violence. Even if there is sure hope of success in the exercise of violence, they will not prefer it to the exercise of nonviolence. We are sure to learn by our mistakes. "We fall to rise, are baffled to fight better, sleep to wake."

CWMG, vol. 72, pp. 248–50

22.
The Best Field for Ahimsa

Last week I wrote about three fields for the operation of ahimsa. I propose to invite attention today to the fourth and the best field for the operation of nonviolence. This is the family field, in a wider sense than the ordinary. Thus members of an institution should be regarded as a family. Nonviolence as between the members of such families should be easy to practice. If that fails, it means that we have not developed the capacity for pure nonviolence. For the love we have to practice toward our relatives or colleagues in our family or institution, we have to practice toward our foes, dacoits, etc. If we fail in one case, success in the other is a chimera. We have generally assumed that, though it may not be possible to exercise nonviolence in the domestic field, it is possible to do so in the political field. This has proved a pure delusion. We have chosen to describe our methods adopted so far as nonviolence, and thus caricatured nonviolence itself. If nonviolence it was, it was such poor stuff that it proved useless at the critical moment. The alphabet of ahimsa is best learnt in the domestic school, and I can say from experience that if we secure success there, we are sure to do so everywhere else. For a nonviolent person the whole world is one family. He will thus fear none, nor will others fear him. It will be retorted that those who satisfy such a test of nonviolence will be few and far between. It is quite likely, but that is no reply to my proposition. Those who profess to believe in nonviolence should know the implications of that belief. And if these scare them away, they are welcome to give up the belief. Now that the Congress Working Committee has made the position clear, it is necessary that those who claim to believe in nonviolence should know what is expected of them. If, as a result, the ranks of the nonviolent army thin down, it should not matter. An army, however small, of truly nonviolent soldiers is likely someday to multiply itself. An army of those who are not truly nonviolent is never likely to yield any use whether it increases or decreases. Let no one understand from the foregoing that a nonviolent army is open only to those who strictly enforce in their lives all the implications of nonviolence. It is open to all those who accept the implications and make an ever-increasing endeavor to observe them. There never will be an army of perfectly nonviolent people. It will be formed of those who will honestly endeavor to observe nonviolence. For the last fifty years I have striven to make my life increasingly nonviolent and to inspire my coworkers in the same direction, and I think I have had a fair amount of success. The growing darkness around, far from damping my zeal and dimming my faith, brightens them, and makes the implications of nonviolence more clearly visible to me.

CWMG, vol. 72, pp. 271–72

23.
How to Cultivate Ahimsa?

Q. *What is the good of your crying "ahimsa, ahimsa" in season and out of season? Will it by itself teach people to be nonviolent? Would it not be better, instead, to tell people how pure ahimsa or the ahimsa of the strong can be cultivated?*

A. Yours is a very timely and opportune question. I have attempted before this on more occasions than one to answer it. But my effort has, I confess, been rather desultory. I have not concentrated upon it, or given it the weight I might have. This was all right while I was devoting all my energy to forging means to give battle to the government. But it had the result of retarding the growth of pure ahimsa, so that today we are not even within ken of the ahimsa of the strong. If we now want to advance further, we ought, at least for some time, to completely forget the idea of offering nonviolent resistance to constituted authority. If nonviolence in the domestic field is successfully achieved, we shall surely see the nonviolence against constituted authority revived in its purified form, and it will be irresistible.

Now that I am no longer in the Congress, I may not offer civil disobedience even in my own person in its name. But I am certainly free to offer civil disobedience in my individual capacity whenever it may be necessary. No one need suppose that all civil disobedience will necessarily be taboo while the country is still being educated in the ahimsa of the strong. But those who may want to join the nonviolent force of my conception should not entertain any immediate prospect of civil disobedience. They should understand that, so long as they have not realized ahimsa in their own person in its pure form, there can be no civil disobedience for them.

Let not the mention of pure ahimsa frighten anybody. If we have a clear conception of it and have a living faith in its matchless efficacy, it will not be found to be so hard to practice as it is sometimes supposed to be. It will be well to remember the immortal Mahabharata verse in this connection. The seer poet therein loudly proclaims to the whole world that dharma includes within itself both legitimate *artha* and *kama*, and asks why men do not follow the royal road of dharma that leads to both earthly and spiritual bliss. Dharma here does not signify mere observance of externals. It signifies the way of truth and nonviolence. The scriptures have given us two immortal maxims. One of these is: "Ahimsa is the supreme law or dharma." The other is: "There is no other law or dharma than truth." These two maxims provide us the key to all lawful *artha* and *kama*. Why should we then hesitate to act up to them? Strange as it may appear, the fact remains that people find the easiest of things oftentimes to be the most difficult to follow. The reason, to borrow a term from the science of physics, lies in our inertia. Physicists tell us that inertia is an essential and, in its own place a most useful, quality of matter. It is that alone which steadies the universe and prevents it from flying off at a tangent. But for it the latter would be a chaos of motion. But inertia becomes an incubus and a vice when it ties the mind down to old ruts. It is this kind of inertia which is responsible for our rooted prejudice that to practice pure ahimsa is difficult. It is up to us to get rid of this incubus. The first step in this direction is firmly to resolve that all untruth and himsa shall hereafter be taboo to us, whatever sacrifice it might seem to involve. For the good these may seem to achieve is in appearance only, but in reality it is deadly poison. If our resolve is firm and our conviction clear, it would mean half the battle won, and the practice of these two qualities would come comparatively easy to us. Let us confine ourselves to ahimsa. We have all along regarded the spinning wheel, village crafts, etc., as the pillars of ahimsa, and so indeed they are. They must stand. But we have now to go a step further. A votary of ahimsa will of course base upon nonviolence, if he has not already done so, all his relations with his parents, his children, his wife, his servants, his dependents, etc. But the real test will come at the time of political or communal disturbances or under the menace of thieves and dacoits. Mere resolve to lay down one's life under the circumstances is not enough. There must be the necessary qualification for making the sacrifice. If I am a Hindu, I must fraternize with the Mussalmans and the rest. In my dealings with them I may not make any distinction between my co-religionists and those who might belong to a different faith. I would seek opportunities to serve them without any feeling of fear or unnaturalness. The word "fear" can have no place in the dictionary of ahimsa. Having thus qualified himself by his selfless service, a votary of pure ahimsa will be in a position to make a fit offering of himself in a communal conflagration. Similarly, to meet the menace of thieves and dacoits, he will need to go among, and cultivate friendly relations with, the communities from which thieves and dacoits generally come. A brilliant example of this kind of work is provided by Ravishanker Maharaj. His work among the criminal tribes in Gujarat has evoked praise even of the Baroda state authorities. There is an almost unlimited field for this kind of work and it does not call for any other talent in one besides pure love. Ravishanker Maharaj is an utter stranger to English. Even his knowledge of Gujarati is barely sufficient for everyday use. But God has blessed him with unlimited neighborly love. His simplicity easily wins all hearts and is the envy of everybody. Let his example provide a cue and inspiration to all those who may be similarly engaged in other fields of satyagraha.

CWMG, vol. 72, pp. 280–82

24.
Nonviolence of the Brave

A correspondent writes:

> *You say nonviolence is for the brave, not for cowards. But, in my opinion, in India the brave are conspicuous by their absence. Even if we claim to be brave, how is the world to believe us when it knows that India has no arms and is therefore incapable of defending herself? What then should we do to cultivate nonviolence of the brave?*

The correspondent is wrong in thinking that in India the brave are conspicuous by their absence. It is a matter for shame that because foreigners once labeled us as cowards we should accept the label. Man often becomes what he believes himself to be. If I keep on saying to myself that I cannot do a certain thing, it is possible that I may end by really becoming incapable of doing it. On the contrary, if I have the belief that I can do it, I shall surely acquire the capacity to do it even if I may not have it at the beginning. Again it is wrong to say that the world today believes us to be cowards. It has ceased to think so since the satyagraha campaign. The Congress prestige has risen very high in the West during the past twenty years. The world is watching with astonished interest the fact that although we have no arms, we are hoping to win swaraj, and

have indeed come very near it. Moreover, it sees in our nonviolent movement rays of hope for peace in the world and its salvation from the hell of carnage. The bulk of mankind has come
to believe that, if ever the spirit of revenge is to vanish and
bloody wars are to cease, the happy event can happen only
through the policy of nonviolence adopted by the Congress.
The correspondent's fear and suspicion are, therefore, un-
founded. It will now be seen that the fact that India is unarmed
is no obstacle in the path of ahimsa. The forcible disarmament
of India by the British government was indeed a grave wrong
and a cruel injustice. But we can turn even injustice to our advantage if God be with us or, if you prefer, we have the skill to
do so. And such a thing has happened in India.

Arms are surely unnecessary for a training in ahimsa. In fact,
the arms, if any, have to be thrown away, as the Khan Saheb
did in the Frontier Province. Those who hold that it is essential
to learn violence before we can learn nonviolence would hold
that only sinners can be saints.

Just as one must learn the art of killing in the training for
violence, so one must learn the art of dying in the training
for nonviolence. Violence does not mean emancipation from
fear but discovering the means of combating the cause of fear.
Nonviolence, on the other hand, has no cause for fear. The votary of nonviolence has to cultivate the capacity for sacrifice of
the highest type in order to be free from fear. He recks not if
he should lose his land, his wealth, his life. He who has not
overcome all fear cannot practice ahimsa to perfection. The
votary of ahimsa has only one fear, that is of God. He who
seeks refuge in God ought to have a glimpse of the atman that
transcends the body; and the moment one has a glimpse of the
imperishable atman, one sheds the love of the perishable body.
Training in nonviolence is thus diametrically opposed to training in violence. Violence is needed for the protection of things
external; nonviolence is needed for the protection of the atman,
for the protection of one's honor.

This nonviolence cannot be learnt by staying at home. It
needs enterprise. In order to test ourselves, we should learn to

dare danger and death, mortify the flesh, and acquire the capacity to endure all manner of hardships. He who trembles or takes to his heels the moment he sees two people fighting is not nonviolent but a coward. A nonviolent person will lay down his life in preventing such quarrels. The bravery of the nonviolent is vastly superior to that of the violent. The badge of the violent is his weapon spear, or sword, or rifle. God is the shield of the nonviolent. This is not a course of training for one intending to learn nonviolence. But it is easy to evolve one from the principles I have laid down. It will be evident from the foregoing that there is no comparison between the two types of bravery. The one is limited, the other is limitless. There is no such thing as out-daring or outfighting nonviolence. Nonviolence is invincible. There need be no doubt that this nonviolence can be achieved. The history of the past twenty years should be enough to reassure us.

CWMG, vol. 72, pp. 415–16

25.
Discussion with a Friend*

Gandhiji questioned the statement that sabotage could be part of the nonviolent program or that it was derivable from the principle of ahimsa as he understood it. The friend, however, persisted that sabotage had come to stay whether one liked it or not.

GANDHIJI: Irresponsible prophesying leads to nowhere. The real question is where we stand, what our attitude toward it is going to be.

FRIEND: *Was destruction of government property violence? You say that nobody has a right to destroy any property not his*

* The discussion took place in May 1944.

own. If so, is not government's property mine? I hold it is mine and I may destroy it.

There is a double fallacy involved in your argument. In the first place, conceding that government property is national property—which today it is not—I may not destroy it because I am dissatisfied with the government. But even a national government will be unable to carry on for a day if everybody claimed the right to destroy bridges, communications, roads, etc., because he disapproved of some of its activities. Moreover, the evil resides not in bridges, roads, etc., which are inanimate objects, but in men. It is the latter who need to be tackled. The destruction of bridges, etc., by means of explosives does not touch this evil but only provokes a worse evil in the place of the one it seeks to end. To sterilize it needs not destruction but self-immolation of the purest type, which would demonstrate that the authorities might break but would not be able to bend a will that has resigned itself to the God of truth.

I agree that the evil is within ourselves, not in the bridge, which can be used for a good purpose as well as an evil one. I also agree that its blowing up provokes counterviolence of a worse type. But it may be necessary from a strategic point of view for the success of the movement and in order to prevent demoralization.

It is an old argument. One used to hear it in old days in defense of terrorism. Sabotage is a form of violence. People have realized the futility of physical violence, but some people apparently think that it may be successfully practiced in its modified form as sabotage. It lacked the quality of nonviolence and could not take the place of full-fledged armed conflict. . . . We have to deal with a power which takes pride in not recognizing defeat. In the early part of the British rule there were powerful risings. In several places the British were actually beaten. But they won in the end. A British statesman used to say, "I do not believe in wooden guns." National struggles could not be won by "wooden guns." It is my conviction that the whole mass of people would not have risen to the height of courage and fearlessness that they have but for the working of full nonviolence. How it works we do not yet fully know. But the fact remains that under nonviolence we have progressed from strength to strength even through our apparent failures and setbacks. On the other hand, terrorism resulted in demoralization. Haste leads to waste.

You characterized the "Quit India" movement as a nonviolent rebellion. Is not nonviolent rebellion a program of seizure of power?

No. A nonviolent rebellion is not a program of seizure of power. It is a program of transformation of relationship ending in a peaceful transfer of power. . . . It will never use coercion. Even those who hold contrary views will receive full protection under it.

We have found that a person who has had a schooling in violent activity comes nearer to true nonviolence than one who has had no such experience.

That can be true only in the sense that having tried violence again and again he has realized its futility. That is all. Would you maintain also that a person who has had a taste of vice is nearer to virtue than the one who had none? For that is what your argument amounts to.

It is no secrecy if the person concerned is boldly prepared to face the consequences of his action. He resorts to secrecy in order to achieve his object. He can refuse to take any part in subsequent interrogations during his trial. He need not make a false statement.

No secret organization, however big, could do any good. Secrecy aims at building a wall of protection around you. Ahimsa disdains all such protection. It functions in the open and in the face of odds, the heaviest conceivable. We have to organize for action a vast people that have been crushed under the heel of unspeakable tyranny for centuries. They cannot be organized by any other than open, truthful means. I have grown up from youth to seventy-six years in abhorrence of secrecy. There must be no watering down of the ideal. Unless we cling to the formula in its fullness, we shall not make any headway. I know we have not always lived up to our ideals. There have been grave lapses. Had our instruments been less imperfect, we would have been nearer our goal. But in spite of our temporizing with our ideal, nonviolence has worked like a silent leaven among the dumb millions. That does not mean that we can afford to go on like this forever. We cannot remain static. We must move forward or we shall slide back.

Are you of opinion then that the August resolution caused a setback in the struggle for independence; that all the heroism and courage which our people showed in the course of it was useless?

No, I do not say that. In the historical process, the country will be found to have advanced toward freedom through every form of struggle, even through the August upheaval. All that I have said is that the progress would have been much greater if we had shown the nonviolent bravery of my conception. In this sense the sabotage activity has retarded the country's freedom. I have the highest admiration for the courage, patriotism, and spirit of self-sacrifice of people, say, like Jayaprakash Narayan. But Jayaprakash cannot be my ideal. If I had to give a medal for heroism, it would go not to him but to his wife, who, though simple and unlearned in politics, typifies in her person the power of satyagraha in its purest form before which even Jayaprakash has to bow. What I have said about the August upheaval is not by way of judgment upon the past—I have consistently refused to condemn it—but as a guidance for the future.

Our people have faith in nonviolence, but they do not know how to make it dynamic. What is the reason for this failure?

By hammering away at it through painful years, people have begun to see that there is a potency in nonviolence, but they have not seen it in all its fullness and beauty. If they had responded to all the steps that had to be taken for the effective organization of nonviolence and carried out in their fullness the various items of the eighteen-fold constructive program, our movement would have taken us to our goal. But today our minds are confused because our faith in constructive work is so weak. I know, one must push forth undaunted by difficulties.

CWMG, vol. 77, pp. 265–68

26.
Interview to Associated Press of America*

CORRESPONDENT: *In view of recent Indian history—1942 unrest, I.N.A. movement and unrest, R.I.N. mutiny, Calcutta-Bombay disturbances, movements in Indian states such as Kashmir, and recent communal riots—can it be said that your creed of nonviolence has failed, insofar as nonviolence has not taken roots in Indian life?*

GANDHIJI: This is a dangerous generalization. All you mention can certainly be called himsa, but that can never mean that the creed of nonviolence has failed. At best it may be said that I have not yet found the technique required for the conversion of the mass mind. But I claim that the millions of the seven hundred thousand villages of India have not participated in the violence alluded to by you. Whether nonviolence has taken roots in Indian life is still an open question which can only be answered after my death. What should one do in his day-to-day life—that is, what is the minimum program—so that one can acquire nonviolence of the brave? The minimum that is required of a person wishing to cultivate the ahimsa of the brave is first to clear his thought of cowardice and in the light of the clearance regulate his conduct in every activity, great or small. Thus the votary must refuse to be cowed down by his superior without being angry. He must, however, be ready to sacrifice his post, however remunerative it may be. Whilst sacrificing his all, if the votary has no sense of irritation against his employer, he has ahimsa of the brave in him. Assume that a fellow passenger threatens my son with assault and I reason with the would-be assailant, who then turns upon me. If then I take his blow with grace and dignity, without harboring any ill will against him, I exhibit the ahimsa of the brave. Such

* The interview took place on board the steamboat *Kiwi* during MKG's journey to interior Bengal on November 6, 1946.

instances are of everyday occurrence and can be easily multiplied. If I succeed in curbing my temper every time and though
able to give blow for blow I refrain, I shall develop the ahimsa
of the brave, which will never fail me and which will compel
recognition from the most confirmed adversaries.

CWMG, vol. 86, pp. 87–88

27.
Talk with Congress Workers*

Only this morning I poured out my anguish before some sisters.
I did not expect that you also would be the cause of similar
pain. It is a bad habit with us that whenever we call a meeting
to discuss some work, we start indulging in personal recrimina-
tion, lose our tempers, and thus waste our time. It seems there
is a growing inconsistency between the public and private life
of a Congress worker. The result is that goondaism, lack of
discipline, and carelessness are increasing day by day. As preparations are afoot for transferring the government into our
hands, our responsibility is also increasing. We must get rid of
anger, intolerance, etc., otherwise we will not be able to stand
on our own. Not only this, we might be caught up in a bigger
bondage. I want a swaraj in which the millions of illiterates in
our country will realize its benefits. You have to cultivate the
strength to achieve that. The government [under swaraj] should
be such that people may clearly see the distinction between the
arbitrary and autocratic British rule and the democratic government run on nonviolent lines. I am an optimist. I maintain that
once the reins of government are transferred to us we will realize our responsibilities and all the artificial barriers existing at
present will vanish. My faith in nonviolence and truth is being
strengthened all the more in spite of the increasing number of

* On April 17, 1947, at Patna.

atom bombs. I have not a shadow of doubt that there is no power superior to the power of truth and nonviolence in the world. See what a great difference there is between the two: one is a moral and spiritual force, and is motivated by infinite soul force; the other is a product of physical and artificial power, which is perishable. The soul is imperishable. This doctrine is not my invention; it is a doctrine enunciated in our Vedas and Shastras. When soul force awakens, it becomes irresistible and conquers the world. This power is inherent in every human being. But one can succeed only if one tries to realize this ideal in each and every act in one's life without being affected in the least by praise or censure.

CWMG, vol. 87, pp. 295–96

28.
Talk with Visitors*

This fight between brother and brother is not going to stop so long as the masses do not get work as well as bread. Order in the society, in fact in the country, cannot possibly be restored unless the indigenous crafts are developed. This is the sole remedy for banishing starvation from the country. The affluent in India can be counted on one's fingers, whereas there are millions who are starving. I fought for India's independence. There were satyagraha movements and as a result we have achieved what the world would consider success (not the kind I would have wished). The partition has come in spite of me. It has hurt me. But it is the way in which the partition has come that has hurt me more. And it is difficult to say what the result of the constant tension will be. I have pledged myself to do or die in the attempt to put down the present conflagration. I love all mankind as I love my own countrymen, because my God dwells in the heart of every human

* On June 9, 1947.

being and I aspire to realize the highest in life through the service of humanity. It is true that the nonviolence that we practiced was the nonviolence of the weak, i.e., no nonviolence at all. But I maintain that this was not what I presented to my countrymen. Nor did I present to them the weapon of nonviolence because they were weak or disarmed or without military training, but because my study of history has taught me that hatred and violence used in howsoever noble a cause only breed their kind and instead of ensuring peace endanger it. There is no miracle except love and nonviolence, which can drive out the poison of hatred. Thanks to the tradition of our ancient seers, sages, and saints, if there is a heritage that India can share with the world, it is this gospel of forgiveness and faith which is her proud possession. I have faith that in time to come India will pit that against the threat of destruction which the world has invited upon itself by the invention of the atom bomb. The weapon of truth and love is infallible, but there is something wrong in us, its votaries, which has plunged us into the present internecine strife. I am, therefore, trying to examine myself because it must be owing to some short-coming in me which it has been my fate to see reflected in the present outburst of violence.

CWMG, vol. 88, pp. 116–17

29.
Question Box*

QUESTION: *You have often stated while you were in Noakh-ali that failure of your mission there would be the failure of your own ahimsa and not of ahimsa itself. In the light of what has been achieved here (Calcutta), do you think that your ahimsa has succeeded or is on the way to success?*

ANSWER: It is a correct statement that has been attributed

* Calcutta, August 31, 1947.

to me. Ahimsa is always infallible. When, therefore, it appears to have failed, the failure is due to the inaptitude of the votary. I have never felt that my ahimsa has failed in Noakhali, nor can it be said that it has succeeded. It is on its trial. And when I talk of my ahimsa, I do not think of it as limited to myself. It must include all my coworkers in Noakhali. Success or failure would, therefore, be attributable to the aggregate of the activities of my coworkers and myself. What I have said about Noakhali applies to Calcutta. It is too early to state that the application of ahimsa to the communal problem in this great city has succeeded beyond doubt. As I have already remarked, it is wrong to contend that the establishment of friendliness between the two communities was a miracle. Circumstances were ready and Shaheed Saheb and I appeared on the scene to take the credit for what has happened. Anyway, it is premature to predicate anything about the application. The first thing naturally is that we, the two partners, have one mind and are believers in ahimsa. That being assured, I would say that if we know the science and its application, it is bound to succeed.

CWMG, vol. 89, p. 121

30.
Letter to Mathuradas Trikumji*

I know that I cannot realize truth if I get impatient. That in the judgment of the world I may seem to have overcome my ego is of little consequence. And if that belief is not true, my realization of ahimsa and truth is imperfect. Then the argument about the success of ahimsa does not arise at all. Where ahimsa is perfect, there can be no failure. One must, therefore, conclude that whenever ahimsa is found to have failed, that ahimsa cannot be perfect. Who is qualified to pass judgment as to its

* November 15, 1947.

success or failure is of course another matter. I myself cannot see the traces of ego and impatience that may be lurking within me. Only other people can observe them to some extent. But God alone sees the whole truth. I should not give the slightest impression, either, that I rebuke the Hindus more than the Muslims.

CWMG, vol. 90, p. 34

31.
Excerpt from a Prayer Speech

As I have admitted earlier, I had been under the delusion that our struggle was truly nonviolent. God had rendered me blind and I was misled. Because the lame, the crippled, the coward cannot be nonviolent. Lame, crippled, and dumb I do not mean literally, for God helps these and they are always nonviolent. Even a child can stand before the world on the strength of nonviolence. Prahlad was an instance. We do not know whether Prahlad was a historical character. To me he was more than a historical character, for I believe in the story. Prahlad's father commanded him not to utter the name of God. But Prahlad insisted that he would continue to utter the name of God. The image of twelve-year-old Prahlad remains before my eyes. Therefore I say that those who are lame and crippled at heart can never be truly nonviolent. So long as the light does not shine in the heart, no one can understand the beauty of nonviolence. What we offered during the struggle was passive resistance, which simply meant that we would not kill the British though in our hearts we wanted to kill them. But we had not the power. When the millions took up passive resistance, it did bring about our freedom. The freedom we have obtained is crippled freedom. It is only partial.

CWMG, vol. 90, p. 292

32.
Two Requests*

A friend suggests that I should resume writing my autobiography† from the point where I left off and, further, that I should write a treatise on the science of ahimsa. I never really wrote an autobiography. What I did write was a series of articles narrating my experiments with truth which were later published in book form. More than twenty years have elapsed since then. What I have done or pondered during this interval has not been recorded in chronological order. I would love to do so, but have I the leisure? I have resumed the publication of *Harijan* in the present trying times as a matter of duty. It is with difficulty that I can cope with this work. How can I find time to bring the remainder of my experiments with truth up-to-date? But if it is God's will that I should write them, He will surely make my way clear.

To write a treatise on the science of ahimsa is beyond my powers. I am not built for academic writings. Action is my domain, and what I understand, according to my lights, to be my duty, and what comes my way, I do. All my action is actuated by the spirit of service. Let anyone who can systematize ahimsa into a science do so, if indeed it lends itself to such treatment. In the event of my inability, the correspondent has suggested three names in order of preference for this task: Shri Vinoba, Shri Kishorelal Mashruwala, Shri Kaka Kalelkar. The first named could do it, but I know he will not. Every hour of his is scheduled for his work and he would regard it as sacrilege to take a single moment therefrom for writing a Shastra. I would

---

* Written on February 25, 1946.

† For an annotated, critical edition of M. K. Gandhi's autobiography, see, M. K. Gandhi, *An Autobiography or The Story of My Experiments with Truth: A Critical Edition*, introduced and annotated by Tridip Suhrud (New Haven: Yale University Press, 2018).

agree with him. The world does not hunger for Shastras. What it craves, and will always crave, is sincere action. He who can appease this hunger will not occupy his time in elaborating a Shastra.

Shri Kishorelal has already written an independent treatise. If his health permits, I know he would like to write further. It may not be correct to call his work a Shastra, but it may be said to be very near to one. In his present state of health, however, I do not think he can shoulder the burden, and I would be the last person to lay it on him. Like Shri Vinoba, he, too, does not allow a moment of his time to be wasted. Much of it is given to help solve the personal problems of a large circle of friends. The end of the day leaves him utterly exhausted.

Shri Kakasaheb, like Shri Thakkar, is an incorrigible nomad. Just now he has made the propagation and development of the national and provincial languages his special concern. Even if he wanted to divert a moment of his time to the writing of a Shastra, I would try to prevent him from doing so.

From the above it may be concluded that there is no need at present for the treatise in question. Any such during my lifetime would necessarily be incomplete. If at all, it could only be written after my death. And even so let me give the warning that it would fail to give a complete exposition of ahimsa. No man has ever been able to describe God fully. The same holds true of ahimsa. I can give no guarantee that I will do or believe tomorrow what I do or hold to be true today. God alone is omniscient. Man in the flesh is essentially imperfect. He may be described as being made in the image of God, but he is far from being God. God is invisible, beyond the reach of the human eye. All that we can do, therefore, is to try to understand the words and actions of those whom we regard as men of God. Let them soak into our being and let us endeavor to translate them into action, but only so far as they appeal to the heart. Could any scientific treatise do more for us?

VI.

LETTER TO HITLER

Is it naive to write to Adolf Hitler intent upon war and holocaust or does belief in the efficacy of nonviolence require one to have faith in all human beings and our capacity to recognize truth from falsehood and have the discernment to distinguish violence and injustice from a situation where all human persons have equal opportunity to realize their potential? This section explores Gandhi's responses to the war in Europe and the engagement of pacifists, war resisters, and devout Christians with Gandhi.

I.
Speech at Friends' House, London*

September 12, 1931

You will not this evening expect me to take up much of your time, or to say much with reference to my mission, but I wish

---

* According to Reuters, MKG arrived in London from Folkestone at 4:10 in the afternoon, and though it was raining, the rush of people was so great that police precautions became necessary. He was driven straight to Friends' House at Euston Road. Lawrence Housman, welcoming him on behalf of the reception committee, said: ". . . Mahatma Gandhi, if I may say so, you are a strange man—to the people of your own country and more so to my people. You are so sincere that you make some of us suspicious. You are so simple that you bewilder some of us. . . ."

to say one thing in a general way. I am here with my friends on a mission of peace. I am, and my friends are, guests of the great English nation. I hope that by the time we have finished our work, you will not consider that we have in any way abused your hospitality. I hope that, as the days go by, you will understand the scope of the mission on which the Congress has sent me. You will also please know that, as an agent holding a power of attorney from the Congress, I shall have my limitations. I have to conduct myself within the four corners of the mandate that I have received from the Congress. There are some words in that mandate which give to me a little measure of freedom of action, but in all respects, in all fundamental respects, I am hidebound. I may not, if I am to be loyal to the trust reposed in me, walk outside the four corners of that mandate. I venture to feel that Congress stands for a good cause, of which any nation would be proud. The Congress wants freedom unadulterated for the dumb and starving millions. In order that Congress may represent them, the Congress has chosen, as its means of vindicating this freedom, truth and nonviolence. I am fully aware that not all congressmen have lived up to the means, and I know that we of the Congress shall deserve the curses of the whole world if, in the name of truth and nonviolence, we do the contrary. But I derive the greatest consolation from the knowledge that I possess that the best workers of the Congress today represent truth and nonviolence in their essence. . . . We have in our midst, I know, a school of violence also. I know many of these young men—I have lived with them, I have mixed with them, I have talked to them also. I have endeavored, as several others of my coworkers have endeavored, to win them from what we hold is an error; but, at the same time, I know that there is a common cause, even between them and ourselves. They are burning to attain the freedom to which India is entitled, which is India's birthright. I repeat what I have told them in public and in private—that their activities embarrass Congress, their activities set back the hands of the clock of progress. The congressmen who are wedded to this creed realize fully that these young men, who resort to violence for the sake of gaining freedom, do harm not only to themselves but to the country, and most of all to the dumb millions to whom I have referred. We may be nationalists, we may be ardent patriots, but immediately we apply these means of truth and nonviolence, our patriotism becomes internationalism. Our patriotism is so conceived that we want our freedom not to injure the freedom of any other country or of any single individual. We believe not in the law that might is right, or the greatest good of the greatest number, but we believe in the greatest good of all, including the meanest of creatures amongst all God's creation. And if India could vindicate her freedom, attain it through these means, do you not think that it would be well, not only with India, but with the whole world? But there is something more. There is the settlement between the government of India and the Congress. That is a sacred thing arrived at through the strivings of that noble Englishman, Lord Irwin. I had repeatedly promised him, if it was humanly possible, that I would come to London and, as soon as I felt the way was open, I have dashed to London.

Recommending the study of the Indian question, Mr. Gandhi realized the difficulty, because the British were rightly preoccupied with home affairs, but [he said:] I wish it were possible for Englishmen and women to realize that the budget will not be honestly balanced, unless the balance between Britain and India is set right. *Concluding, Mr. Gandhi asked the audience to work for the fulfillment of his mission, for it would be for the good not only of India but of the world.*

CWMG, vol. 48, p. 2–4

2.
Answers to Questions*

LAUSANNE, December 8, 1931

Q. *How can East and West be brought together to work for peace?*

A. This question was asked me some five years ago. And this was my answer: I, who belong to a subject nation, did not know how I could work for peace except by working for freedom, and if India could be helped to win freedom through peaceful means, it would be a very good combination for peace. I have said this after having attempted the deliverance of my country through absolutely nonviolent and truthful means.

Q. *Must we admit that, parallel to the use of nonviolence in India, there should be a movement here also for use of nonviolence for political ends?*

A. If you are convinced that the means adopted in India are day by day bringing about the results we desire, and if you are convinced that India is doing so through spiritual means, then do so here, too. Though there is greater difference in Europe. Friends have told me there were special difficulties in Europe to adopt nonviolent means. Europe consists of martial races, unlike India. Here all know how to wield arms. All the male population has at one time or another wielded arms. It is difficult for you to understand the efficacy and beauty of nonretaliation. Why not punish the wrongdoer—and in an exemplary manner?—that is what is asked everywhere here. Thus nonviolence is quite foreign to Europe. For people belonging to such a country, it is difficult to strike out on a new path. Your economic life is so constructed that it is not possible, generally speaking, for an ordinary man to get out of the ordinary rut unless he faces poverty. And the fourth difficulty is that in

* Excerpts.

Catholic Europe the iron discipline allows very little free play to the intellect. These are the four difficulties we have not to face in India, which you have to face. If India becomes free through nonviolent means, it won't enter upon war. But if she does, God will give me strength to fight India single-handed.

Q. *What do you think of Einstein's call to military people not to take part in war?*

A. My answer can only be one. That, if Europe can take up this method enthusiastically like me, I can only say Einstein has stolen the method from me. But if you want me to elaborate the thing, I would like to elaborate the method a little deeper. To refuse to render military service when a particular individual's time comes is to do the thing after all the time for combating the evil is practically gone. The disease is deeper. I suggest to you that those who are not on the register for military service are equally participating in the crime. He or she, therefore, who supports a state so organized is, whether directly or indirectly, participating in the sin. It is fraught with immediate danger. Seeing that each man, old or young, takes part in this sin by contributing to the state (by paying the tax to the state), I said so long as I ate wheat supplied by the navy, whilst I was doing everything short of being a soldier, it was best for me to be shot; otherwise I should go to the mountains and eat food grown by nature. Similarly, all those who want to stop military service can do so by withdrawing all military co-operation. Refusal of military service is much more superficial than noncooperation with a whole system which supports the state. But then your opportunity becomes so swift and so effective that you run the risk of not only being marched to jail, but of being thrown on the street. This was the position of Tolstoy.

CWMG, vol. 48, pp. 401–2

3.
Excerpts from a Speech at a Meeting in Lausanne*

Q. *What is the difference between nonresistance and your resistance without violence?*

A. It has been often said that the doctrine of nonviolence I owe to Tolstoy. It is not the whole truth, but there again I derive the greatest strength from his writings. But as Tolstoy himself admitted, the nonresistance method I had cultivated and elaborated in South Africa was different from the nonresistance Tolstoy had written upon and recommended. This I say in no derogation of Tolstoy's fame. He is not an apt pupil who will not build upon foundations laid by his teacher for him. He only deserves a good teacher who would add to the legacy that teacher would leave for him. I should be an unworthy son to my father if I should not add to my inheritance, and so I have always regarded it as a matter of pride that, thanks be to God, what I had learned from Tolstoy has fructified a hundredfold. Tolstoy talked of passive resistance largely, but nonresistance elaborated in Transvaal was a force infinitely more active than resistance that an armed man can devise, and I am glad to recall the fact that in a long letter he wrote to me unsolicited he said that his eyes were fixed upon me wherever I was. And if you will study the movements in South Africa and India, you will find how this thing is capable of infinite expansion.

Q. *Is not nonresistance submission?*

A. Passive resistance is regarded as the weapon of the weak, but the resistance for which I had to coin a new name altogether for want of a phrase in the English language and not to have this mixed up with nonresistance, namely, "satyagraha," is not conceived in any shape or form as a weapon of the weak but as a weapon of the strongest. But its matchless beauty is

* This meeting took place on December 8, 1931.

that it can be wielded by the weak in body, [by the] oldest, and even by children if they have strong hearts and, since resistance through satyagraha is offered through self-suffering, it is a weapon open preeminently to women. And we found in actual experience in India last year that women in many instances surpassed men in suffering. And children also—thousands—played a noble part in this campaign. For the idea of self-suffering became contagious and they embarked upon amazing acts of self-denial. Supposing that women of Europe and children of Europe became fired with love of humanity and said our men are doing wrong by arming, they would take them by storm and reduce militarism to nothingness in an incredibly short time. And the underlying idea is that children, women, and others have the same identical soul, same potentiality. The question is of drawing out the limitless power of truth. But I must again call a halt to this fascinating subject.

CWMG, vol. 48, pp. 407–8

4.
Excerpts from a Speech at a Meeting*

Q. *How could workers obtain justice without violence? If capitalists use force, why should not workers use pressure?*

A. This is the old law, the law of the jungle—blow against blow—and I have told you that I am endeavoring to make this experiment essentially to substitute the law of the jungle, which is foreign to man. You may not know that I am supposed to be the chief adviser to a labor union in Ahmedabad, which has commanded the testimony of labor experts. Through this labor union we have been endeavoring to enforce methods of nonviolence for solving questions arising between the employers and the employed. Therefore, what I am now about to

---

* This meeting took place on December 10, 1931, in Geneva.

tell you is based upon actual experience—in the very line about which the question has been asked. In my humble opinion, labor can always vindicate itself provided it is united and self-sacrificing. No matter how oppressive capitalism may be, I am convinced that those who are connected with labor and guiding labor have no idea of the resources that labor can command and capitalism can never command. If labor would only understand and recognize that capital is perfectly helpless without labor, labor would easily come to its own. We have unfortunately come under the hypnotic suggestion and influence of capital that capital is all in all on earth. But a moment's thought would show that labor has at its disposal a capital that capitalists never possess. Ruskin taught in his age that labor had unrivaled opportunity. But he spoke above our heads. At the present moment an Englishman is making the same experiment. He is an economist and also a capitalist, but through economic researches he has come to the same conclusions that Ruskin arrived at intuitively and he has brought back a vital message. He says it is wrong to think that a piece of metal constitutes capital; it is also wrong to think that so much produce is capital. He adds that, if we go to the source, it is labor that is capital and that living capital cannot be reduced in terms of economics and it is inexhaustible. It is upon that law and truth we are conducting the labor union in Ahmedabad and fighting the government and it is that law the recognition of which delivered 1,700,000 people in Champaran from age-long tyranny. I must not tarry to tell you what that tyranny was, but those who are interested in that problem will be able to study every one of the facts which I have put before them. Now I tell you what we have done. There is in the English language a very potent word—all languages have it: "No." And the secret is that when capital wants labor to say "Yes," labor roars out "No." And immediately labor comes to recognize that it has choice before it of saying "No" when it wants to say "No," it has nothing to fear and it would not matter in the slightest degree that capital has guns and poison gas at its disposal. Capital will still be perfectly helpless if labor will assert its dignity making good its "No." Then labor does not need to retaliate, but stands defiant receiving the bullets and poison gas and still insists upon its "No." But I tell you why labor so often fails. Instead of sterilizing capital as I have suggested labor should do (I say this as a laborer myself), it wants to seize capital and become capitalist itself in the worst sense of the term. And therefore the capitalist who is properly entrenched and organized, finding in labor a desire for the same objective, makes use of labor to suppress labor. And if we were really not under the hypnotic spell, every one of us—man and woman—would recognize this rock-bottom truth without the slightest difficulty. Having achieved brilliant successes in various departments of life, I am saying this with authority. I have placed before you something not superhuman but within the grasp of every laborer. You will see that what labor is called upon to do is nothing more than what Swiss soldiers are doing, for undoubtedly the Swiss soldier carries his own destruction in his pocket. I want labor to copy the courage of the soldier without copying the brute in the soldier, viz., the ability to inflict death, and I suggest to you that a laborer who courts death without carrying arms shows a courage of a much higher degree than the man who is armed from top to toe. Though this is a fascinating subject, I must reluctantly leave this point and go to the fourth question.

Q. *What is the difference between your message and the Christian, which we prefer to keep?*

A. I do not profess to give any original message at all. My message is as old as this earth and I do not know that it is at all different from the Christian message. If you mean by it nonviolence, I should be sorry to discover that you have given up the teaching of the Sermon on the Mount. Nothing will give me greater pleasure than that the Christians of Europe were translating in their lives the message of Jesus. The second question betrays ignorance. Shall I answer it in biblical language—you cannot save yourself unless you are prepared to lose yourself.

CWMG, vol. 48, pp. 418–19

5.
Letter to Adolf Hitler*

As AT WARDHA,
C. P.,
INDIA.

July 23, 1939

DEAR FRIEND,

Friends have been urging me to write to you for the sake of humanity. But I have resisted their request, because of the feeling that any letter from me would be an impertinence. Something tells me that I must not calculate and that I must make my appeal for whatever it may be worth. It is quite clear that you are today the one person in the world who can prevent a war which may reduce humanity to the savage state. Must you pay that price for an object however worthy it may appear to you to be? Will you listen to the appeal of one who has deliberately shunned the method of war not without considerable success? Anyway, I anticipate your forgiveness, if I have erred in writing to you.†

---

* The government did not allow the letter to be dispatched.

† In a statement to the press on September 5, 1939, MKG mentioned this letter and further stated: "How I wish that even now he would listen to reason and the appeal from almost the whole of thinking mankind, not excluding the German people themselves. I must refuse to believe that Germans contemplate with equanimity the evacuation of big cities like London for fear of destruction to be wrought by man's inhuman ingenuity. They cannot contemplate with equanimity such destruction of themselves and their own monuments. I am not therefore just now thinking of India's deliverance. It will come, but what will it be worth if England and France fall, or if they come out victorious over Germany ruined and humbled? Yet it almost seems as if Herr Hitler knows no God but brute force and, as Mr. Chamberlain says, he will listen to nothing else."

I remain,

Your sincere friend,
M. K. GANDHI

HERR HITLER
BERLIN, GERMANY

CWMG, vol. 70, pp. 20–21

6.
Letter to Adolf Hitler*

WARDHA,

December 24, 1940

DEAR FRIEND,

That I address you as a friend is no formality. I own no foes. My business in life has been for the past thirty-three years to enlist the friendship of the whole of humanity by befriending mankind, irrespective of race, color, or creed. I hope you will have the time and desire to know how a good portion of humanity who have been living under the influence of that doctrine of universal friendship view your action. We have no doubt about your bravery or devotion to your fatherland, nor do we believe that you are the monster described by your opponents. But your own writings and pronouncements and those of your friends and admirers leave no room for doubt that many of your acts are monstrous and unbecoming of human dignity, especially in the estimation of men like me who believe in universal friendliness. Such are your humiliation of Czechoslovakia, the rape of Poland, and the swallowing of Denmark. I am aware that your

* This letter, too, was suppressed by the colonial government.

view of life regards such spoliations as virtuous acts. But we
have been taught from childhood to regard them as acts degrading humanity. Hence we cannot possibly wish success to your
arms. But ours is a unique position. We resist British imperialism no less than Nazism. If there is a difference, it is in degree.
One-fifth of the human race has been brought under the British
heel by means that will not bear scrutiny. Our resistance to it
does not mean harm to the British people. We seek to convert
them, not to defeat them on the battlefield. Ours is an unarmed
revolt against the British rule. But whether we convert them or
not, we are determined to make their rule impossible by nonviolent noncooperation. It is a method in its nature indefensible. It
is based on the knowledge that no spoliator can compass his end
without a certain degree of cooperation, willing or compulsory,
of the victim. Our rulers may have our land and bodies but not
our souls. They can have the former only by complete destruction of every Indian—man, woman, and child. That all may not
rise to that degree of heroism and that a fair amount of fright-
fulness can bend the back of revolt is true, but the argument
would be beside the point. For, if a fair number of men and
women be found in India who would be prepared without any
ill will against the spoliators to lay down their lives rather than
bend the knee to them, they would have shown the way to freedom from the tyranny of violence. I ask you to believe me when
I say that you will find an unexpected number of such men and
women in India. They have been having that training for the
past twenty years. We have been trying for the past half a century to throw off the British rule. The movement of independence has been never so strong as now. The most powerful
political organization, I mean the Indian National Congress, is
trying to achieve this end. We have attained a very fair measure
of success through nonviolent effort. We were groping for the
right means to combat the most organized violence in the world,
which the British power represents. You have challenged it. It
remains to be seen which is the better organized, the German
or the British. We know what the British heel means for us and
the non-European races of the world. But we would never wish
to end the British rule with German aid. We have found in

nonviolence a force which, if organized, can without doubt match itself against a combination of all the most violent forces in the world. In nonviolent technique, as I have said, there is no such thing as defeat. It is all "do or die" without killing or hurting. It can be used practically without money and obviously without the aid of science of destruction which you have brought to such perfection. It is a marvel to me that you do not see that it is nobody's monopoly. If not the British, some other power will certainly improve upon your method and beat you with your own weapon. You are leaving no legacy to your people of which they would feel proud. They cannot take pride in a recital of cruel deed, however skillfully planned. I, therefore, appeal to you in the name of humanity to stop the war. You will lose nothing by referring all the matters of dispute between you and Great Britain to an international tribunal of your joint choice. If you attain success in the war, it will not prove that you were in the right. It will only prove that your power of destruction was greater. Whereas an award by an impartial tribunal will show as far as it is humanly possible which party was in the right. You know that not long ago I made an appeal to every Briton to accept my method of nonviolent resistance. I did it because the British know me as a friend though a rebel. I am a stranger to you and your people. I have not the courage to make you the appeal I made to every Briton. Not that it would not apply to you with the same force as to the British. But my present proposal is much simple because much more practical and familiar. During this season when the hearts of the peoples of Europe yearn for peace, we have suspended even our own peaceful struggle.* Is it too much to ask you to make an effort for peace during a time which may mean nothing to you personally but which must mean much to the millions of Europeans whose dumb cry for peace I hear, for my ears are attuned to hearing the dumb millions? I had intended to address a joint appeal to you and Signor

* On December 17, 1940, MKG had asked for the suspension of the satyagraha movement to mark the Christmas from December 24 to January 4.

Mussolini, whom I had the privilege of meeting* when I was in Rome during my visit to England as a delegate to the Round Table Conference. I hope that he will take this as addressed to him also with the necessary changes.

I am,

Your sincere friend,
M. K. GANDHI

CWMG, vol. 73, pp. 253–55

7.
Interview to a Professor[†]

PROFESSOR: *How is it that many of the English pacifists are talking of defense and elaborate plans of defense? . . . May it not be possible to carry pacifism too far? Supposing Abyssinia had simply nonresisted and said to Italy, "Do your worst," would the Italians have been ashamed and desisted from their design? Lansbury said they would.*

GANDHI: I shall take up the Abyssinian question first. I can answer it only in terms of active resistant nonviolence. Now nonviolence is the activest force on earth, and it is my conviction that it never fails. But if the Abyssinians had adopted the attitude of nonviolence of the strong, i. e., the nonviolence which breaks to pieces but never bends, Mussolini would have had no interest in Abyssinia. Thus if they had simply said: "You are welcome to reduce us to dust or ashes, but you will not find one Abyssinian ready to cooperate with you," what would Mussolini have done? He did not want a desert.

---

* On December 12, 1931.

[†] Not identified in the source, but probably a professor at Edwardes College, Peshawar, where MKG gave a lecture on May 5, 1938.

Mussolini wanted submission and not defiance, and if he had met with the quiet, dignified, and nonviolent defiance that I have described, he would certainly have been obliged to retire. Of course it is open to anyone to say that human nature has not been known to rise to such heights. But if we have made unexpected progress in physical sciences, why may we do less in the science of the soul? Now about the English pacifists. I know there are some great and sincere men amongst them, but they are thinking in terms of pacifism as distinguished from unadulterated nonviolence. I am essentially a nonviolent man, and I believe in war bereft of every trace of violence. An essentially nonviolent man does not calculate the consequences. The English pacifists you are talking of calculate, and when they speak of pacifism they do so with the mental reservation that when pacifism fails, arms might be used. With them not nonviolence but arms are the ultimate sanction, as was the case with Woodrow Wilson's Fourteen Points*. No, someone has to arise in England with the living faith to say that England, whatever happens, shall not use arms. They are a nation fully armed, and if they, having the power, deliberately refuse to use arms, theirs will be the first example of Christianity in active practice on a mass scale. That will be a real miracle.

CWMG, vol. 67, pp. 75–76

8.
If I Were a Czech

If I have called the arrangement with Herr Hitler "peace without honor," it was not to cast any reflection on British or French statesmen. I have no doubt that Mr. Chamberlain could

---

* Outlined by him in a speech before the U.S. Congress on January 8, 1918, they became the basis of the armistice between Germany and the Allies and the subsequent peace treaty signed at Versailles.

not think of anything better. He knew his nation's limitations. He wanted to avoid war, if it could be avoided at all. Short of going to war, he pulled his full weight in favor of the Czechs. That it could not save honor was no fault of his. It would be so every time there is a struggle with Herr Hitler or Signor Mussolini. It cannot be otherwise. Democracy dreads to spill blood. The philosophy for which the two dictators stand calls it cowardice to shrink from carnage. They exhaust the resources of poetic art in order to glorify organized murder. There is no humbug about their word or deed. They are ever ready for war. There is nobody in Germany or Italy to cross their path. Their word is law. It is different with Mr. Chamberlain or M. Daladier*. They have their parliaments and chambers to please. They have parties to confer with. They cannot maintain themselves on a perpetual war footing if their language is to have a democratic accent about it. Science of war leads one to dictatorship pure and simple. Science of nonviolence can alone lead one to pure democracy. England, France, and America have to make their choice. That is the challenge of the two dictators. Russia is out of the picture just now. Russia has a dictator who dreams of peace and thinks he will wade to it through a sea of blood. No one can say what Russian dictatorship will mean to the world. It was necessary to give this introduction to what I want to say to the Czechs and through them to all those nationalities which are called "small" or "weak." I want to speak to the Czechs because their plight moved me to the point of physical and mental distress and I felt that it would be cowardice on my part not to share with them the thoughts that were welling up within me. It is clear that the small nations must either come or be ready to come under the protection of the dictators or be a constant menace to the peace of Europe. In spite of all the goodwill in the world, England and France cannot save them. Their intervention can only mean bloodshed and destruction such as has never been seen before. If I were a Czech, therefore, I would free these two nations from the obligation to defend my country. And yet I must live.

---

* Edouard Daladier, then prime minister of France.

I would not be a vassal to any nation or body. I must have absolute independence or perish. To seek to win in a clash of arms would be pure bravado. Not so, if in defying the might of one who would deprive me of my independence I refuse to obey his will and perish unarmed in the attempt. In so doing, though I lose the body, I save my soul, i.e., my honor. This inglorious peace should be my opportunity. I must live down the humiliation and gain real independence. But, says a comforter, "Hitler knows no pity. Your spiritual effort will avail nothing before him." My answer is, "You may be right. History has no record of a nation having adopted nonviolent resistance. If Hitler is unaffected by my suffering, it does not matter. For I shall have lost nothing worth [preserving]. My honor is the only thing worth preserving. That is independent of Hitler's pity. But as a believer in nonviolence, I may not limit its possibilities. Hitherto he and his likes have built upon their invariable experience that men yield to force. Unarmed men, women, and children offering nonviolent resistance without any bitterness in them will be a novel experience for them. Who can dare say that it is not in their nature to respond to the higher and finer forces? They have the same soul that I have." But says another comforter, "What you say is all right for you. But how do you expect your people to respond to the novel call? They are trained to fight. In personal bravery they are second to none in the world. For you now to ask them to throw away their arms and be trained for nonviolent resistance, seems to me to be a vain attempt." "You may be right. But I have a call I must answer. I must deliver my message to my people. This humiliation has sunk too deep in me to remain without an outlet. I, at least, must act up to the light that has dawned on me." This is how I should, I believe, act if I was a Czech. When I first launched out on satyagraha, I had no companion. We were thirteen thousand men, women, and children against a whole nation capable of crushing the existence out of us. I did not know who would listen to me. It all came as in a flash. All the thirteen thousand did not fight. Many fell back. But the honor of the nation was saved. New history was written by the South African satyagraha. A more apposite instance, perhaps, is that

of Khan Saheb Abdul Ghaffar Khan, the servant of God as he
calls himself, the pride of Afghan, as the Pathans delight to call
him. He is sitting in front of me as I pen these lines. He has
made several thousands of his people throw down their arms.
He thinks he has imbibed the lesson of nonviolence. He is not
sure of his people. Elsewhere I reproduce the pledge that his
soldiers of peace make. I have come to the Frontier Province,
or rather he has brought me, to see with my own eyes what his
men here are doing. I can say in advance and at once that these
men know very little of nonviolence. All the treasure they have
on earth is their faith in their leader. I do not cite these soldiers
of peace as at all a finished illustration. I cite them as an honest
attempt being made by a soldier to convert fellow soldiers to
the ways of peace. I can testify that it is an honest attempt, and
whether in the end it succeeds or fails, it will have its lessons
for satyagrahis of the future. My purpose will be fulfilled if I
succeed in reaching these men's hearts and making them see
that if their nonviolence does not make them feel much braver
than the possession of arms and the ability to use them, they
must give up their nonviolence, which is another name for
cowardice, and resume their arms, which there is nothing but
their own will to prevent them from taking back. I present Dr.
Benes* with a weapon not of the weak but of the brave. There
is no bravery greater than a resolute refusal to bend the knee to
an earthly power, no matter how great, and that without bitterness of spirit and in the fullness of faith that the spirit alone
lives, nothing else does.

CWMG, vol. 67, pp. 404–7

---

* Eduard Benes, the president of the then Czechoslovakia.

9.
Logical Consequence

One must feel happy that the danger of war has been averted for the time being. Is the price paid likely to be too great? Is it likely that honor has been sold? Is it a triumph of organized violence? Has Herr Hitler discovered a new technique of organizing violence which enables him to gain his end without shedding blood? I do not profess to know European politics. But it does appear to me that small nationalities cannot exist in Europe with their heads erect. They must be absorbed by their larger neighbors. They must become vassals. Europe has sold her soul for the sake of a seven days' earthly existence. The peace Europe gained at Munich is a triumph of violence; it is also its defeat. If England and France were sure of victory, they would certainly have fulfilled their duty of saving Czechoslovakia or of dying with it. But they quailed before the combined violence of Germany and Italy. But what have Germany and Italy gained? Have they added anything to the moral wealth of mankind? In penning these lines, my concern is not with the great powers. Their height dazes me. Czechoslovakia has a lesson for me and us in India. The Czechs could not have done anything else when they found themselves deserted by their two powerful allies. And yet I have the hardihood to say that if they had known the use of nonviolence as a weapon for the defense of national honor, they would have faced the whole might of Germany with that of Italy thrown in. They would have spared England and France the humiliation of suing for a peace which was no peace; and to save their honor they would have died to a man without shedding the blood of the robber. I must refuse to think that such heroism, or call it restraint, is beyond human nature. Human nature will only find itself when it fully realizes that to be human it has to cease to be beastly or brutal. Though we have the human form, without the attainment of the virtue of nonviolence we still share the qualities of our remote reputed ancestor, the orangutan. These are not idle words I am writing. Let the Czechs know that the Working Committee wrung itself with pain while their doom was being decided.* The pain was quite selfish in a way. But on that account it was the more real. For though numerically we are a big nation, in terms of Europe, i.e., in terms of organized scientific violence, we are smaller than Czechoslovakia. Our liberty is not merely threatened, we are fighting to regain it. The Czechs are fully armed; we are wholly unarmed. And so the committee sat to deliberate what its duty was by the Czechs, what part the Congress was to play if the war cloud burst on us. Were we to bargain with England for our liberty and appear to befriend Czechoslovakia, or were we to live up to the creed of nonviolence and say in the hour of trial for afflicted humanity that, consistent with our creed, we could not associate ourselves with war even though it might ostensibly be for the defense of Czechoslovakia, whose very existence was threatened for no fault of hers, or for the only fault that she was too small to defend herself single-handed? The Working Committee had almost come to the conclusion that it would deny itself the opportunity of striking a bargain with England but would make its contribution to the world peace, to the defense of Czechoslovakia, and to India's freedom by declaring to the world by its action that the way to peace with honor did not lie through the mutual slaughter of the innocents, but that it lay only and truly through the practice of organized nonviolence even unto death. And this was but the logical and natural step the Working Committee could have taken, if it was

---

* The Congress Working Committee's resolution on Czechoslovakia read: "The Working Committee has been following with great interest the events as they have been developing in Europe. It views with great concern the unabashed attempt that is being made by Germany to deprive Czechoslovakia of its independence or reduce it to impotence. The Working Committee sends its profound sympathy to the brave people of Czechoslovakia in their struggle to preserve their freedom. Being themselves engaged in a war—nonviolent but nonetheless grim and exacting— against the greatest imperialist power on earth, India cannot but be deeply interested in the protection of Czechoslovak freedom. The committee hopes that the better part of humanity will still assert itself and save humanity from the impending catastrophe."

to prove true to its creed. If India could gain her freedom through nonviolence, as congressmen are to believe they can, she could also defend her freedom by the same means, and hence, a fortiori, could a smaller nation like Czechoslovakia. I do not know what actually the Working Committee would have done if the war had come. But the war is only postponed. During the breathing time, I present the way of nonviolence for acceptance by the Czechs. They do not yet know what is in store for them. They can lose nothing by trying the way of nonviolence. The fate of Republican Spain is hanging in the balance. So is that of China. If in the end they all lose, they will do so not because their cause is not just, but because they are less skilled in the science of destruction or because they are under-manned. What would Republican Spain gain if it had Franco's resources, or China if she had Japan's skill in war, or the Czechs if they had the skill of Herr Hitler? I suggest that if it is brave, as it is, to die to a man fighting against odds, it is braver still to refuse to fight and yet to refuse to yield to the usurper. If death is a certainty in either case, is it not nobler to die with the breast bared to the enemy without malice against him within?

CWMG, vol. 67, pp. 413–15

10.
Two Thought-Provoking Letters

A friend writes thus: *When you asked for the names of out-and-out believers in nonviolence, I wanted very much to send in mine, but something within compelled me to refrain. First because I felt there was lack of ahimsa in my personal conduct, and secondly because there was the opposite of love for the English in my heart. I rejoice when I read in the papers of the destruction wrought on London and Britain, and I inwardly want the British to be defeated in the war. I am impelled to confess this, for I could not deceive you.*

The second letter is from South Africa. I take a few sentences from it: *I am puzzled as to what should be the attitude of Indians at the present juncture. The "White" races are so utterly callous in regard to "Colored" people, and in spite of the war color prejudice continues unabated. Why then should we give our lives for them? Quite recently an Indian student who returned here from Europe was telling us that in spite of the fact that the steamer was not crowded, the British company hesitated to give accommodation to Indians. Such treatment leads us and also the African people to believe that there is no difference between the Nazis, the Boers, and the British so far as we are concerned. If there were Nazi rule in South Africa, we could not be treated worse than we are today. Many of us think that the British are sweet-tongued, but they pursue their own ruthless policy in spite of honeyed words, whereas Hitler would be more frank. He at any rate says exactly what he feels. Is there not truth in this? Anyhow we ought to know where we stand. Please tell us.*

Though differently worded the two letters betray the same thought. It is difficult for those who suffer at British hands to shed either their dislike of or a disinclination to help them. But the present is a real testing time for ahimsa, which alone can throw light on our path. First of all we must distinguish between the British people and their policy. We must have full liberty thoughtfully and with reason to criticize the latter, but we may not dislike them. To err is human. All have their good as well as bad points. It is in human nature, even if we are in the wrong, to resent bitter, often unjust, criticism. But if we were lovingly shown our faults, we would perhaps be willing to listen. We must behave thus toward the British. Let us tell them where they are in the wrong, but let us not wish them any harm. We may demand a mental and heart change in their outlook, but we may not pray for their downfall. Such an attitude is indispensable in satyagraha, which demands that, while we may neither speak evil of wrongdoers nor wish them ill, we must at the same time show them the error of their ways and noncooperate with them in their wrongdoing. The Congress has been trying to follow this great principle for the last twenty years. I believe that we have benefited greatly therefrom. Moreover, there is no reason why we should wish the British to be defeated in this war. The writer from South Africa rightly says that there is not much to choose between the British and the Nazis. This is as clear as daylight in South Africa, in particular, where colored races are treated as definitely inferior in every way. What more than this could the Nazis say or do? The defeat of the British would connote the victory of the Nazis, which, again, we do not and must not desire. Therefore, we should be impartial. We are desirous of our own independence. For that there is no reason why we should want the destruction of Germany. We have to achieve as well as maintain our freedom through our own strength. We do not need British or any outside help for it. Those of us who have full faith in ahimsa believe that we can win it through nonviolence and keep it thereby also. There is, however, a section amongst us who believe in winning and maintaining our independence through force of arms. Their position is a difficult one. As a matter of fact, we have still to gain our freedom. If we win it through violence, we will not do so by helping Britain in the war. For if we help the war effort, we really come more under their sway than we are today. And if in spite of our help they lose, we would then come under the rule of another foreign power. So that if Britain and India were jointly defeated, we would, so to speak, be jumping from the frying pan into the fire. Moreover, India has no enmity toward any nation. Hitler and others have no illusions. They know full well that India is not a willing partner in the war, that we are a slave country and that our wishes do not count. It was really the Congress who raised this question because the Congress has adopted nonviolence as its weapon. At the same time we have no quarrel with those who do not believe in nonviolence. Each of us must go his own way. By doing so we shall know where India stands. If the Congress had not spoken out its mind, it would have committed suicide, that is to say, it would have given up its right to follow out its policy of nonviolence. It is its duty to keep itself alive. Therefore the Congress has to take some action. What that action

will be will shortly become known. I suggest to the two writers
that they should try to rid their hearts of all anger and hatred.
These are in reality signs of weakness. Nonviolence is an active
force. If they were to follow it, they would be active and they
would be spreading the leaven of ahimsa. The Congress demand is not for itself only. It extends far beyond even India and
embraces the world. Let us therefore wish well from the bottom of our hearts to all the warring nations.

CWMG, vol. 73, pp. 84–86

II.
Working of Nonviolence

*I have been very much interested in reading the recent numbers
of Harijan and your observations on the European crisis and the
N. W. F. Province.* But there is one aspect of the nonviolence
problem, which I should have discussed with you at Segaon if
there had been time, to which you seldom or never refer. You say
that nonviolent noncooperation, as you have developed it, is the
answer to the violence which is now threatening the whole world
with ruin. There is no doubt as to the immense effect such spirit
and action could produce. But must not the nonviolent spirit of
selfless love for all, enemies and friends alike, express itself, if it
is to succeed, in a liberal, democratic, and constitutional form of
government? Society cannot exist without law and government.
International peace cannot exist unless the nations accept a system of constitutional government which will give them unity
and law and end anarchy among them. No doubt someday the
law of God will be so "written on the hearts and minds" of men
that they become individually the expression of it, and will need
no human law or government. But that is the end. The beginning of progress toward that heavenly goal must take the form at*

---

* North West Frontier Province.

first of a willingness among races, religions, and nations to unite under a single constitution, through which their unity and membership one of another is established, the laws under which they live are promulgated after public discussion and by some form of majority decision and are enforced, where it is not voluntarily obeyed, not by war but by police force, where persuasion and example have not sufficed. As between sovereign nations the operation of a constructive nonviolence spirit must lead to some form of federation. It cannot succeed until it has done so. The proof that it exists effectively will be the appearance of a federal system. Thus the only real solution for the European problem is the federation of its twenty-five peoples and nations under a single democratic constitution, which will create a government which can look at and legislate for the problems of Europe, not as a set of rival and conflicting nations but as a single whole with autonomous parts. In the same way the only solution to the Indian problem is the substitution of a democratic constitution for the control of Great Britain. And what is true for Europe and India is true, in the long run, for the whole world and is the only final method of ending war.

Nonviolent noncooperation may be the best, perhaps the only, method of bringing about the change of mind and heart which will make acceptance of a federal democratic constitution by the nation possible. But attainment to democratic federation is the necessary attainment whereby its success is assured and without which it cannot succeed. It is always a matter of interest and indeed of surprise to me that you appear to think that nonviolent noncooperation is enough in itself, and that you never proclaim that a democratic system of government unifying men, races, religions, and nations is the goal to which it must lead, though that attainment is only possible as the result of a spiritual change of heart and cannot be reached by force or violence or chicanery. I do not write this as a kind of indirect argument for the Indian constitution, though it obviously has a bearing on that problem also. The Government of India Act is clearly a very imperfect application of the principle of democratic federation and must necessarily evolve rapidly if it is to work. The main argument I have always urged for it is

that in present conditions it represents the only constitutional
compromise uniting provinces, states, Muslims, and Hindus
which can be made to work and that it has far more seeds of
evolution within it than is generally recognized. If your spiritual
gospel informed the people, it would rapidly and easily evolve.
My object is not to elicit any opinion from you about the con-
stitutional problem but an answer to the larger question set
forth in the early part of the letter.

Thus writes Lord Lothian. The letter was received early in January, but urgent matters prevented my dealing earlier with the important question raised in it. I have purposely refrained from dealing with the nature of government in a society based deliberately on nonviolence. All society is held together by nonviolence, even as the earth is held in her position by gravitation. But when the law of gravitation was discovered, the discovery yielded results of which our ancestors had no knowledge. Even so when society is deliberately constructed in accordance with the law of nonviolence, its structure will be different in material particulars from what it is today. But I cannot say in advance what the government based wholly on nonviolence will be like. What is happening today is disregard of the law of nonviolence and enthronement of violence as if it were an eternal law. The democracies, therefore, that we see at work in England, America, and France are only so called because they are no less based on violence than Nazi Germany, Fascist Italy, or even Soviet Russia. The only difference is that the violence of the last three is much better organized than that of the three democratic powers. Nevertheless we see today a mad race for outdoing one another in the matter of armaments. And if when the clash comes, as it is bound to come one day, the democracies win, they will do so only because they will have the backing of their people who imagine that they have a voice in their own government, whereas in the other three cases the people might rebel against their own dictatorships. Holding the view that without the recognition of nonviolence on a national scale, there is no such thing as a constitutional or democratic government, I devote my energy to the propagation of nonviolence as the law of our life—individual, social, political, national, and international. I fancy that I have seen the light, though dimly. I write cautiously, for I do not profess to know the whole of the law. If I know the successes of my experiments, I know also my failures. But the successes are enough to fill me with undying hope. I have often said that if one takes care of the means, the end will take care of itself. Nonviolence is the means; the end for every nation is complete independence. There will be an international league only when all the nations, big or small, composing it are fully independent. The nature of that independence will correspond to the extent of nonviolence assimilated by the nations concerned. One thing is certain. In a society based on nonviolence, the smallest nation will feel as tall as the tallest. The idea of superiority and inferiority will be wholly obliterated. It follows from this that the Government of India Act is merely a makeshift and has to give way to an act coined by the nation itself. So far as provincial autonomy is concerned, it has been found possible to handle it somewhat. My own experience of its working is by no means happy. The congress governments have not that nonviolent hold over the people that I had expected they would have. But the federal structure is inconceivable to me because it contemplates a partnership, however loose, among dissimilars. How dissimilar the states are is being demonstrated in an ugliness for which I was unprepared. Therefore the federal structure, as conceived by the Government of India Act, I hold to be an utter impossibility. Thus the conclusion is irresistible that for one like me, wedded to nonviolence, constitutional or democratic government is a distant dream so long as nonviolence is not recognized as a living force, an inviolable creed, not a mere policy. While I prate about universal nonviolence, my experiment is confined to India. If it succeeds, the world will accept it without effort. There is, however, a big BUT. The pause does not worry me. My faith is brightest in the midst of impenetrable darkness.

CWMG, vol. 68, pp. 388–91

12.
What to Do?

Here is an important letter* from a principal who wishes to remain anonymous:

A troubled conscience seeks the reasoned opinion of others to help to solve the following pressing question: Is the carrying out of the pledge of the Peace Pledge Union (the late Dick Shepard's organization for opposing war by the refusal to resort to violence under any circumstances whatever) a right and a practicable course of action in the present conditions of our world? On the side of "Yea" there are the following arguments:

1. The world's greatest spiritual teachers have taught and exemplified in their own lives that an evil thing can only be destroyed by good means, and never by evil means, and any sort of violence . . . is undoubtedly an evil means, whatever may be the motive. . . .

2. The real causes of the present violence and misery can never be removed by war. . . .

3 . . . War . . . , even if it ends in victory, means . . . destruction of such liberties as remain to us . . . for no modern war can be waged . . . without the complete regimentation. . . . It is better to die in conscientiously resisting oppression nonviolently than to live as a pawn in the regimented society. . . . On the side of "Nay" there are the following arguments:

1. Nonviolent resistance can only be effective in resisting people who are capable of being moved by moral and

---

* Only extracts were reproduced in the source.

*humanitarian considerations. Fascism . . . has no scruple . . .
in employing any degree of brutality. . . .*

2. *To refuse cooperation in violent resistance . . . in defense of democratic liberty is tantamount to helping those
who are destroying that liberty. Fascist aggression has
undoubtedly been encouraged by the knowledge that the
democracies contain numbers of people who are unwill-
ing to fight in their defense, and who would even oppose
(and thus obstruct) their own governments. . . . This being
so, the conscientious objector to violent means of defense
becomes not merely ineffective in promoting peace, but
actually helpful to those who are breaking it.*

3. *War may destroy liberty, but if the democracies survive
there is at least some possibility of regaining part of it,
whereas if the Fascists are allowed to rule the world, there
is no chance at all. . . .*

*The solution of this question is obviously terribly pressing. . . .
But is it not really just as pressing for those in other countries,
say South Africa, Egypt, or Australia, which may have to face
the possibility of invasion, or in an India, which in the event
of "complete independence" might be faced with the possibility of invasion by Japan or by a pan-Islamic combination? In
the face of such possibilities (say rather probabilities), ought
not even every keen conscience (whether in a young body or
in an old) to be certain exactly what is the right and practical
way of action? . . .*

Nothing need be said about the arguments in favor of the peace
pledger's resistance. Those against resistance deserve careful
examination. The first argument, if it is valid, cuts at the very
root of the antiwar movement. It is based on the assumption
that it is possible to convert Fascists and Nazis. They belong to
the same species as the so-called democracies or, better still,
war resisters themselves. They show in their family circles the
same tenderness, affection, consideration, and generosity that

war resisters are likely to show even outside such circles. The difference is only of degree. Indeed Fascists and Nazis are a revised edition of so-called democracies if they are not an answer to the latters' misdeeds. Kirby Page in his brochure on the toll of the late war has shown that both the combatants were guilty of falsehoods, exaggerations, and inhumanities. The Versailles Treaty was a treaty of revenge against Germany by the victors. The so-called democracies have before now misappropriated other people's lands and have resorted to ruthless repression. What wonder if Messrs. Hitler and company have reduced to a science the unscientific violence their predecessors had developed for exploiting the so-called backward races for their own material gain? It is therefore a matter of rule of three to find out the exact amount of nonviolence required to melt the harder hearts of the Fascists and the Nazis, if it is assumed, as it is, that the so-called democracies melt before a given amount of nonviolence. Therefore, we must eliminate from consideration the first and the fatal argument if it could be proved to have any content in it. The other two arguments are practical. The pacifists may not do anything to weaken their own governments so as to compel defeat. But for fear of so doing they may not miss the only effective chance they have of demonstrating their undying faith in the futility of all war. If their own governments go mad and make martyrs of war resisters, they [the governments] must suffer the consequence of the unrest of their own creation. The democracies must respect the liberty of individual nonviolent conscience however inconvenient it may be. From that respect there will spring hope for the world. This means that they put their conscience and truth before their country's so-called interest. For, regard for one's conscience, if it is really such, has never yet injured any legitimate cause or interest. Therefore, it comes to this that a pacifist must resist when he feels strongly that, whether so-called democracies live or die, the tug of war will never end war and that it will only end when at the crucial moment a body of pacifists have at any cost testified their living faith by suffering, if need be, the extreme penalty. I know the point for me to consider is not how to avoid the extreme penalty but how to behave so as to achieve the object in view. Where the very disturbing but potent factor of faith is part of one's conduct, human calculations are of no avail. A true pacifist is a true satyagrahi. The latter acts by faith and therefore is not concerned about the result, for he knows that it is assured when the action is true. After all, what is the gain if the so-called democracies win? War certainly will not end. Democracies will have adopted all the tactics of the Fascists and the Nazis including conscription and all other forcible methods to compel and exact obedience. All that may be gained at the end of the victory is the possibility of comparative protection of individual liberty. But that protection does not depend upon outside help. It comes from the internal determination to protect it against the whole world. In other words, the true democrat is he who with purely nonviolent means defends his liberty and therefore his country's and ultimately that of the whole of mankind. In the coming test pacifists have to prove their faith by resolutely refusing to do anything with war whether of defense or offense. But the duty of resistance accrues only to those who believe in nonviolence as a creed—not to those who will calculate and will examine the merits of each case and decide whether to approve of or oppose a particular war. It follows that such resistance is a matter for each person to decide for himself and under the guidance of the inner voice, if he recognizes its existence.

CWMG, vol. 69, pp. 121–23

13.
On Trial

In the course of the conversation with the members of the Working Committee, I discovered that their nonviolence had never gone beyond fighting the British government with that weapon. I had hugged the belief that congressmen had appreciated the

logical result of the practice of nonviolence for the past twenty
years in fighting the biggest imperialist power in the world. But
in great experiments like that of nonviolence, hypothetical questions have hardly any play. I myself used to say in answer to
questions that when we had actually acquired independence we
would know whether we could defend ourselves nonviolently or
not. But today the question is no longer hypothetical. Whether
there is on the part of the British government a favorable declaration or not, the Congress has to decide upon the course it
would adopt in the event of an invasion of India. For, though
there may be no settlement with the government, the Congress
has to declare its policy and say whether it would fight the in-
vading host violently or nonviolently. So far as I can read the
Working Committee's mind after a fairly full discussion, the
members think that congressmen are unprepared for nonviolent
defense against armed invasion. This is tragic. Surely the means
adopted for driving an enemy from one's house must, more or
less, coincide with those to be adopted for keeping him out of
the house. If anything, the latter process must be easier. The
fact, however, is that our fight has not been one of nonviolent
resistance of the strong. It has been one of passive resistance of
the weak. Therefore there is no spontaneous response in our
hearts, at this supreme moment, to an undying faith in the efficacy of nonviolence. The Working Committee, therefore, wisely
said that they were not ready for the logical step. The tragedy of
the situation is that if the Congress is to throw in its lot with
those who believe in the necessity of armed defense of India, the
past twenty years will have been years of gross neglect of the
primary duty of congressmen to learn the science of armed warfare. And I fear that history will hold me, as the general of the
fight, responsible for the tragedy. The future historian will say
that I should have perceived that the nation was learning not
nonviolence of the strong but merely passivity of the weak and I
should have, therefore, provided for congressmen's military
training. Being obsessed with the idea that somehow or other
India will learn true nonviolence, it would not occur to me to
invite my coworkers to train themselves for armed defense. On

the contrary, I used to discountenance all swordplay and the display of stout lathis. Nor am I even now repentant for the past. I have the unquenchable faith that, of all the countries in the world, India is the one country which can learn the art of nonviolence, that if the test were applied even now, there would be found, perhaps, thousands of men and women who would be willing to die without harboring malice against their persecutors. I have harangued crowds and told them repeatedly that they might have to suffer much, including death by shooting. Did not thousands of men and women brave hardships during the salt campaign equal to any that soldiers are called upon to bear? No different capacity is required from what has been already evinced, if India has to contend against an invader. Only it will have to be on a vaster scale. One thing ought not to be forgotten. India unarmed would not require to be destroyed through poison gas or bombardment. It is the Maginot line that has made the Siegfried line necessary, and vice versa. Defense of India by the present methods has been necessary because she is an appendage of Britain. Free India can have no enemy. And if her people have learnt the art of saying resolutely "No" and acting up to it, I daresay, no one would want to invade her. Our economy would be so modeled as to prove no temptation for the exploiter. But some congressmen will say: "Apart from the British, India has so many martial races within her border that they will want to put up a fight for the country, which is as much theirs as ours." This is perfectly true. I am, therefore, talking for the moment only of congressmen. How would they act in the event of an invasion? We shall never convert the whole of India to our creed unless we are prepared to die for it. The opposite course appalls me. Already the bulk of the army is manned by the Mussalmans of the north, Sikhs, and Gurkhas.

If the masses of the south and the center wish to become militarized, the Congress, which is supposed to represent them, will have to enter into competition with them. The Congress will then have to be party to an enormous military budget. There may be all these things without the Congress's consent. It will make all the difference in the world whether the Congress is party to them or not. The world is looking for something new and unique from India. The Congress will be lost in the crowd if it wears the same old outworn armor that the world is wearing today. The Congress has a name because it represents nonviolence as a political weapon par excellence. If the Congress helps the Allies as a representative of nonviolence, it will give to the Allied cause a prestige and a power which will be invaluable in deciding the ultimate fate of the war. But the members of the Working Committee have honestly and bravely not made the profession of such nonviolence. My position is, therefore, confined to myself alone. I have to find out whether I have any fellow travelers along the lonely path. If I am in the minority of one, I must try to make converts. Whether one or many, I must declare my faith that it is better for India to discard violence altogether even for defending her borders. For India to enter into the race for armaments is to court suicide. With the loss of India to nonviolence, the last hope of the world will be gone. I must live up to the creed I have professed for the last half a century and hope to the last breath that India will make nonviolence her creed, preserve man's dignity, and prevent him from reverting to the type from which he is supposed to have raised himself.

CWMG, vol. 70. pp. 243–45

14.
Discussion with Pacifists

On or before February 19, 1940

Q. *Supposing in the presence of superior brute force one feels helpless, would one be justified in using just enough force to prevent the perpetration of wrong?*

A. Yes, but there need not be that feeling of helplessness if there is real nonviolence in you. To feel helpless in the presence of violence is not nonviolence but cowardice. Nonviolence should not be mixed up with cowardice.

Q. *Suppose someone came and hurled insults at you, should you allow yourself to be thus humiliated?*

A. If you feel humiliated, you will be justified in slapping the bully in the face or taking whatever action you might deem necessary to vindicate your self-respect. The use of force, under the circumstances, would be the natural consequence if you are not a coward. But there should be no feeling of humiliation in you if you have assimilated the nonviolence spirit. Your nonviolent behavior would then either make the bully feel ashamed of himself and prevent the insult or make you immune against it so that the insult would remain only in the bully's mouth and not touch you at all. Supposing there is a person with a diseased mind—a lunatic run amok, bent upon murder, or you arrive on the scene of trouble when the situation has already advanced too far. An infuriated mob has got out of hand and you feel helpless, would you justify the use of physical force to restrain the lunatic in the first case or allow the use, say, of teargas in the latter? I will excuse it for all time. But I would not say it is justified from the nonviolent standpoint. I would say that there was not that degree of nonviolence in you to give you confidence in purely nonviolent treatment. If you had, your simple presence would be sufficient to pacify the lunatic. Nonviolence carries within it its own sanction. It is not a mechanical thing. You do not become nonviolent by merely saying, "I shall not use force." It must be felt in the heart. There must be within you an upwelling of love and pity toward the wrongdoer. When there is that feeling, it will express itself through some action. It may be a sign, a glance, even silence. But such as it is, it will melt the heart of the wrongdoer and check the wrong. The use of teargas is not justified in terms of the nonviolent ideal. But I would defend its use against the whole world if I found myself in a corner when I could not save a helpless girl from violation or prevent an infuriated crowd from indulging in madness except by its use. God would not excuse me if, on the Judgment Day, I were to plead before Him that I could not prevent these things from

happening because I was held back by my creed of nonviolence. Nonviolence is self-acting. A fully nonviolent person is
by nature incapable of using violence or rather has no use for
it. His nonviolence is all-sufficing under all circumstances.
Therefore, when I say that the use of force is wrong in whatever degree and under whatever circumstances, I mean it in a
relative sense. It is much better for me to say I have not sufficient nonviolence in me than to admit exceptions to an eternal
principle. Moreover, my refusal to admit exceptions spurs me
to perfect myself in the technique of nonviolence. I literally believe in Patanjali's aphorism that violence ceases in the presence of nonviolence.

Q. *Can a state carry on strictly according to the principle of
nonviolence?*

A. A government cannot succeed in becoming entirely nonviolent because it represents all the people. I do not today conceive of such a golden age. But I do believe in the possibility of
a predominantly nonviolent society. And I am working for it.
A government representing such society will use the least
amount of force. But no government worth its name can suffer
anarchy to prevail. Hence I have said that even under a government based primarily on nonviolence a small police force will
be necessary.

CWMG, vol. 71, pp. 224–26

15.
Interview to *The New York Times*

[Before April 22, 1940]

Q. *You have seen in your lifetime more devastation by war
than there has been at any time in the world's history. And yet
do you still believe in nonviolence as the basis of a new civilization? Are you satisfied that your own countrymen accept it*

*without reservation? You continue to harp on your conditions
being fulfilled before starting civil disobedience. Do you still
hold to them?*

A. You are right in pointing out that there is unheard-of devastation going on in the world. But that is the real moment for
testing my faith in nonviolence. Surprising as it may appear to
my critics, my faith in nonviolence remains absolutely un-
dimmed. Of course nonviolence may not come in my lifetime
in the measure I would like to see it come, but that is a different
matter. It cannot shake my faith, and that is why I have become unbending so far as the fulfillment of my conditions
prior to the starting of civil disobedience is concerned; because, at the risk of being the laughingstock of the whole
world, I adhere to my belief that there is an unbreakable connection between the spinning wheel and nonviolence so far as
India is concerned. Just as there are signs by which you can
recognize violence with the naked eye, so is the spinning wheel
to me a decisive sign of nonviolence. But nothing can deter me
from working away in hope. I have no other method for solving the many baffling problems that face India.

*Q. Supposing India does become free in your lifetime, what
will you devote the rest of your years to?*

A. If India becomes free in my lifetime and I have still energy
left in me, of course I would take my due share, though outside
the official world, in building up the nation on a strictly nonviolent basis.

CWMG, vol. 72, p. 12

16.
How to Combat Hitlerism

Whatever Hitler may ultimately prove to be, we know what
Hitlerism has come to mean. It means naked, ruthless force reduced to an exact science and worked with scientific precision.

In its effect it becomes almost irresistible. In the early days of satyagraha, when it was still known as passive resistance, *The Star* of Johannesburg, stirred by the sight of a handful of Indians, wholly unarmed and incapable of organized violence even if they wished it, pitting themselves against an overwhelmingly armed government, had a cartoon in which the latter was depicted as a steamroller representing irresistible force and passive resistance was depicted as an elephant unmoved and comfortably planting himself in his seat. This was marked immovable force. The cartoonist had a true insight into the duel between the irresistible and the immovable force. It was then a stalemate. The sequel we know. What was depicted and appeared to be irresistible was successfully resisted by the immovable force of satyagraha—call it suffering without retaliation. What became true then can be equally true now. Hitlerism will never be defeated by counter-Hitlerism. It can only breed superior Hitlerism raised to nth degree. What is going on before our eyes is a demonstration of the futility of violence as also of Hitlerism. Let me explain what I mean by failure of Hitlerism. It has robbed the small nations of their liberty. It has compelled France to sue for peace*. Probably by the time this is in print Britain will have decided upon her course. The fall of France is enough for my argument. I think French statesmen have shown rare courage in bowing to the inevitable and refusing to be party to senseless mutual slaughter. There can be no sense in France coming out victorious if the stake is in truth lost. The cause of liberty becomes a mockery if the price to be paid is wholesale destruction of those who are to enjoy liberty. It then becomes an inglorious satiation of ambition. The bravery of the French soldier is world-known. But let the world know also the greater bravery of the French statesmen in suing for peace. I have assumed that the French statesmen have

---

* The French request for armistice was sent to Hitler on June 16. Hitler's terms were delivered to the French on June 20. On June 22 the German terms were accepted and three days later on June 25 the armistice became effective.

taken the step in a perfectly honorable manner as behooves true soldiers. Let me hope that Herr Hitler will impose no humiliating terms but show that, though he can fight without mercy, he can at least conclude peace not without mercy. But to resume the thread of the argument. What will Hitler do with his victory? Can he digest so much power? Personally he will go as empty-handed as his not very remote predecessor Alexander. For the Germans he will have left not the pleasure of owning a mighty empire but the burden of sustaining its crushing weight. For they will not be able to hold all the conquered nations in perpetual subjection. And I doubt if the Germans of future generations will entertain unadulterated pride in the deeds for which Hitlerism will be deemed responsible. They will honor Herr Hitler as a genius, as a brave man, a matchless organizer, and much more. But I should hope that the Germans of the future will have learnt the art of discrimination even about their heroes. Anyway, I think it will be allowed that all the blood that has been spilled by Hitler had added not a millionth part of an inch to the world's moral stature. As against this imagine the state of Europe today if the Czechs, the Poles, the Norwegians, the French, and the English had all said to Hitler: "You need not make your scientific preparation for destruction. We will meet your violence with nonviolence. You will therefore be able to destroy our nonviolent army without tanks, battleships, and airships." It may be retorted that the only difference would be that Hitler would have got without fighting what he has gained after a bloody fight. Exactly. The history of Europe would then have been written differently. Possession might (but only might) have been then taken under nonviolent resistance, as it has been taken now after perpetration of untold barbarities. Under nonviolence only those would have been killed who had trained themselves to be killed, if need be, but without killing anyone and without bearing malice toward anybody. I daresay that in that case Europe would have added several inches to its moral stature. And in the end I expect it is the moral worth that will count. All else is dross. I have written these lines for the European powers. But they are meant for ourselves. If my argument has gone home, is it not time for us to declare our changeless faith in nonviolence of the strong and say we do not seek to defend our liberty with the force of arms, but we will defend it with the force of nonviolence?

CWMG, vol. 72, pp. 187–89

17.
Letter to *The Times of India*

SEVAGRAM,
WARDHA.

February 10, 1941

SIR,

Your word to me written so earnestly in your issue of February 7 demands a reply. In spite of your disbelief, I must adhere to my faith in the possibility of the most debased human nature to respond to nonviolence. It is the essence of nonviolence that it conquers all opposition. That I may not express myself that measure of nonviolence, and the rest may express less is highly probable. But I will not belittle the power of nonviolence or distrust the Führer's capacity to respond to true nonviolence. The illustrations you have cited in support of your disbelief are all unhappy because wholly inapplicable. A man is not necessarily nonviolent because he lays down his arms. The Czechs, the Danes, the Austrians, and the Poles may have all acted most wisely, but certainly not nonviolently. If they could have put up successful armed resistance, they would have done so and would have deserved well of their countrymen. Nor is it for me to blame them for submission when resistance became vain. It was, however, in order to meet such

contingencies and in order to enable even the physically weakest persons not to feel powerless against physically strong persons fully armed with modern weapons of destruction that
satyagraha was discovered and applied in South Africa in
1907. And it has since been successfully applied under varying
and even baffling circumstances. You will please excuse me for
refusing to draw a distinction in kind between the forces I have
had to cope with hitherto and what I may have to cope with if
the Führer attacked India. The prospect of his killing every
satyagrahi causes neither terror nor despair. If India has to go
through such a purgatory and if a fair number of satyagrahis
face the Führer's army and die without malice in their breasts,
it would be a new experience for him. Whether he responds or
not, I am quite clear that these satyagrahis facing the army will
go down in history as heroes and heroines at least equal to
those of whom we learn in fables or cold history. You are,
however, on less weak ground when you doubt the honesty or
nonviolence of my companions. You are entitled to throw the
Poona resolution in my face. I have already confessed that the
Poona resolution would not have been passed but for my momentary weakness. As to the want of honesty or defective nonviolence, I can only say that the future alone will show whether
satyagrahis were only so-called or as honest and true as human
beings can be. I can only assert that every care has been taken
in making the selection to ensure a fair standard of nonviolence. I admit, however, that hypocrites have undoubtedly
crept in. But I entertain the belief that the vast majority will be
found to be true. The Congress president has been frank
enough to define the limitations of his nonviolence. But so far
as I know his mind—and nobody does if I do not—his nonviolence will be proof against any temptation within the limits
defined by him. I should undertake to engage in nonviolent resistance to the Führer if I had companions with the Maulana
Saheb's circumscribed belief. Whether such nonviolence can
stand the test or not is a moot question. I have achieved success
till now with such material.

    You are incorrect in attributing to me a demand for unfettered liberty of the press or speech.* What I have said is that there should be unfettered liberty provided that it is not inconsistent with nonviolence. I am not aware that Congress ministers' restrictive action went beyond the proviso. If it did, it was certainly against the declared Congress policy and can be no guide or criterion for me. The unkindest cut is contained in the insinuation that my demand for free speech, subject to the proviso mentioned, was "a device for squeezing political concessions from the British." There would be nothing politically wrong if political concessions were demanded even at the point of civil disobedience. But it is a matter of public knowledge that the Poona resolution has lapsed. And insofar as I am concerned, it remains lapsed so long as the war lasts. Civil disobedience would certainly be withdrawn if free speech is genuinely recognized and the status quo restored. I have never stated during previous movements that they were likely to be long drawn out. But I have done so this time because I believe that there can be no settlement with the Congress, short of complete independence during the pendency of the war, for the simple reason that the Congress cannot commit itself to active help in war with men and money. That would mean a reversal of the policy of nonviolence which the Congress has pursued for the last twenty years. And independence cannot come through any settlement while the war lasts. Therefore so far as I know, the Congress will be satisfied with the fullest freedom to grow in nonviolence. The Congress demand concerns all persons and parties. You ask me in the face of all these facts whether it is "fair or morally right to pursue his (my) present campaign." You have answered the question yourself in the negative. But I may not accept your answer. In the first place, as shown above, I do not subscribe to your facts. Secondly, to accept your

* *The Times of India* had argued: "He demands the unfettered liberty of the press and the right of the individual to say what he likes. These so-called rights do not exist anywhere in the world; they did not prevail when Mr. Gandhi's Congress governments were in office in the Indian provinces. Bombay and Madras bear witness to that fact. Is Mr. Gandhi justified in demanding for himself and others a privilege that even Congress ministers denied to the public?"

answer will be to declare my utter insolvency. I would be untrue to the faith I have unwaveringly held now for nearly half
a century in the efficacy of nonviolence. I may seemingly fail,
but even at the risk of being completely misunderstood, I must
live and act according to my faith and belief that I am serving
India, Britain, and humanity. I do not wish well to India at the
expense of Britain, as I do not wish well to Britain at the expense of Germany. Hitlers will come and go. Those who believe that when the Führer dies or is defeated his spirit will die,
err grievously. What matters is how we react to such a spirit,
violently or nonviolently. If we react violently, we feed that evil
spirit. If we act nonviolently, we sterilize it. You ask me to devote myself to internal unity. Well, my passion for it is as old as
that for nonviolence. Indeed, my first nonviolent experiment
outside the domestic circle was to promote that unity. And I
had considerable success. I ask you, therefore, to believe me
that my effort for unity is not suspended but intensified by the
present movement. The great beauty of nonviolent effort lies in
the fact that its failure can only harm those who are in it, while
its success is sure to promote all-round good.

M. K. GANDHI

CWMG, vol. 73, pp. 321–24

VII.

CONUNDRUMS OF AHIMSA

The lived ideal of nonviolence required Gandhi to face questions of conduct in everyday life, his own and that of the community. Truth and nonviolence are not occasional aspirations; they require a daily practice, incessant vigilance, and seeking answers to problems. This section contains the most fundamental of the conundrums of ahimsa: When is it an act of nonviolence to take life?

I.
"The Fiery Ordeal"

The killing of an ailing calf in the Ashram under circumstances described below having caused a great commotion in certain circles in Ahmedabad and some angry letters having been addressed to Gandhiji on the subject, Gandhiji has critically examined the question in the light of the principle of nonviolence in an article in Navajivan, *the substance of which is given below. P.**

---

* Pyarelal Nayar, MKG's secretary who translated the essay originally written in Gujarati.

I

WHEN KILLING MAY BE AHIMSA

An attempt is being made at the Ashram to run a small model dairy and tannery on behalf of the Goseva Sangha. Its work in this connection brings it up, at every step, against intricate moral dilemmas that would not arise but for the keenness to realize the Ashram ideal of seeking truth through the exclusive means of ahimsa.

For instance, some days back a calf having been maimed lay in agony in the Ashram. Whatever treatment and nursing was possible was given to it. The surgeon whose advice was sought in the matter declared the case to be past help and past hope. The suffering of the animal was so great that it could not even turn [on] its side without excruciating pain.

In these circumstances I felt that humanity* demanded that the agony should be ended by ending life itself. I held a preliminary discussion with the managing committee, most of whom agreed with my view. The matter was then placed before the whole Ashram. At the discussion a worthy neighbor vehemently opposed the idea of killing even to end pain and offered to nurse the dying animal. The nursing consisted in cooperation with some of the Ashram sisters in warding the flies off the animal and trying to feed it. The ground of the friend's opposition was that one has no right to take away life, which one cannot create. His argument seemed to me to be pointless here. It would have [a] point if the taking of life was actuated by self-interest. Finally, in all humility but with the clearest of convictions, I got in my presence a doctor kindly to administer the calf a quietus by means of a poison injection. The whole thing was over in less than two minutes.

I knew that public opinion especially in Ahmedabad would not approve of my action and that it would read nothing but himsa in it. But I know, too, that performance of one's duty should be independent of public opinion. I have all along held

* The Gujarati original has "ahimsa."

that one is bound to act according to what to one appears to be right even though it may appear wrong to others. And experience has shown that that is the only correct course. I admit that there is always a possibility of one's mistaking right for wrong and vice versa, but often one learns to recognize wrong only through unconscious error. On the other hand, if a man fails to follow the light within for fear of public opinion or any other similar reason, he would never be able to know right from wrong and in the end lose all sense of distinction between the two. That is why the poet has sung:

> *The pathway of love is the ordeal of fire,*
> *The shrinkers turn away from it.*

The pathway of ahimsa, that is, of love, one has often to tread all alone. But the question may very legitimately be put to me: Would I apply to human beings the principle I have enunciated in connection with the calf? Would I like it to be applied in my own case? My reply is yes; the same law holds good in both the cases. The law of "as with one so with all" admits of no exceptions, or the killing of the calf was wrong and violent. In practice, however, we do not cut short the sufferings of our ailing dear ones by death because as a rule we have always means at our disposal to help them and because they have the capacity to think and decide for themselves. But supposing that in the case of an ailing friend I am unable to render any aid whatever and recovery is out of the question and the patient is lying in an unconscious state in the throes of fearful agony, then I would not see any himsa in putting an end to his suffering by death. Just as a surgeon does not commit himsa but practices the purest ahimsa when he wields his knife on his patient's body for the latter's benefit, similarly one may find it necessary under certain imperative circumstances to go a step further and sever life from the body in the interest of the sufferer. It may be objected that whereas the surgeon performs his operation to save the life of the patient, in the other case we do just the reverse. But on a deeper analysis it will be found that the ultimate object sought to be served in both the cases is

the same, viz., to relieve the suffering soul within from pain.
In the one case you do it by severing the diseased portion from
the body, in the other you do it by severing from the soul the
body that has become an instrument of torture to it. In either
case, it is the relief of the soul within from pain that is aimed
at, the body without the life within being incapable of feeling
either pleasure or pain. Other circumstances can be imagined
in which not to kill would spell himsa, while killing would be
ahimsa. Suppose, for instance, that I find my daughter—whose
wish at the moment I have no means of ascertaining—is threatened with violation and there is no way by which I can save
her, then it would be the purest form of ahimsa on my part to
put an end to her life and surrender myself to the fury of the
incensed ruffian. But the trouble with our votaries of ahimsa is
that they have made of ahimsa a blind fetish and put the greatest obstacle in the way of the spread of true ahimsa in our
midst. The current (and in my opinion, mistaken) view of
ahimsa has drugged our conscience and rendered us insensible
to a host of other and more insidious forms of himsa like harsh
words, harsh judgments, ill will, anger and spite, and lust of
cruelty; it has made us forget that there may be far more himsa
in the slow torture of men and animals, the starvation and exploitation to which they are subjected out of selfish greed, the
wanton humiliation and oppression of the weak, and the killing of their self-respect that we witness all around us today
than in mere benevolent taking of life. Does anyone doubt for
a moment that it would have been far more humane to have
summarily put to death those who in the infamous lane of Amritsar were made by their torturers to crawl on their bellies like
worms? If anyone desires to retort by saying that these people
themselves today feel otherwise, that they are none the worse
for their crawling, I shall have no hesitation in telling him that
he does not know even the elements of ahimsa. There arise occasions in a man's life when it becomes his imperative duty to
meet them by laying down his life; not to appreciate this fundamental fact of man's estate is to betray an ignorance of the
foundation of ahimsa. For instance, a votary of truth would
pray to God to give him death to save him from a life of

falsehood. Similarly, a votary of ahimsa would on bent knees implore his enemy to put him to death rather than humiliate him or make him do things unbecoming the dignity of a human being. As the poet has sung:

> The way of the Lord is meant for heroes,
> Not for cowards.

It is this fundamental misconception about the nature and scope of ahimsa, this confusion about the relative values, that is responsible for our mistaking mere non-killing for ahimsa and for the fearful amount of himsa that goes on in the name of ahimsa in our country. Let a man contrast the sanctimonious horror that is affected by the so-called votaries of ahimsa at the very idea of killing an ailing animal to cut short its agony with their utter apathy and indifference to countless cruelties that are practiced on our dumb cattle world. And he will begin to wonder whether he is living in the land of ahimsa or in that of conscious or unconscious hypocrisy. It is our spiritual inertia, lack of moral courage—the courage to think boldly and look facts squarely in the face—that is responsible for this deplorable state of affairs. Look at our *pinjrapoles* and *goshalas*, many of them represent today so many dens of torture to which as a sop to conscience we consign the hapless and helpless cattle. If they could only speak, they would cry out against us and say, "Rather than subject us to this slow torture give us death." I have often read this mute appeal in their eyes. To conclude then, to cause pain or wish ill to or to take the life of any living being out of anger or a selfish intent is himsa. On the other hand, after a calm and clear judgment to kill or cause pain to a living being with a view to its spiritual or physical benefit from a pure, selfless intent may be the purest form of ahimsa. Each such case must be judged individually and on its own merits. The final test as to its violence or nonviolence is after all the intent underlying the act.

II

WHEN KILLING IS HIMSA

I now come to the other crying problem that is confronting the Ashram today. The monkey nuisance has become very acute and an immediate solution has become absolutely necessary. The growing vegetables and fruit trees have become a special mark of attention of this privileged fraternity and are now threatened with utter destruction. In spite of all our efforts we have not yet been able to find an efficacious and at the same time nonviolent remedy for the evil. The matter has provoked a hot controversy in certain circles and I have received some angry letters on the subject. One of the correspondents has protested against the "killing of monkeys and wounding them by means of arrows in the Ashram." Let me hasten to assure the reader that no monkey has so far been killed in the Ashram, nor has any monkey been wounded by means of "arrows" or otherwise as imagined by the correspondent. Attempts are undoubtedly being made to drive them away and harmless arrows have been used for the purpose. The idea of wounding monkeys to frighten them away seems to me unbearable though I am seriously considering the question of killing them in case it should become unavoidable. But this question is not so simple or easy as the previous one. I see a clear breach of ahimsa even in driving away monkeys; the breach would be proportionately greater if they have to be killed. For any act of injury done from self-interest whether amounting to killing or not is doubtless himsa. All life in the flesh exists by some himsa. Hence the highest religion has been defined by a negative word "ahimsa." The world is bound in a chain of destruction. In other words himsa is an inherent necessity for life in the body. That is why a votary of ahimsa always prays for ultimate deliverance from the bondage of flesh. None, while in the flesh, can thus be entirely free from himsa because one never completely renounces the will to live. Of what use is it to force the flesh merely if the spirit refuses to cooperate? You may starve even unto death, but if at the same time the mind continues to hanker after objects of the sense, your fast is a sham and a delusion. What then is the poor help-less slave to the will to live to do? How is he to determine the exact nature and the extent of himsa he must commit? Society has no doubt set down a standard and absolved the individual from troubling himself about it to that extent. But every seeker after truth has to adjust and vary the standard according to his individual need and to make a ceaseless endeavor to reduce the circle of himsa. But the peasant is too much occupied with the burden of his hard and precarious existence to have time or energy to think out these problems for himself, and the cul-tured class instead of helping him chooses to give him the cold shoulder. Having become a peasant myself, I have no clear-cut road to go by and must therefore chalk out a path for myself and possibly for fellow peasants. And the monkey nuisance being one of the multitude of ticklish problems that stare the farmer in the face, I must find out some means by which the peasant's crops can be safeguarded against it with the mini-mum amount of himsa. I am told that the farmers of Gujarat employ special watchmen whose very presence scares away the monkeys and saves the peasant from the necessity of killing them. That may be, but it should not be forgotten that what-ever efficacy this method might have, it is clearly dependent upon some measure of destruction at some time or other. For these cousins of ours are wily and intelligent beings. The mo-ment they discover that there is no real danger for them, they refuse to be frightened even by gunshots and only gibber and howl the more when shots are fired. Let nobody therefore imagine that the Ashram has not considered or left any method of dealing with the nuisance untried. But none of the methods that I have known up to now is free from himsa. Whilst there-fore I would welcome any practical suggestions from the read-ers of *Navajivan* for coping with this problem, let the intending advisers bear in mind what I have said above and send only such solutions as they have themselves successfully tried and cause the minimum amount of injury.

2.
The Tangle of Ahimsa

My article "The Fiery Ordeal" has brought down upon me the ire of many an incensed critic. Some of them seem to have made the violence of their invective against me a measure of their solicitude for ahimsa. Others, as if to test my capacity for ahimsa, have cast all decorum and propriety to the winds and have poured upon me the lava of their unmeasured and acrimonious criticism, while still some others have felt genuinely grieved at what seems to them a sad aberration on my part and have written to me letters to unburden their grief to me. I have not the time to reply to all the letters that have been sent to me, nor do I feel it to be necessary. As for the acrimonious letters, the only possible purpose that they can serve is to provide me with some exercise in forbearance and nonviolence. Leaving aside such letters, therefore, I shall here try to examine some arguments that I have been able to glean from other and soberly written communications. I am always prepared to give my best consideration to letters that are brief and to the point and are neatly written out in ink in a clear legible hand. For I claim to be a humble seeker after truth and am conducting *Navajivan* not merely to teach but also to learn. To come now to the objections and the counsels addressed to me by my correspondents, they may be summed up as follows:

1. You should now retire from the field of ahimsa.

2. You should confess that your views about ahimsa are imported from the West.

3. You must not express views even when they are correct if there is a possibility of their being misused.

4. If you believe in the law of karma, then your killing of the calf was a vain attempt to interfere with the operation of that law.

5. What warrant had you for believing that the calf was bound not to recover? Have you not heard of cases of recovery after the doctors have pronounced them to be hopeless?

Whether I should retire or not from the field of ahimsa, or for the matter of that from any other field, is essentially and solely for me to judge. A man can give up a right, but he may not give up a duty without being guilty of a grave dereliction. Unpopularity and censure are often the lot of a man who wants to speak and practice the truth. I hold it to be the bounden duty of a satyagrahi openly and freely to express his opinions which he holds to be correct and of benefit to the public even at the risk of incurring popular displeasure and worse. So long as I believe my views on ahimsa to be correct, it would be a sin of omission on my part not to give expression to them. I have nothing to be ashamed of if my views on ahimsa are the result of my Western education. I have never tabooed all Western ideas, nor am I prepared to anathematize everything that comes from the West as inherently evil. I have learnt much from the West and I should not be surprised to find that I had learnt something about ahimsa, too, from the West. I am not concerned what ideas of mine are the result of my foreign contacts. It is enough for me to know that my views on ahimsa have now become a part and parcel of my being. I have publicly discussed my views in the matter of the calf, not necessarily because I believe them to be correct, but because they are to the best of my knowledge based on pure ahimsa and as such likely to throw light on the tangled problem of ahimsa. As for the problem of the monkeys, I have discussed it publicly, because I do not know my duty in the matter, and I am anxious to be enlightened. Let me assure the readers that my effort has not been in vain and I have already received several helpful suggestions from my correspondents. Let me further assure them that I would not proceed to the extreme length of killing unless I am absolutely driven to it. It is because I am anxious to be spared this painful necessity that I have invited suggestions for dealing with these persistent and unwelcome guests. I firmly believe in the law of karma, but I believe, too, in human endeavor. I regard as the *summum bonum* of life the attainment of salvation through karma by annihilating its effects by detachment. If it is a violation of the law of karma to cut short the agony of an ailing animal by putting an end to its life, it is no less so to minister to the sick or try to nurse them back to life. And yet if a man were to refuse to give medicine to a patient or to nurse him on the ground of karma, we would hold him to be guilty of inhumanity and himsa. Without therefore entering into a discussion about the eternal controversy regarding predestination and free will, I will simply say here that I deem it to be the highest duty of man to render what little service he can. I admit that there was no guarantee that the calf would not recover. I have certainly known cases that were pronounced by doctors to be hopeless and were cured afterward. But even so I hold that a man is bound to make the utmost use of his reason, circumscribed and poor as undoubtedly it is, and to try to penetrate the mists of ignorance by its light and try to act accordingly. And that is precisely what we do in countless cases in our everyday life. But strangely paradoxical as it may seem, it is nevertheless a fact that the moment we come to think of death, the very idea frightens us out of our wits and entirely paralyzes our reasoning faculty, although as Hindus we ought to be the least affected by the thought of death, since from the very cradle we are brought up on the doctrines of the immortality of the spirit and the transitoriness of the body. Even if it were found that my decision to poison the calf was wrong, it could have done no harm to the soul of the animal. If I have erred, I am prepared to take the consequences of my error, but I refuse to go into hysterics because by my action I possibly cut short the painful existence of a dying calf say by a couple of hours. And the rule that I have applied to the calf I am prepared to apply in the case of my own dear ones as well. Who knows how often we bring those we love to a premature end by our coddling, infatuation, wrong diagnosis, or wrong treatment? The letters that I have received from my correspondents more than ever confirm me in my conviction that in our effusiveness over matters like this we forget the elementary duty of kindness, are led away from the path of true love, and discredit our ahimsa. The fear of death is thus the greatest obstacle in the way of our realizing the true nature of ahimsa.

CWMG, vol. 37, pp. 338–41

3.
More About Ahimsa

I

A correspondent writes:

> *I have read your article "The Fiery Ordeal" over and over again, but it has failed to satisfy me. Your proposal about the killing of monkeys has taken me aback. I believed that a person like you with his being steeped in ahimsa would never swerve from the right path even though the heavens fell. And now you say that you might kill off the monkeys to protect your Ashram against their inroads. Maybe that my first impression about you was wrong. But I cannot describe what a shock your proposal about the killing of the monkeys has given me, and may I also confess, how angry it has made me feel against you? Would you kindly help me out of my perplexity?*

I have received several other letters, too, in the same strain. I am afraid people have formed an altogether exaggerated estimate of me. These good people seem to think that because I am trying to analyze and define the ideal of ahimsa I must have fully attained that ideal. My views regarding the calf and the monkeys seem happily to have shattered this illusion of theirs. Truth to me is infinitely dearer than the "mahatmaship" which is purely a burden. It is my knowledge of my limitations and my nothingness which has so far saved me from the oppressiveness of the "mahatmaship." I am painfully aware of the fact that my desire to continue life in the body involves me in constant himsa, that is why I am becoming growingly indifferent to this physical body of mine. For instance, I know that in the act of respiration I destroy innumerable invisible germs floating in the air. But I do not stop breathing. The consumption of vegetables involves himsa, but I find that I cannot give them up. Again, there is himsa in the use of antiseptics, yet I cannot bring myself to discard the use of disinfectants like kerosene, etc., to rid myself of the mosquito pest and the like. I suffer snakes to be killed in the Ashram when it is impossible to catch and put them out of harm's way. I even tolerate the use of the stick to drive the bullocks in the Ashram. Thus there is no end of *himsa* which I directly and indirectly commit. And now I find myself confronted with this monkey problem. Let me assure the reader that I am in no hurry to take the extreme step of killing them. In fact, I am not sure that I would at all be able finally to make up my mind to kill them. As it is, friends are helping me with useful suggestions and the adoption of some of them may solve the difficulty at least temporarily without our having to kill them. But I cannot today promise that I shall never kill the monkeys even though they may destroy all the crops in the Ashram. If as a result of this humble confession of mine, friends choose to give me up as lost, I would be sorry, but nothing will induce me to try to conceal my imperfections in the practice of ahimsa. All I claim for myself is that I am ceaselessly trying to understand the implications of great ideals like ahimsa and to practice them in thought, word, and deed and that not without a certain measure of success as I think. But I know that I have a long distance yet to cover in this direction. Unless therefore the correspondent in question can bring himself to bear with my imperfections, I am sorry I can offer him but little consolation.

II

Another correspondent writes:

Supposing my elder brother is suffering from a terrible and painful malady and doctors have despaired of his life and I, too, feel likewise, should I in the circumstances put him out of life?

My reply is in the negative. I am afraid some of my correspondents have not even taken the trouble to understand my article. In propounding their conundrums, they forget that whilst I have certainly compared the case of an ailing human being with that of an ailing calf and recommended the killing of the former in exactly similar circumstances, in actual practice such a complete analogy is hardly ever to be found. In the first place, the human body being much more manageable in bulk is always easier to manipulate and nurse; secondly, man being gifted with the power of speech more often than not is in a position to express his wishes and so the question of taking his life without his consent cannot come within the rule. For I have never suggested that the life of another person can be taken against his will without violating the principle of ahimsa. Again, we do not always despair of the life of a person when he is reduced to a comatose state and even when he is past all hope he is not necessarily past all help. More often than not it is both possible and practicable to render service to a human patient till the very end. Whilst, therefore, I would still maintain that the principle enunciated regarding the calf applies equally to man and bird and beast, I should expect an intelligent person to know the obvious natural difference between a man and an animal. To recapitulate the conditions the fulfillment of all of which alone can warrant the taking of life from the point of view of ahimsa:

1. The disease from which the patient is suffering should be incurable.

2. All concerned have despaired of the life of the patient.

3. The case should be beyond all help or service.

4. It should be impossible for the patient in question to express his or its wish.

So long as even one of these conditions remains unfulfilled, the taking of life from the point of view of ahimsa cannot be justified.

III

A third correspondent writes:

> Well, the killing of the calf is all right so far as it goes. But have you considered that your example is likely to afford a handle to those who indulge in animal sacrifices and thus accentuate the practice; do you not know that even those who commit these deeds argue that the animals sacrificed gain merit in the life to follow?

Such abuse of my action is quite possible and inevitable so long as there are hypocrisy and ignorance in this world. What crimes have not been committed in the world in the sacred name of religion? One therefore need not be deterred from doing what one considers to be right merely because one's conduct may be misunderstood or misinterpreted by others. And as for those who practice animal sacrifice, surely they do not need the authority of my example to defend their conduct since they profess to take their stand on the authority of the Shastras. My fear, however, is that proceeding on my analogy some people might actually take it into their head summarily to put to death those whom they might imagine to be their enemies on the plea that it would serve both the interests of society and the "enemies" concerned if the latter were killed. In fact, I have often heard people advance this argument. But it is enough for my purpose to know that my interpretation of ahimsa affords no basis whatever for such an argument, for in the latter case there is no question of serving or anticipating the wishes of the victims concerned. Finally, even if it were admitted that it was in the interest of the animal or the enemy in question to be summarily dispatched, the act would still be spelt as himsa because it would not be altogether disinterested. The fallacy is so obvious. But who can help people who seeing see not or are bent upon deceiving themselves?

CWMG, vol. 37, pp. 408–11

4.
Jain Ahimsa?*

A Jain friend who is reputed to have made a fair study of the Jain philosophy as also of the other systems has addressed me a long letter on ahimsa. It deserves a considered reply. He says in effect:

> *Your interpretation of ahimsa has caused confusion. In the ordinary sense of the term himsa means to sever life from body and not to do so is ahimsa. Refraining from causing pain to any living creature is only an extension of the original meaning, which cannot by any stretch of language be made to cover the taking of life. You would not understand me to mean from this that I regard all taking of life as wrong in every possible circumstance; for I do not think that there is any ethical principle in this world that can be regarded as absolute and admitting of no exception whatever. The maxim "Ahimsa is the highest or the supreme duty" embodies a great and cardinal truth, but it does not cover the entire sum of human duties. Whilst therefore what you have termed "nonviolent killing" may be a right thing, it cannot be described as ahimsa.*

* Excerpted from the original.

I am of opinion that just as life is subject to constant change and development, the meanings of terms, too, are constantly undergoing a process of evolution, and this can be amply proved by illustrations from the history of any religion. The word "yajna" or sacrifice in the Hindu religion, for instance, is an illustration in point. Sir J. C. Bose's discoveries are today revolutionizing the accepted connotations of biological terms. Similarly, if we will fully realize ahimsa, we may not fight shy of discovering fresh implications of the doctrine of ahimsa. We cannot improve upon the celebrated maxim "Ahimsa is the highest or the supreme duty," but we are bound, if we would retain our spiritual inheritance, to explore the implications of this great and universal doctrine. But I am not particular about names. I do not mind whether the taking of life in the circumstances I have mentioned is called ahimsa or not, so long as its correctness is conceded.

. . . The fourth poser is as follows: The Jain view of ahimsa rests on the following three principles:

> "No matter what the circumstances are or how great the suffering, it is impossible for anyone deliberately to renounce the will to live or to wish another to put him out of pain. Therefore the taking of life cannot in any circumstances be morally justified.
>
> "In a world full of activities which necessitate himsa, an aspirant for salvation should try to follow ahimsa, engaging in the fewest possible activities.
>
> "There are two kinds of himsa—direct such as that involved in agriculture, and indirect as that involved in the eating of agricultural produce. Where one cannot altogether escape from either, a votary of ahimsa should try to avoid direct himsa."

I would earnestly request you critically to examine and discuss these three Jain principles of ahimsa in Navajivan. I notice that there is a vital difference between your view of ahimsa and that of the Jains. Whereas your view of ahimsa is based on the philosophy of action, that of the Jains is based on that of renunciation of action. The present is an era of action. If the principle of ahimsa be an eternal and universal principle untrammelled by time and place, it seems to me that there is a great need to *stimulate the people's mind to think out for themselves as to how the principle of ahimsa that has so far been confined to the field of renunciation only can be worked in present-day life of action and what form it will take when applied to this new environment.*

It is with the utmost reluctance that I have to enter into a discussion of these principles. I know the risks of such discussion. But I see no escape from it. As for the first principle, I have already expressed my opinion on it in a previous portion of this article. It is my firm conviction that the principle of clinging to life in all circumstances betrays cowardice and is the cause of much of the himsa that goes on around us and blind adherence to this principle is bound to increase instead of reducing himsa. It seems to me that if this Jain principle is really as it is here enunciated, it is a hindrance to the attainment of salvation. For instance, a person who is constantly praying for salvation will never wish to continue his life at the expense of another's. Only a person steeped in ignorance who cannot even remotely understand what salvation means would wish to continue life on any terms. The sine qua non of salvation is a total annihilation of all desire. How dare, then, an aspirant for salvation be sordidly selfish or wish to preserve his perishable body at all cost? Descending from the field of salvation to that of the family, one's country, or the world of humanity, we again find innumerable instances of men and women who have dedicated themselves to the service of their family, their country, or the world at large in entire disregard of their own life, and this ideal of utter self-sacrifice and self-abnegation at present is being inculcated throughout the world. To hang on to life at all cost seems to me the very height of selfishness. Let, however, nobody understand me to mean that one may try to wean another even from such sordid egoism by force. I am adducing the argument merely to show the fallacy of the doctrine of will to live at all cost. As for the second, I do not know whether it can at all be described as a principle. But be that as it may, to me it represents a truism and I heartily endorse it. Coming to the third principle in the form in which it is enunciated by the

friend, it suffers from a grave defect. The most terrible consequence of this principle to me seems to be this: that if we accept
it, then a votary of ahimsa must renounce agriculture although
he knows that he cannot renounce the fruits of agriculture and
that agriculture is an indispensable condition for the existence
of mankind. The very idea that millions of the sons of the soil
should remain steeped in himsa in order that a handful of men
who live on the toil of these people might be able to practice
ahimsa seems to me to be unworthy of and inconsistent with
the supreme duty of ahimsa. I feel that this betrays a lack of
perception of the inwardness of ahimsa. Let us see, for instance,
to what it leads to if pushed to its logical conclusion. You may
not kill a snake, but if necessary, according to this principle,
you may get it killed by somebody else. You may not yourself
forcibly drive away a thief, but you may employ another person
to do it for you. If you want to protect the life of a child en-
trusted to your care from the fury of a tyrant, somebody else
must bear the brunt of the tyrant's fury for you. And you thus
refrain from direct action in the sacred name of ahimsa! This in
my opinion is neither religion nor ahimsa. So long as one is not
prepared to take the risks mentioned and to face the consequences, one cannot be free from fear, and so long as a man has
not shed all fear, he is ipso facto incapable of practicing ahimsa.
Our scriptures tell us that ahimsa is all conquering. That before
it, even the wild beasts shed their ferocity and the most hard-
hearted of tyrants forget their anger. Utterly inadequate and
imperfect as my own practice of ahimsa has been, it has enabled me to realize the truth of this principle. I cannot once
more help expressing my doubt that Jainism subscribes to the
third principle of ahimsa as enunciated by this friend. But even
if Jain doctrine is just as it is stated by the friend, I must say, I
for one cannot reconcile myself to it. Now to come to the question of renunciation versus action: I believe in the doctrine of
renunciation, but I hold that renunciation should be sought for
in and through action. That action is the sine qua non of life in
the body, that the wheel of life cannot go on even for a second
without involving some sort of action goes without saying. Renunciation can therefore in these circumstances only mean

detachment or freedom of the spirit from action, even while the body is engaged in action. A follower of the path of renunciation seeks to attain it not by refraining from all activity but by carrying it on in a perfect spirit of detachment and altruism as a pure trust. Thus a man may engage in farming, spinning, or any other activity without departing from the path of renunciation provided one does so merely for selfless service and remains free from the taint of egoism or attachment. It remains for those therefore who like myself hold this view of renunciation to discover for themselves how far the principle of ahimsa is compatible with life in the body and how it can be applied to acts of everyday life. The very virtue of a dharma is that it is universal, that its practice is not the monopoly of the few but must be the privilege of all. And it is my firm belief that the scope of truth and ahimsa is worldwide. That is why I find an ineffable joy in dedicating my life to researches in truth and ahimsa and I invite others to share it with me by doing likewise.

CWMG, vol. 37, pp. 381–86

5.
How to Observe Ahimsa

Can we kill a snake? Can we use violence against a ruffian attempting to rape a woman? Can we plow a field, though knowing that we kill germs thereby? A votary of ahimsa need not concern himself with such problems. Let them solve themselves when they will. If we lose ourselves in this labyrinth, we shall forget ahimsa. Those who are sincere in their desire to follow ahimsa will examine their own hearts and look at their neighbors. If one finds ill will and hatred in one's heart, one may know that one has not climbed the first step toward the goal of ahimsa. If a person does not observe ahimsa in his relations with his neighbors and his associates, he is thousands of miles away from ahimsa. A votary of ahimsa, therefore, should ask himself every day when retiring: "Did I speak harshly today to any coworker? Did I give him inferior khadi and keep better khadi for myself? Did I give him imperfectly baked *rotli* and reserve for myself a fully baked one? Did I shirk my duty and throw the burden on my coworker? Did I neglect serving the neighbor who was ill today? Did I refuse water to a thirsty passerby who asked for it? Did I not care even to greet the guest who had arrived? Did I scold a laborer? Did I go on exacting work from him without thinking that he might be tired? Did I goad bullocks with spiked sticks? Did I get angry in the kitchen because the rice was half cooked?" All these are forms of intense violence. If we do not observe ahimsa spontaneously in such daily acts, we shall never learn to observe it in other fields and, if at all we seem to observe it, our ahimsa will be of little or no value. Ahimsa is a great force which is active every moment of our lives. It is felt in our every action and thought. He who takes care of his pennies may rest assured that his pound is safe. But he who does not take care of pennies will lose them, and as for the pound he never had it.

CWMG, vol. 50, p. 96

6.
"Is This Humanity?" (Series of Eight Essays)

I.

The Ahmedabad Humanitarian League has addressed me a letter from which I take the relevant portions:

The talk of the whole city of Ahmedabad is the destruction of sixty dogs on his mill premises at the instance of Seth. . . . Many

a humanitarian heart is considerably agitated over the incident.
When Hinduism forbids the taking of the life of any living
being, when it declares it to be a sin, do you think it right to kill
rabid dogs for the reason that they would bite human beings
and by biting other dogs make them also rabid? Are not the man
who actually destroys the dogs as also the man at whose in-
stance he does so both sinners? A deputation of three gentlemen
from our society waited on the Seth on the twenty-eighth ul-
timo. He confessed in the course of the interview that he had to
take the course in question to save human life. He also said: "I
myself had no sleep on the night I took that decision. I met Ma-
hatmaji the next morning and ascertained his view in the mat-
ter. He said, 'What else could be done?'" Is that a fact? And if
so, what does it mean? We hope you will express your views in
the matter and set the whole controversy at rest and prevent hu-
manitarianism from being endangered by the shocks given to it
by distinguished men like the Seth. The Ahmedabad municipal-
ity, we have heard, is soon going to have before it a resolution
for the castration of stray dogs. Is it proper? Does religion sanc-
tion the castration of an animal? We should be thankful if you
would give your opinion in this matter also.

Ahmedabad knows the name of the mill owner, but as *Nava-*
jivan is being read outside Ahmedabad also, I have omitted to
mention his name in accordance with my practice to avoid per-
sonalities whilst discussing a principle. The question raised by
the humanitarian society is an intricate one. I had been thinking of discussing the question ever since and even before the
incident, but on second thought dropped the idea. But the letter
of the society now compels me, makes it my duty, to enter into
a public discussion of the question. I must say that my relations
with the mill owner have been sweet and, if I may say so,
friendly. He came to me and expressed his distress in having
had to order destruction of the dogs, and asked my opinion
about it. He also said: "When the government, the municipality, and the *mahajan* all alike failed to guide me, I was driven to
this course." I gave him the reply that the society's letter attributes to me. I have since thought over the matter and feel that

my reply was quite proper. Imperfect, erring mortals as we are, there is no course open to us but the destruction of rabid dogs. At times we may be faced with the unavoidable duty of killing a man who is found in the act of killing people. If we persist in keeping stray dogs undisturbed, we shall soon be faced with the duty of either castrating them or killing them. A third alternative is that of having a special *pinjrapole* for dogs. But it is out of the question. When we cannot cope with all the stray cattle in the city, the very proposal of having a *pinjrapole* for dogs seems to me to be chimerical. There can be no two opinions on the fact that Hinduism regards killing a living being as sinful. I think all religions are agreed on the principle. There is generally no difficulty in determining a principle. The difficulty comes in when one proceeds to put it into practice. A principle is the expression of a perfection, and as imperfect beings like us cannot practice perfection, we devise every moment limits of its compromise in practice. So Hinduism has laid down that killing for sacrifice is no himsa [violence]. This is only a half-truth. Violence will be violence for all time, and all violence is sinful. But what is inevitable is not regarded as a sin, so much so that the science of daily practice has not only declared the inevitable violence involved in killing for sacrifice as permissible but even regarded it as meritorious. But unavoidable violence cannot be defined. For it changes with time, place, and person. What is regarded as excusable at one time may be inexcusable at another. The violence involved in burning fuel or coal in the depth of winter to keep the body warm may be unavoidable and, therefore, a duty for weak-bodied man, but fire unnecessarily lit in midsummer is clearly violence. We recognize the duty of killing microbes by the use of disinfectants. It is violence and yet a duty. But why go even as far as that? The air in a dark, closed room is full of little microbes, and the introduction of light and air into it by opening it is destruction indeed. But it is ever a duty to use that finest of disinfectants—pure air. These instances can be multiplied. The principle that applies in the instances cited applies in the matter of killing rabid dogs. To destroy a rabid dog is to commit the minimum amount of violence.

A recluse, who is living in a forest and is compassion incarnate, may not destroy a rabid dog. For in his compassion he has the virtue of making it whole. But a city dweller who is responsible for the protection of lives under his care and who does not possess the virtues of the recluse, but is capable of destroying a rabid dog, is faced with a conflict of duties. If he kills the dog, he commits a sin. If he does not kill it, he commits a graver sin. So he prefers to commit the lesser one and save himself from the graver. I believe myself to be saturated with ahimsa nonviolence. Ahimsa and Truth are as my two lungs. I cannot live without them. But I see every moment, with more and more clearness, the immense power of ahimsa and the littleness of man. Even the forest dweller cannot be entirely free from violence in spite of his limitless compassion. With every breath he commits a certain amount of violence. The body itself is a house of slaughter, and therefore moksha and eternal bliss consist in perfect deliverance from the body and, therefore, all pleasure, save the joy of moksha, is evanescent, imperfect. That being the case, we have to drink, in daily life, many a bitter draught of violence. It is therefore a thousand pities that the question of stray dogs, etc., assumes such a monstrous proportion in this sacred land of ahimsa. It is my firm conviction that we are propagating himsa in the name of ahimsa owing to our deep ignorance of the great principle. It may be a sin to destroy rabid dogs and such others as are liable to catch rabies. But we are responsible, the *mahajan* is responsible, for this state of things. The *mahajan* may not allow the dogs to stray. It is a sin, it should be a sin, to feed stray dogs, and we should save numerous dogs if we had legislation making every stray dog liable to be shot. Even if those who feed stray dogs consented to pay a penalty for their misdirected compassion, we should be free from the curse of stray dogs. Humanity is a noble attribute of the soul. It is not exhausted with saving a few fish or a few dogs. Such saving may even be sinful. If I have a swarm of ants in my house, the man who proceeds to feed them will be guilty of a sin. For God has provided their grain for the ants, but the man who feeds them might destroy me and my family. The *mahajan* may feel itself safe and believe that it has saved their lives by dumping dogs near my field, but it will have committed the greater sin of putting my life in danger. Humaneness is impossible without thought, discrimination, charity, fearlessness, humility, and clear vision. It is no easy thing to walk on the sharp sword edge of ahimsa in this world which is so full of himsa. Wealth does not help; anger is the enemy of ahimsa; and pride is a monster that swallows it up. In this straight and narrow observance of this religion of ahimsa, one has often to know so-called himsa as the truest form of ahimsa. Things in this world are not what they seem and do not seem as they really are. Or if they are seen as they are, they so appear only to a few who have perfected themselves after ages of penance. But none has yet been able to describe the reality, and no one can.

CWMG, vol. 31, pp. 486–89

II.

When I wrote the article on this subject, I knew that I was adding one more to my already heavy burden of troubles. But it could not be helped. Angry letters are now pouring in. At an hour when after a hard day's work I was about to retire to bed, three friends invaded me, infringed the religion of ahimsa in the name of humanity, and engaged me in a discussion on it. They had come in the name of humanity. How could I refuse to see them? So I met them. One of them, I saw, betrayed anger, bitterness, and arrogance. He did not seem to me to have come with a view to getting his doubts solved. He had come rather to correct me. Everyone has a right to do so, but whoever undertakes such a mission must know my position. This friend had taken no trouble to understand my position. But he was not to blame for it. This impatience which is but a symptom of violence is to be found everywhere. The violence in this case was painful to me as it was betrayed by an advocate of nonviolence. He claimed to be a Jain. I have made a fair study of Jainism. This visitor's ahimsa was a distortion of the reality as I

have known it in Jainism. But the Jains have no monopoly of
ahimsa. It is not the exclusive peculiarity of any religion. Every
religion is based on ahimsa; its application is different in different religions. I do not think that the Jains of today practice
ahimsa in any better way than others. I can say this because of
my acquaintance with Jains, which is so old that many take me
to be a Jain. Mahavir was an incarnation of compassion, of
ahimsa. How I wish his votaries were votaries also of his
ahimsa! Protection of little creatures is indeed an essential part
of ahimsa, but it does not exhaust itself with it. Ahimsa begins
with it. Besides, protection may not always mean mere refraining from killing. Torture or participation, direct or indirect, in
the unnecessary multiplication of those that must die is himsa.
The multiplication of dogs is unnecessary. A roving dog without an owner is a danger to society and a swarm of them is a
menace to its very existence. If we want to keep dogs in towns
or villages in a decent manner, no dog should be suffered to
wander. There should be no stray dogs even as we have no
stray cattle. Humanitarian societies should find a religious solution of such questions. But can we take individual charge of
these roving dogs? And if we cannot, can we have a *panjrapol*
for them? If both these things are impossible, there seems to
me to be no alternative except to kill them. Connivance or putting up with the status quo is no ahimsa; there is no thought or
discrimination in it. Dogs will be killed whenever they are a
menace to society. I regard this as unavoidable in the life of a
householder. To wait until they get rabid is not to be merciful
to them. We can imagine what the dogs would wish if a meeting could be called of them, from what we would wish under
the same circumstances. We will not choose to live anyhow.
That many of us do so is no credit to us. A meeting of wise
men will never resolve that men may treat one another as they
treat rabid or stray dogs. What shall we expect of them if there
were to be some beings lording it over us as we do over dogs?
Would we not rather prefer to be killed than to be treated as
dogs? We offend against dogs as a class by suffering them to
stray and live on crumbs or savings from our plates that we
throw at them and we injure our neighbors also by doing so. I

admit that there is the duty of suffering dogs to live even at the cost of one's life. But that religion is not for the householder who desires to live, who procreates, who would protect society. The householder can but practice the middle path of taking care of a few dogs. Our domestics of today are the wild animals of yesterday. The buffalo is a domestic only in India. It is a sin to domesticate wild animals inasmuch as man does so for his selfish purposes. That he has domesticated the cow and the buffalo is not out of mercy for them; it is for his own use. He, therefore, does not allow a cow or a buffalo to stray. The same duty is incumbent regarding dogs. I am, therefore, strongly of opinion that, if we would practice the religion of humanity, we should have a law making it obligatory on those who would have dogs to keep them under guard, and not allow them to stray, and making all the stray dogs liable to be destroyed after a certain date. If the *mahajan* has really any mercy for the dogs, it should take possession of all the stray dogs and distribute them to those who want to keep them. It seems to me to be impossible to protect dogs as we can protect cows. But there is a regular science of dog keeping which the people in the West have formulated and perfected. We should learn it from them and devise measures for the solution of our own problem. The work cannot be done without patience, wisdom, and perseverance. So much about dogs. But with ahimsa in its comprehensive aspect I propose to deal on another occasion.

CWMG, vol. 31, pp. 505–7

III.

Whilst I admit the possibility of having made a mistake in giving the opinion that the destruction by Mr. Ambalal's order of sixty dogs was unavoidable, I do not regret having expressed that opinion. The result so far is all to the good. We shall perhaps now understand more clearly our duty to such animals. Much wrong has been done partly out of ignorance, partly from hypocrisy, and partly for fear of public opinion. All that should now cease. But if the good is to be maintained, a clear understanding is necessary between the readers and myself. I have received quite a pile of letters on the subject, some friendly, some sharp, and some bitter. They do not seem to have understood my attitude on the destruction of dogs by Mr. Ambalal. I have often had the misfortune to be misunderstood. In South Africa my life was in peril over an action which was quite consistent with my avowed principles but which, as was proved later, was rashly regarded as contrary to them.* The so-called Himalayan blunder of Bardoli is a recent memory. The Bombay government very kindly imprisoned me at Yeravda and saved me the trouble of much writing by way of explaining and clearing my position. The Bardoli decision, I still hold, was not wrong. It was, on the contrary, an act of purest ahimsa and of invaluable service to the country. I feel just as clear about my opinion regarding the present question. I hold that the opinion is perfectly in accord with my conception of ahimsa. The critics, whether friendly or hostile, should bear with me. Some of the hostile critics have transgressed the limits of decorum. They have made no attempt to understand my position. It seems they cannot for a moment tolerate my opinion. Now they must be one of two things. They are either my teachers or they regard me as one. In the latter case, they should be courteous and patient and should have faith in me and ponder over what I write. In the former case, they should be indulgent to me and try to reason with me as lovingly and patiently as they can. I teach the children under my care not by being angry with them, but I teach them, if at all, by loving them, by allowing for their ignorance, and by playing with them. I expect the same love, the same consideration, and the same sportsmanlike spirit from my angry teachers. I have given my opinion with regard to the dogs with the best of motives and as a matter of duty. If I am mistaken, let the critics who would teach me reason with me

* The reference is to the assaults made on MKG in 1908 by his Indian followers under the belief that he had compromised with the Smuts government; vide *CWMG*, vol. VIII, pp. 75–76.

patiently and logically. Angry and irrelevant argument will not convince me. A gentleman called on me the other evening at a late hour. He knew that my time was completely occupied. He engaged me in a discussion, used hard and bitter language, and poured vials of wrath on me. I answered his questions in good humor and politely. He has published the interview in a leaflet which he is selling. It is before me. It has crossed the limits of truth, obviously of decorum. He had neither obtained my permission to publish the interview nor showed it to me before publication. Does he seek to teach me in this manner? He who trifles with truth cuts at the root of ahimsa. He who is angry is guilty of himsa. How can such a man teach me ahimsa? Even so, the hostile critics are doing me a service. They teach me to examine myself. They afford me an opportunity to see if I am free from the reaction of anger. And when I go to the root of their anger, I find nothing but love. They have attributed to me ahimsa as they understand it. Now they find me acting in a contrary manner and are angry with me. They once regarded me as a mahatma; they were glad that my influence on the people was according to their liking. Now I am an *alpatma* [a little soul] in their opinion; my influence on the people they now regard as unwholesome and they are pained by the discovery; and as they cannot control themselves, they turn the feeling of pain into one of anger. I do not mind this outburst of anger, as I appreciate the motive behind it. I must try to reason with them patiently, and if they would help me in my attempt, I request them to calm their anger. I am a votary of truth and seeker after it. If I am convinced that I am mistaken I shall admit my mistake (as I always love to do), and shall promptly mend it. It is the word of the scriptures that the mistakes of a votary of truth never harm anybody. That is the glorious secret of truth. Just a word to friendly critics: I have preserved your letters. I usually reply to my correspondents individually. But the number of letters I have received this time and have been still getting is so large and they are so inordinately long that I cannot possibly reply to them individually. I cannot, I fear, make time even to acknowledge them. Some of the correspondents ask me to publish their letters in *Navajivan*. I hope they will not press the request. I shall try to answer all the arguments that are relevant as well as I can, and hope that that will satisfy them. I bespeak the indulgence of the reader for this necessary preface. I shall now take up some of the letters before me. A friend says: You ask us not to feed stray dogs. But we do not invite them. They simply come. How can they be turned back? It will be time enough when there is a plethora of them. But is there any doubt that feeding dogs cultivates the impulse of compassion and turning them away hardens our hearts? We are all sinners. Why should we not practice what little kindness we can? It is from this false feeling of compassion that we encourage himsa in the name of ahimsa. But as ignorance is no excuse before man-made law, even so is it no excuse before the divine law. But let us analyze the argument. We cast a morsel at the beggar come to our door and feel that we have earned some merit, but we really thereby add to the number of beggars, aggravate the evil of beggary, encourage idleness, and consequently promote irreligion. This does not mean that we should starve the really deserving beggars. It is the duty of society to support the blind and the infirm, but everyone may not take the task upon himself. The head of the society, i.e., the *mahajan* or the state where it is well organized, should undertake the task, and the philanthropically inclined should subscribe funds to such an institution. If the *mahajan* is pure-minded and wise, it will carefully investigate the condition of beggars and protect the deserving ones. When this does not happen, i.e., when relief is indiscriminate, scoundrels disguised as beggars get the benefit of it and the poverty of the land increases. If it is thus a sin on the part of an individual to undertake feeding beggars, it is no less a sin for him to feed stray dogs. It is a false sense of compassion. It is an insult to the starving dog to throw a crumb at him. Roving dogs do not indicate the civilization or compassion of the society, they betray, on the contrary, the ignorance and lethargy of its members. The lower animals are our brethren. I include among them the lion and the tiger. We do not know how to live with these carnivorous beasts and poisonous reptiles because of our ignorance. When man knows himself better, he will learn to

befriend even these. Today he does not even know how to befriend a man of a different religion or from a foreign country.
The dog is a faithful companion. There are numerous instances
of the faithfulness of dogs and horses. But that means that we
should keep them and treat them with respect as we do our
companions and not allow them to roam about. By aggravat-
ing the evil of stray dogs we shall not be acquitting ourselves
of our duty to them. But if we regard the existence of stray
dogs as a shame to us and, therefore, refuse to feed them, we
shall be doing the dogs as a class a real service and make them
happy. What, then, can a humane man do for stray dogs? He
should set apart a portion of his income and send it on to a society for the protection of those animals if there be one. If such
a society is impossible—and I know it is very difficult even if it
is not impossible—he should try to own one or more dogs. If
he cannot do so, he should give up worrying about the question of dogs and direct his humanity toward the service of
other animals. "But you are asking us to destroy them?" is the
question angrily or lovingly asked by others. Now, I have not
suggested the extirpation of dogs as an absolute duty. I have
suggested the killing of some dogs as a "duty in distress" and
under certain circumstances. When the state does not care for
stray dogs, nor does the *mahajan*, and when one is not prepared to take care of them oneself, then, and if one regards
them as a danger to society, one should kill them and relieve
them from a lingering death. This is a bitter dose, I agree. But
it is my innermost conviction that true love and compassion
consist in taking it. The dogs in India are today in as bad a
plight as the decrepit animals and men in the land. It is my firm
conviction that this sorry plight is due to our misconception of
ahimsa, is due to our want of ahimsa. Practice of ahimsa cannot have as its result impotence, impoverishment, and famine.
If this is a sacred land, we should not see impoverishment
stalking it. From this state of things some rash and impatient
souls have drawn the conclusion that ahimsa is irreligion. But
I know that it is not ahimsa that is wrong, it is its votaries that
are wrong. Ahimsa is the religion of a Kshatriya. Mahavira
was a Kshatriya, Buddha was a Kshatriya, Rama and Krishna

were Kshatriyas, and all of them were votaries of ahimsa. We want to propagate ahimsa in their name. But today ahimsa has become the monopoly of timid Vaisyas and that is why it has been besmirched. Ahimsa is the extreme limit of forgiveness. But forgiveness is the quality of the brave. Ahimsa is impossible without fearlessness. Cows we cannot protect; dogs we kick about and belabor with sticks, their ribs are seen sticking out, and yet we are not ashamed of ourselves and raise a hue and cry when a stray dog is killed. Which of the two is better—that five thousand dogs should wander about in semi-starvation, living on dirt and excreta, and drag on a miserable existence, or that fifty should die and keep the rest in a decent condition? It is admittedly sinful always to be spurning and kicking the dogs. But it is possible that the man who kills the dogs that he cannot bear to see tortured thus may be doing a meritorious act. Merely taking life is not always himsa; one may even say that there is sometimes more himsa in not taking life. We must examine this position in another article.

CWMG, vol. 31, pp. 520–21

IV.

Taking life may be a duty. Let us consider this position. We do destroy as much life as we think is necessary for sustaining the body. Thus for food we take life, vegetable and other, and for health we destroy mosquitoes and the like by the use of disinfectants, etc., and we do not think that we are guilty of irreligion in doing so. This is as regards one's own self. But for the sake of others, i.e., for the benefit of the species, we kill carnivorous beasts. When lions and tigers pester their villages, the villagers regard it a duty to kill them or have them killed. Even manslaughter may be necessary in certain cases. Suppose a man runs amok and goes furiously about, sword in hand, and killing anyone that comes his way, and no one dares to capture him alive. Anyone who dispatches this lunatic will earn the gratitude of the community and be regarded a benevolent man.

From the point of view of ahimsa, it is the plain duty of every-one to kill such a man. There is, indeed, one exception if it can be so called. The yogi who can subdue the fury of this danger-ous man may not kill him. But we are not here dealing with beings who have almost reached perfection; we are considering the duty of the society, of the ordinary erring human beings.

There may be a difference of opinion as regards the apposite-ness of my illustrations. But if they are inadequate, others can be easily imagined. What they are meant to show is that re-fraining from taking life can in no circumstances be an abso-lute duty. The fact is that ahimsa does not simply mean non-killing. Himsa means causing pain to or killing any life out of anger or from a selfish purpose, or with the intention of injuring it. Refraining from so doing is ahimsa. The physician who prescribes bitter medicine causes you pain but does no himsa. If he fails to prescribe bitter medicine when it is neces-sary to do so, he fails in his duty of ahimsa. The surgeon who, from fear of causing pain to his patient, hesitates to amputate a rotten limb is guilty of himsa. He who refrains from killing a murderer who is about to kill his ward (when he cannot pre-vent him otherwise) earns no merit but commits a sin; he prac-tices no ahimsa but himsa out of a fatuous sense of ahimsa. Let us now examine the root of ahimsa. It is uttermost selflessness. Selflessness means complete freedom from a regard for one's body. When some sage observed man killing numberless crea-tures, big and small, out of a regard for his own body, he was shocked at his ignorance. He pitied him for thus forgetting the deathless soul, encased within the perishable body, and for thinking of the ephemeral physical pleasure in preference to the eternal bliss of the spirit. He therefrom deduced the duty of complete self-effacement. He saw that if man desired to realize himself, i.e., truth, he could do so only by being completely de-tached from the body, i.e., by making all other beings feel safe from him. That is the way of ahimsa. A realization of this truth shows that the sin of himsa consists not in merely taking life but in taking life for the sake of one's perishable body. All destruction therefore involved in the process of eating, drink-ing, etc., is selfish and, therefore, himsa. But man regards it to be unavoidable and puts up with it. But the destruction of bodies of tortured creatures being for their own peace cannot be regarded as himsa, or the unavoidable destruction caused for the purpose of protecting one's wards cannot be regarded as himsa. This line of reasoning is liable to be most mischievously used. But that is not because the reasoning is faulty but because of the inherent frailty of man to catch at whatever pretexts he can get to deceive himself to satisfy his selfishness or egoism. But that danger may not excuse one from defining the true nature of ahimsa. Thus we arrive at the following result from the foregoing:

1. It is impossible to sustain one's body without the destruction of other bodies to some extent.

2. All have to destroy some life
    (a) for sustaining their own bodies;
    (b) for protecting those under their care; or
    (c) sometimes for the sake of those whose life is taken.

3. (a) and (b) in (2) mean himsa to a greater or less extent. (c) means no himsa, and is therefore ahimsa. Himsa in (a) and (b) is unavoidable.

4. A progressive ahimsaist will, therefore, commit the himsa contained in (a) and (b) as little as possible, only when it is unavoidable, and after full and mature deliberation and having exhausted all remedies to avoid it. The destruction of dogs that I have suggested comes under (4) and can, therefore, be resorted to only when it is unavoidable, when there is no other remedy and after mature deliberation. But I have not the slightest doubt that refraining from that destruction when it is unavoidable is worse than destruction. And, therefore, although there can be no absolute duty to kill dogs, etc., it becomes a necessary duty for certain people at certain times and under certain circumstances. I shall now try to take up one by one some of the questions that have been asked me. Some correspondents

demand personal replies and in case I fail to do so threaten to publish their views. It is impossible for me to reach every individual correspondent by a personal reply. Those that are necessary I shall deal with here. I have no right, nor desire, to stop people from carrying on the controversy in other papers. I may remind the correspondents, however, that threats and impatience have no place in a sober and religious discussion. A correspondent asks: How did you hit upon the religion of destroying dogs at the old age of fifty-seven? If it had occurred to you earlier than this, why were you silent so long? Man proclaims a truth only when he sees it and when it is necessary, no matter even if it be in his old age. I have long recognized the duty of killing such animals within the limits laid down above, and have acted up to it on occasions. In India the villagers have long recognized the duty of destroying intruding dogs. They keep dogs who scare away intruders and kill them if they do not escape with their lives. These watchdogs are purposely maintained with a view to protecting the village from other dogs, etc., as also from thieves and robbers whom they attack fearlessly. The dogs have become a nuisance only in cities, and the best remedy is to have a law against stray dogs. That will involve the least destruction of dogs and ensure the protection of citizens. Another correspondent asks: Do you expect to convince people by logical argument in a matter like that of ahimsa? The rebuke contained in this is not without some substance. But I wanted to convince no one. Being a student and practicer of ahimsa, I have had to give expression to my views when the occasion demanded it. I have an opinion based on experience that logic and reasoning have some place, no doubt very small, in a religious discussion.

CWMG, vol. 31, pp. 544–47

V.

A friend writes a long letter mentioning his difficulties and pointing out what Jainism has to say to him, a *shrawak*, in the matter. One of his questions is:

> You say that if we can neither take individual charge of roving dogs nor have a pinjrapole for them, the only alternative is to kill them. Does that mean that every roving dog should be killed, although it may not be rabid? Don't you agree that we leave unmolested all harmful beasts, birds, and reptiles, so long as they do not actually harm us? Why should the dogs be an exception? Where is the humanity of shooting innocent dogs whenever they are found roving? How can one wishing well to all living beings do this?

The writer has misunderstood my meaning. I would not suggest even the destruction of rabid dogs for the sake of it, much less that of innocent roving dogs. Nor have I said that these latter should be killed wherever they are found. I have only suggested legislation to that effect, so that as soon as the law is made, humane people might wake up in the matter and devise measures for the better management of stray dogs. Some of these might be owned, some might be put in quarantine. The remedy, when it is taken, will be once for all. Stray dogs do not drop down from heaven. They are a sign of the idleness, indifference, and ignorance of society. When they grow into a nuisance, it is due to our ignorance and want of compassion. A stray dog is bound to take to his heels if you do not feed him. The measure that I have suggested is actuated no less by a consideration of the welfare of the dogs than by that of society. It is the duty of a humanitarian to allow no living being aimlessly to roam about. In performance of that duty it may be his duty once in a way to kill some dogs. Here is another question: I agree that the dogs are sure to be killed by man whenever they become a menace to society. But you say, "To wait until they get rabid is not to be merciful to them." This means that every dog is potentially rabid and that therefore it should be killed as a matter of precaution. I met a friend from the Ashram who assured me that you did not mean this, and that you had suggested it only as a last resort when dogs had become a menace. This is not clear from your articles. Will you make it clear? My previous articles and my answer to the first question leave nothing to be cleared. I must explain what I mean when you say that you cannot wait on until the dog gets rabid. Every stray dog is harmful. The harm is [not] confined to cities alone and it must stop. We do not wait until the serpent bites us. The rabies of the dog is concealed in its capacity to bite. A friend has sent me figures of cases of hydrophobia treated in the Civil Hospital, Ahmedabad:

PERIOD	CASES FROM THE CITY	CASES FROM THE DISTRICT	TOTAL
Jan. to Dec. '25	194	923	1117
Jan. to Sept. '26	295	695	990

These figures must alarm everyone who is interested in the welfare of the community, especially if he is a humanitarian. I admit that all the cases may not have been of hydrophobia. But it is difficult to say whether a dog is or is not rabid, and many run in fear to the hospital, because most dogs are found to be rabid afterward. There is only one remedy to relieve them of this fear and it is not to allow dogs to roam about. I was in England forty years ago when effective measures were taken to stamp out rabies. There were, of course, no stray dogs there. But even for the dogs which had regular owners, an order was passed that dogs found without collars with the name and address of the owner thereon and without muzzles would be killed. The measure was taken purely in the public interest. Practically the next day all the dogs in London were found to be with collars and muzzles. It was, therefore, necessary to kill only a very few. If anyone thinks that the people in the West are innocent of humanity, he is sadly mistaken. The ideal of humanity in the West is perhaps lower, but their practice of it

is very much more thorough than ours. We rest content with a
lofty ideal and are slow or lazy in its practice. We are wrapped
in deep darkness, as is evident from our paupers, cattle, and
other animals. They are eloquent of our irreligion rather than
of religion.

Here is a third question:

> You have different definitions of religion for the individual and
> for society. But why should not religion in both cases be the
> same? The ideal ought to be the same for both. That it may be
> impossible to carry it out is a different matter. For, even in case
> of the individual, only the occasion can show how far he has
> been able to carry out his ideal in practice. You yourself have
> said that your ideal is to save even a cruel animal at the risk of
> your life, but you could not say what you would actually do
> when faced by such an animal. There is no reason why society
> should not similarly have a lofty ideal and leave the individuals
> free to practice it according to their capacity.

My definition of religion for the individual and for society is
the same. The ideal must always be the same, but the practice
I have conceived to be different in the case of the individual
and the society. Truly speaking, practice differs in case of every
individual. I do not know of two men having the same extent
of the practice of ahimsa, though their definition of ahimsa is
the same. The extent of practice in case of society is the average of the different capacities of its members. Thus, for instance, where a section of the society is milk-arian and the
other fruitarian, the practice for the society extends to the use
of milk and fruit.

The writer next sets out two Jain doctrines as follows:

> Jainism is based on the doctrine of syadvada-manysidedness of
> reality. As is aptly said: "No absolute rule is correct; only the
> relative rule is the correct rule." Which means that an act which
> may be described as himsa under certain circumstances may be

ahimsa under other circumstances. Man should always use his discrimination in determining his conduct. There are two classes of Jains. Sadhus [the monks] and shrawaks [the laity]. Their code of conduct is thus defined: The sadhu is always non-violent. He may not eat to save himself, may not cook for himself, may not walk even a step for his own purpose—all his activity is for the welfare of the community and it should be as harmless as possible. He has to avoid the forty-two infringements laid down in the Shastras. The sadhu is described as nirgrantha-free from bonds. So far as I know there is no sadhu today who can satisfy the definition of a sadhu given above. The shrawak may not kill or injure any living being except when it is essential for himself. He is a worldly man and he cannot take his humanity farther than this. So if 20 percent compassion is expected of the sadhu, 1.25 percent is expected of the shrawak. If the latter goes beyond the measure expected of him, he approaches the state of a sadhu, but as a shrawak nothing more is expected of him.

I knew the substance of this distinction. I am quite conscious that the Jain doctrine is not contrary to the opinion I have expressed in these articles. If the Jains accept the interpretation given above, the opinion expressed by me can be deduced from it. But whether they accept it or not, I humbly submit that my opinion is capable of being, and has been, independently justified.

CWMG, vol. 32, pp. 14–17

VI.

A friend has sent a long letter containing a number of questions and raising a number of difficulties. He has also sent me his copies of *Navajivan* with profuse marginal notes on this series of articles. Some of his questions have been already answered in these pages. Without reproducing here the rest of his questions, I propose merely to give my answers. I think I have been considering the whole question quite dispassionately. I do not think I could be accused of any partiality for himsa or for my own peculiar views in the matter. My partiality is all for truth, which I seek to find out through ahimsa. It is my conviction that it cannot be found out in any other way. The question in dispute for me is not whether truth is our goal or not, nor whether ahimsa is or is not the only way to it. There is no possibility of my ever doubting these fundamental principles. The question before me is about the practice of these principles. Every day I see fresh aspects opening out to me. There is every possibility of my making mistakes in the practice of ahimsa and, though I am taking every precaution possible to avoid them, it is possible that I may err occasionally. Let not friends, therefore, impute partiality to me when I cannot agree with them. Let them believe me to be unconsciously in error and bear with me. I now proceed to give the answers.

1. The question to solve is not what is hydrophobia and how to treat it.

2. The municipality or the government will find a remedy not in accordance with ahimsa but with what they conceive to be public interest. The *mahajan* can find the right remedy if they are truly nonviolent. Government will never subscribe to the absolute principle of nondestruction of animals (dogs in the present case). Municipalities have members belonging to different faiths and different communities. They cannot, therefore, be expected to insist on a nonviolent remedy.

3. The duty of finding a nonviolent remedy is the *mahajan*'s. It is a mistake to think that the *mahajan* is blameless or helpless.

4. For the purpose of the discussion, I make no distinction between a rabid dog and a man who has run amok and is in the act of dealing death. Habitual violence is a disease. The habitually violent man goes on in his murderous career only because he is beside himself. Both a rabid dog and a rabid man are worthy of pity. When they are found in the act of injuring others,

and when there is no other remedy than to take their life, it becomes a duty to do so to arrest their activity. The duty is all the greater in case of a votary of ahimsa.

5. I have never meant that everyone should own a dog. What I have said is that the dogs should in no case be ownerless. Not that the owned dogs will be immune, but the owners will be responsible for them if they are diseased or get rabies.

6. The ownerless stray dogs are not innocent as lambs. They were never so. Owned dogs are generally so. The purpose of the present controversy is to make all the dogs innocuous.

7. I have never suggested that roving dogs should be killed wherever found. I have suggested enabling legislation in the interest of the dogs themselves. That will make humanely inclined people alive to their sense of duty and they will then either own dogs or find out some other remedy and thus make the existence of stray dogs impossible. In refusing alms to the beggar, the purpose is not to starve him but to teach him self-help, to make him a man. The duty of killing dogs arises in the circumstances and to the extent I have indicated in the previous articles. To say that it is a sin to extirpate dogs is not to contradict me. For I have never expressed a contrary opinion.

8. It is idle to discuss whether Mr. Ambalal's conduct was or was not proper, or whether my opinion about it was or was not correct. The public is not in full possession of the details of the incident. The broader question of ahimsa is the main issue, and to bring in Mr. Ambalal in the discussion is to cloud the issue.

9. The issue is: Whether, in consonance with the principle of ahimsa, it may be a duty to kill certain dogs under certain circumstances when no other alternative is possible. I submit that it may be and I hold that there cannot be two opinions in the matter. There may be a difference as to whether particular circumstances justify the act. The consolation for a votary of

ahimsa lies in the fact that, from his standpoint, such circumstances can only be rare.

10. But I can see one difference of opinion that must for the time being remain. In the letter under consideration as also in many others, I see that there is an instinctive horror of killing living beings under any circumstances whatsoever. For instance, an alternative has been suggested in the shape of confining even rabid dogs in a certain place and allowing them to die a slow death. Now, my idea of compassion makes this thing impossible for me. I cannot for a moment bear to see a dog, or for that matter any other living being, helplessly suffering the torture of a slow death. I do not kill a human being thus circumstanced because I have more hopeful remedies. I should kill a dog similarly situated, because in its case I am without a remedy. Should my child be attacked by rabies and there was no hopeful remedy to relieve his agony, I should consider it my duty to take his life. Fatalism has its limits. We leave things to fate after exhausting all the remedies. One of the remedies, and the final one to relieve the agony of a tortured child, is to take his life. But I shall not labor this point. What to my mind is impotence of the votaries of ahimsa is an obstacle to a true understanding of this dharma. I hope therefore that those who differ from me will for the present bear with me. So much about the thoughtful letter of a friend. I shall now deal with an angry letter.

The letter says: *You have been so much under the Western influence that you have learnt to think it proper to kill lower beings for the sake of man. It is better for you to confess your error and apologize to the world. You should have made up your mind in this matter after exhaustless [sic] sifting. Instead, you have passionately taken sides and discredited yourself.*

This is the least offensive sentence I have picked up from letters of this type. I submit I have not formed my opinion without much deliberation. It is not an opinion I have recently formed. Neither is it hasty. One should not let one's so-called

greatness come in the way of the formation of opinion, otherwise one cannot arrive at truth. I do not think that everything
Western is to be rejected. I have condemned the Western civilization in no measured terms. I still do so, but it does not mean
that everything Western should be rejected. I have learnt a
great deal from the West and I am grateful to it. I should think
myself unfortunate if contact with and the literature of the
West had no influence on me. But I do not think I owe my
opinion about the dogs to my Western education or Western
influence. The West (with the exception of a small school of
thought) thinks that it is no sin to kill the lower animals for
what it regards to be the benefit of man. It has, therefore, encouraged vivisection. The West does not think it wrong to
commit violence of all kinds for the satisfaction of the palate. I
do not subscribe to these views. According to the Western
standard, it is no sin, on the contrary it is a merit, to kill animals that are no longer useful. Whereas I recognize limits at
every step. I regard even the destruction of vegetable life as
himsa. It is not the teaching of the West. *Argumentum ad ho-
minem* has no place in a discussion of principles and their
practice. My opinions should be considered as they are, irrespective of whether they are derived from the West or the East.
Whether they are based on truth or untruth, himsa or ahimsa,
is the only thing to be considered. I firmly believe that they are
based on truth and ahimsa.

CWMG, vol. 32, pp. 40–43

VII.

Some of my correspondents do not seem to realize the fundamental consideration underlying my suggestion for the destruction of dogs under certain circumstances. Thus, for instance, I
have not made the suggestion in a purely utilitarian spirit. The
utility to society incidentally accrues from the act, but the principal consideration is the relief of the long-drawn-out agony of
the creatures whose present condition it is simply impossible for

me to tolerate. In the articles in this series, there has not been even the remotest suggestion that man has the right of disposal over the lower animals and that he may, therefore, kill them for his own comfort or pleasure. One of the writers betrays a strange confusion of thought when he says that the characteristic of an exalted soul is that he remains unaffected by the misery around him. He is callous, rather than exalted, who has not learnt to melt at others' woe, who has not learnt to see himself in others and others in himself. Intense longing for the happiness of others was the mother of the discovery of ahimsa. And the sage who was the embodiment of compassion found his soul's delight in renouncing his own physical comfort and stopped killing for his pleasure the dumb creation about him. A correspondent reminds me of the advice given me by Shri Rajchandra when I approached him with a doubt as to what I should do if a serpent threatened to bite me. Certainly his advice was that, rather than kill the serpent, I should allow myself to be killed by it. But the correspondent forgets that it is not myself that is the subject matter of the present discussion but the welfare of society in general as also of the suffering animals. If I had approached Raychandbhai with the question whether I should or should not kill a serpent writhing in agony, and whose pain I could not relieve otherwise, or whether I should or should not kill a serpent threatening to bite a child under my protection, if I could not otherwise turn the reptile away, I do not know what answer he would have given. For me the answer is clear as daylight and I have given it. A studious correspondent confronts me with some verses from a Jain philosopher and asks if I agree with the position taken up in them.

One of the verses says: *One should not kill even beasts of prey in the belief that by killing one such, one saves the lives of many.*

Another says: *Nor should one kill them out of a compassionate feeling that if they were suffered to live longer they might sink deeper into sin.*

The third verse says: *Nor should one kill distressed creatures presuming that one would thereby shorten the length of their agony.*

To me the meaning of the verses is clear. And it is this that a particular theory should not be the spring of action in any case. You may commit himsa, not in order that you thereby realize in practice a pet theory of yours, but because you are driven to it as an imperative duty. Work which spontaneously comes to one's lot, or action without attachment, in the words of the Gita, is the duty of a seeker after moksha. Confine your energy to work that comes your way, I conceive the Jain philosopher to say, never seek fresh fields of activity. The verses, to me, define the mental attitude of detachment that should govern one's action in cases where himsa seems to be imperative and unavoidable. But I have arrived at my present views independently of any authority, though originally they may have been drawn from various sources, and I submit that they are in perfect consonance with ahimsa, even though they may be proved to be contrary to the teaching of the philosopher.

CWMG, vol. 32, pp. 72–73

VIII.

Letters on this subject are still pouring in, but I fail to discover in them any new question or any fresh argument advanced. I would therefore ask those who have been thinking on this subject to read this series of articles over and over again. I do so without the slightest hesitation, inasmuch as they are the result not of ideas hastily formed but of experience of many years. I have presented no new principles but have tried to restate old principles. I cannot say how far the presentation is correct, but as it represents my honest conviction, and as many friends expect me to solve intricate problems in ahimsa, I can only ask them to turn to the series I have been writing. Some of my correspondents wrench my own sentences from their contexts and quote them against me, some quote part of them and omit the most essential remainder. Thus I have never advocated the extirpation of dogs as a class. On the contrary, my suggestions have been made for their betterment. I have repeatedly said that I have suggested the destruction of certain dogs under certain circumstances. Even this may be open to question. If it is, the objector should address himself only to that and nothing more. I continue to be the same votary of ahimsa that I was before. I still continue to hold life not only in man and animal, but in plant and flower, as sacred, and yet make use of vegetables and flowers and fruit. Only the spirit behind the use is: "He that soweth to his flesh shall of the flesh reap corruption; but he that soweth to the spirit shall of the spirit reap life everlasting." Destruction of dogs, even as that of plant or vegetable, is advised only when it is a matter of imperative duty, and only when it is meant not to sow to the flesh, but to the spirit. What torments me is the impotence of the votary of ahimsa. Ahimsa is not impotence. Ahimsa is not powerlessness. Ahimsa is unconquerable power. We shrink from it as we are dazed by its overpowering luster. Only very few of us can catch a glimpse of it. Ahimsa is the distinguishing characteristic of an untrammeled spirit. It is at the root of a number of other qualities—discrimination, detachment, penance, equability, and knowledge. It is the way of the brave, not of shrinkers. He who would understand ahimsa must understand the meaning of the inevitable himsa one sees about oneself. This statement, I know, is liable to abuse. But what is there free from this danger? Is not even God's name turned to the worst account? Have not rivers of blood been made to flow in His name? Have we not worshipped the Devil in His name? But that does not diminish His glory. That does not mean that we shall take His name in a secret corner. All action is tainted inasmuch as it presupposes himsa. And yet we free ourselves from the bondage of action through action itself. This body is the receptacle of sin, and yet we seek to achieve salvation by making of that abode of sin God's own sanctuary. Even so with himsa. And this himsa, calculated to take us on the onward path, must be spontaneous, must be the lowest minimum, must be rooted in compassion, must have discrimination, restraint, detachment at its back, and must lead us every moment onward to the path of ahimsa. I propose to conclude this series with a brief reference by way of illustration to the

way in which we are trying to solve the dog problem in the
Ashram. The problem is as old as the Ashram itself. The activity of the *mahajan* has made it more serious, and we have put
up with it not without reluctance. It is our practice to destroy
rabid dogs. Two or three such cases have occurred during the
last ten years. Healthy dogs have not been destroyed. They
are being refused food. I see that if the rule is strictly observed
we would be all happy, but we cannot do so. Every inmate does
not yet realize the necessity of it, and those who do are not sufficiently alive to the observance of the rule. And there are also
employees in the Ashram—how can they be made to observe
the rule? Some dogs we feed, there being no other alternative.
Two bitches and their puppies are being maintained at present.
The puppies have been kept in cozy boxes or baskets to keep
them from cold and are being given milk, and the dams get
specially prepared food. On the other hand, we have applied to
the *mahajan* to remove stray dogs from here. The request has
been accepted, though their cart has not yet come. I have explained to the best of my light our duty to the dogs. Everyone
has to act according to his own light. Let no one learn from me
the duty of destruction. He may under certain circumstances
permit himself to have recourse to it. I have laid down the limits. Everyone observes and will observe the law according to
his own capacity. I have referred to the present practice at the
Ashram simply to serve as an illustration of what my opinion
means. The religion of ahimsa consists in allowing others the
maximum of convenience at the maximum of inconvenience to
us, even at the risk of life. Everyone has to determine for himself the amount of inconvenience he is capable of putting up
with. No third party can determine it for him. Religion, even
as the soul, is both one and many.

VIII.

DARK NIGHT OF THE SOUL

As the Indian subcontinent approached freedom from colonial rule and attendant partition, the Hindus and Muslims turned against each other in a macabre orgy of violence. The lifelong efforts of Gandhi at Hindu-Muslim unity and collective non-violence began to unravel. These were perhaps the darkest and also the most sublime months of Gandhi's life as he embarked upon a lonely path seeking to regain and rebuild his faith in company with those who were both victims and perpetrators alike. This section contains documents from a period where Gandhi saw no consolation.

I.
Statement to the Press

November 20, 1946

I find myself in the midst of exaggeration and falsity. I am unable to discover the truth. There is terrible mutual distrust. Oldest friendships have snapped. Truth and ahimsa, by which I swear, and which have, to my knowledge, sustained me for sixty years, seem to fail to show the attributes I have ascribed to them.

To test them or, better, to test myself, I am going to a village called Srirampur, cutting myself away from those who have been with me all these years and who have made life easy for

me. I am taking Professor Nirmal Kumar Bose as my Bengali
teacher and interpreter and Shri Parasuram, who has been my
most devoted, selfless, and silent stenographer.

The other workers, whom I have brought with me, will each
distribute themselves in other villages of Noakhali to do the
work of peace, if it is at all possible, between the two communities. They are, unfortunately, all non-Bengalis except little
Abha. They will, therefore, be accompanied by one Bengali
worker each as teacher and interpreter, even like Prof. N. K.
Bose will be to me.

Distribution work and selection work will be done by Shri
Satis Chandra Das Gupta of the Khadi Pratishthan. My ideal
is to live in a local Muslim League family, but I see that I must
not wait for that happy day. I must meanwhile establish such
contacts with the Muslims as I can in their own villages. My
suggestion to the league ministers is that they should give me
one honest and brave Muslim to accompany one equally honest and brave Hindu for each affected village. They should
guarantee, at the cost of their lives if need be, the safety of the
returning Hindu refugees. I am sorry to have to confess that
without some such thing it seems to me difficult to induce them
to return to their villages.

From all accounts received by me, life is not as yet smooth
and safe for the minority community in the villages. They,
therefore, prefer to live as exiles from their own homes, crops,
plantations, and surroundings and live on inadequate and ill-
balanced doles.

Many friends from outside Bengal have written to me to
allow them to come for peace work, but I have strongly dis-
suaded them from coming. I would love to let them come if and
when I see light through this impenetrable darkness.

In the meantime, both Pyarelal and I have decided to suspend all other activities in the shape of correspondence, including the heavy work of the *Harijan* and the allied weeklies. I
have asked Shri Kishorelal, Shri Kakasaheb, Shri Vinoba, and
Shri Narahari Parikh to edit the weeklies jointly and severally.
Pyarelal and I may, if our work permits, send stray contribu-

tions from our respective villages. Correspondence will be attended to from Sevagram.

How long this suspense will last is more than I can say. This much, however, I can. I do not propose to leave East Bengal till I am satisfied that mutual trust has been established between the two communities and the two have resumed the even tenor of their life in their villages. Without this there is neither Pakistan nor Hindustan—only slavery awaits India, torn asunder by mutual strife and engrossed in barbarity. No one need at present be disturbed about my low diet. On receipt of the following wire from Dr. Rajendra Prasad: "Letter received. Have already wired quiet. There have been no incidents for a week now. Situation satisfactory. Most earnestly desire resumption of normal diet. Myself going Delhi 19th." I resumed goat's milk from yesterday and propose to revert to normal diet as early as the system permits. The future is in God's keeping.

CWMG, vol. 86, pp. 138–39

2.
Letter to Sevagram Ashram Inmates*

I am afraid you must give up all hope of my returning early or returning at all to the Ashram. The same applies to my companions. It is a Herculean task that faces me. I am being tested. Is the satyagraha of my conception a weapon of the weak or really that of the strong? I must either realize the latter or lay down my life in the attempt to attain it. That is my quest. In pursuit of it I have come to bury myself in this devastated village. His will be done.

CWMG, vol. 86, p. 143

* Written on or before November 20, 1946.

3.
Excerpts from a Letter to G. D. Birla

November 26, 1946

CHI. GHANSHYAMDAS,

You know I am staying at Srirampur all by myself, with only Professor Nirmal Kumar Bose and Parasuram as my companions. The people with whom I am putting up are gentlemen. There is only one Hindu family in the entire village, the rest are all Muslims. They all stay widely separated from each other. The hundreds of villages here do not maintain much contact with each other through any conveyance after the water dries up. The result is that work is possible only on foot. Therefore, only desperadoes, hooligans, or able-bodied men can maintain contact among themselves. I am living in one such village at present and intend to spend more time in another village similar to this. It is my intention to stay on here so long as the Hindus and Muslims do not start living together as sincere friends. God alone can keep man's resolve unshaken. At the moment I have forgotten Delhi, Sevagram, Uruli, and Panchgani. My only desire is to do or die. This will test my nonviolence, too. I have come here determined to emerge successful from this ordeal. . . .

. . . Friends will also do well to bear in mind that what I am doing here is not in the name of the Congress. Nor is there any thought of associating it with this work. What I am doing is only from my personal view of nonviolence. Anybody, if he so desires, can publicly oppose my work. That in fact is his right; it may even be his duty. Therefore, whosoever wishes to do anything or say anything, let him do so fearlessly. If anybody wants to warn me of anything, let him do that, too. Please send a copy of this to Sardar so that he may tell the others named above. Or you can get copies made and send them to the five friends yourself. Do express whatever you wish to. Write to me direct so that

I may reply. Pyarelal, Sushila, etc., all are in different villages. Pyarelal has been ill since yesterday. I hope you are all right.

Blessings from
Bapu

CWMG, vol. 86, pp. 162–63

4.
Excerpts from a Discussion with Amiya Chakravarty*

I am groping for light. I am surrounded by darkness; but I must act or refrain as guided by truth. I find that I have not the patience and the technique needed in these tragic circumstances; suffering and evil often overwhelms me and I stew in my own juice. Therefore, I have told my friends that they should bear with me and work or refrain as guided by wisdom, which is now utterly demanded of us. This darkness will break and, if I see light even those who created the tragedy of the recent communalism in Bengal, will.

CWMG, vol. 86, p. 192

5.
Note to Pyarelal†

I am still groping. I see I have not the knack. I have not yet quite found the key to ahimsa. Here I am out to perform a stupendous yajna, but my unfitness for the task is being demonstrated at every step. There can, however, be no running away. And where

---

* This discussion took place on December 4, 1946.

† Written after December 4, 1946.

can I run away? Success or failure is not in our hands. It is enough if we do our part well. I am leaving no stone unturned. Ours is but to strive. In the end it will be as He wishes.

CWMG, vol. 86, p. 195

6.
Excerpts from a Letter to Agatha Harrison

As FROM KHADI PRATISHTHAN,
SODEPUR, CAMP: SRIRAMPUR.

December 5, 1946

DEAR AGATHA,

Ramakrishna Bajaj has sent me your welcome letter. Carl Heath did write to me and I wrote to him at once. I have no doubt he will share that letter with you. I, therefore, say no more about the subject matter of the letter, important though it is. Here I am in an inaccessible part of Bengal and dealing with the most difficult part of my mission in life. I have never been in such darkness as I am in today. And the darkness does not come from outside. It is due to my limitations. My faith in ahimsa has never burned brighter and yet I feel that there is something wanting in my technique of it that I feel as though I were on an unbeaten track. . . . If my mission succeeds here, I shall be fit enough for further work. Anyway, so far as I know, I have to bury myself here till mutual confidence and friendship between the communities are restored. What happens here will happen throughout India, because Bengal is the nerve center.

Love,
BAPU

CWMG, vol. 86, p. 196

7.
Excerpts from a Letter to Narandas Gandhi

SRIRAMPUR,
NOAKHALI.

December 5, 1946

Your letter calls for a reply. I have resumed my normal food. Hence there is no cause at all now for worry. Really, speaking worry has no place in a thoughtful life. The present mission is the most complicated of all I have undertaken in my life. "I cannot see my path in the thick darkness of the night, take this your child under your protecting care. Light up the path of my life." I can sing these lines with perfect truth. I do not remember to have experienced such darkness in my life ever before, and the night seems long. My only consolation is that I have not accepted defeat or given way to despair. His will be done. I mean to do or die here. "To do" means to restore amity between Hindus and Muslims; or I should perish in the attempt. This is difficult to achieve. But it will be as God wills.

CWMG, vol. 86, pp. 197–98

8.
Excerpts from a Talk with Manu Gandhi*

During the last eight days, since I sent you to the hospital, I have been constantly thinking where I stand, what God demands of me, where He will ultimately lead me. . . . Though I

---

* This talk took place on May 22, 1947. Manu Gandhi was operated upon for her appendicitis.

have no longer the desire to live for 125 years, as I have said again and again of late, my striving to meet death unafraid with Ramanama on my lips continues. I know my striving is incomplete; your operation is a proof. But if I should die of lingering illness, it would be your duty to proclaim to the whole world that I was not a man of God but an impostor and a fraud. If you fail in that duty, I shall feel unhappy wherever I am. But if I die taking God's name with my last breath, it will be a sign that I was what I strove for and claimed to be.

CWMG, vol. 87, pp. 521–22

Suggestions for Further Reading

Mohandas Karamchand Gandhi's writings have been compiled in ninety-seven volumes (with three other volumes of indices and prefaces) in *The Collected Works of Mahatma Gandhi*. These are available in an open-source internet archive, the Gandhi Heritage Portal: www.gandhi heritageportal.org. This site is also a large resource for other writings, Gandhi's journals, photographs, films, and recordings of his voice.

Gandhi's autobiography remains for many readers their first introduction to his life's strivings: M. K. Gandhi, *An Autobiography or The Story of My Experiments with Truth: A Critical Edition*, introduced with notes by Tridip Suhrud (New Haven and London: Yale University Press, 2018; and New Delhi: Penguin Random House India, 2018).

The other key philosophical work is the *Hind Swaraj: M K Gandhi's Hind Swaraj: A Critical Edition*, annotated and edited by Suresh Sharma and Tridip Suhrud (Hyderabad, India: Orient Blackswan, 2009).

The biographical corpus on Gandhi is large. Some of the more insightful biographical studies are:

Ashe, Geoffrey. *Gandhi: A Biography*. New York: Cooper Square Press, 2000.

Desai, Narayan. *My Life Is My Message*. Volumes 1 to 4. Translated from the original Gujarati by Tridip Suhrud. New Delhi: Orient Blackswan, 2009.

DiSalvo, Charles R. *M. K. Gandhi, Attorney at Law: The Man Before the Mahatma*. New Delhi: Random House India, 2012.

Gandhi, Rajmohan. *Mohandas: A True Story of a Man, His People and an Empire*. New Delhi: Viking Penguin India, 2007.

Guha, Ramachandra. *Gandhi Before India*. New Delhi: Allen Lane, 2013, and New York: Knopf, 2014.

———. *Gandhi: The Years That Changed the World: 1914–1948*. New Delhi: Allen Lane, 2018, and New York: Knopf, 2018.

Tendulkar, D. G. *Mahatma: Life of Mohandas Karamchand Gandhi: Volumes 1-8.* Rev. ed. New Delhi: Publications Division, Government of India, 1963.

ON SATYAGRAHA AND NONVIOLENCE

Bhana, Surendra, and Neelima Shukla-Bhatt. *A Fire That Blazed in the Ocean: Gandhi and the Poems of Satyagraha in South Africa, 1909–1911.* 2nd ed. New Delhi: Promilla and Co., 2011.

Brown, Judith M., and Anthony Parel, eds. *The Cambridge Companion to Gandhi.* New York: Cambridge University Press, 2011.

Chatterjee, Margaret. *Gandhi's Religious Thought.* London: Palgrave Macmillan, 1983.

Devji, Faisal. *The Impossible Indian: Gandhi and the Temptation of Violence.* Cambridge, MA: Harvard University Press, 2012.

Erikson, Erik H. *Gandhi's Truth: On the Origins of Militant Nonviolence.* New York: W. W. Norton & Co., 1969.

Ganguly, Debjani, and John Docker, eds. *Rethinking Gandhi and Nonviolent Relationality.* New York: Routledge, 2007.

Hardiman, David. *The Nonviolent Struggle for Indian Freedom, 1905–19.* New Delhi: Viking, 2018, and New York: Oxford University Press, 2018.

———, ed. *Nonviolence in Modern Indian History.* New Delhi: Orient Blackswan, 2017.

Hunt, James D. *Gandhi and the Nonconformists: Encounters in South Africa.* New Delhi: Promilla and Co., 1986.

Juergensmeyer, Mark. *Gandhi's Way: A Handbook of Conflict Resolution.* New Delhi: Oxford University Press, 2003.

Mukherji, Gangeya, ed. *Learning Non-Violence.* New Delhi: Oxford University Press, 2016.

Reddy, E. S., and Kalpana Hiralal. *Pioneers of Satyagraha: Indian South Africans Defy Racist Laws, 1907–1914.* Ahmedabad: Navajivan, 2017.

Richards, Glyn. *Gandhi's Philosophy of Education.* New Delhi: Oxford University Press, 2001.

Suhrud, Tridip, and Peter Ronald deSouza, eds. *Speaking of Gandhi's Death.* New Delhi: Orient Blackswan, 2010.

Weber, Thomas. *The Shanti Sena: Philosophy, History and Action.* New Delhi: Orient Blackswan, 2009.

———. *On the Salt March: The Historiography of Mahatma Gandhi's March to Dandi.* New Delhi: HarperCollins India, 1997.